To all drug addicts and alcoholics
who have not yet found a way to stop...

To Jommy a great
friend, a marvellous
and this fine musician
but a special person
why thee learned
about life from him
and also one of the
most honest men I've
ever know

Woody

HOPE TO DIE
a memoir of jazz and justice

Schaffner Press, Inc.
Tucson. Arizona

Book design by Kay Sather
Front Cover Photo: Darren Clark
Back Cover Photo: Jackie Keller and Lori Innes

ISBN 978-0-97-105984-9

First Edition
PRINTED IN THE UNITED STATES

Schaffner Press, Inc.
PO Box 87648
Tucson, AZ 85745

CONTENTS

FOREWORD

John Irwin, PhD, author of *The Felon, The Jail, Prisons in Turmoil*

I 've known Verdi Woodward (Woody) since 1952, when he and I started our first adult prison sentence at the Chino Guidance Center. We walked the yard together, shooting the shit and getting to know each other. He came with a reputation. Many of my friends knew him in Preston, the youth joint, where he was known as the toughest guy there. I learned that he could also tell a story with a unique command of the lingo, and his timing, inflections, phrasing, and gestures were just right. He didn't just talk; he spouted, roared, guffawed and gesticulated, and as he spoke he radiated energy.

We were sent to Soledad although we didn't hang together because we were following different strategies for doing time. I was getting healthy, getting educated, and learning Spanish while he was playing the saxophone, playing sports and trying to score dope. He was always in the yard, telling stories, listening to stories, laughing, "jiving," and thumping on the chest and shoulders of anybody who was near him. I kept a little distance, but I liked the guy and kept my eye on him.

When I got out, I went to college and got a PhD in sociology. As research for my dissertation, a study of the prison, I formed a group of convict "experts" in San Quentin to help me gather data. Woody, back on another robbery beef, was in the group along with several other convict friends. He entertained us with his stories.

When Woody was released, I was organizing a prisoners' union, and he came by several times. He worked a bit in San Francisco, and then moved to L.A. I occasionally heard from him over the next fifteen years or so. He got hooked up with Narcotics Anonymous and stayed pretty clean.

At one of those meetings he told me he was writing this book, and had a publisher. I introduced him to a criminologist colleague, prominent author Lewis Yablonsky, who read Woody's book and immediately phoned to tell me I should read it. I couldn't put it down. It rang true from the first page, like when you hear some singer hit a few notes and you immediately feel that not only are the notes true, the timing and phrasing are just right.

Woody writes in tune. I've read a lot of books by ex-convicts, ex-thieves, ex-dope fiends, some of them damn good. But Woody's descriptions of this life ring truer than any I've read. This is a hell of a book.

—J. I.
San Francisco, 2006

PROLOGUE

SANTA MONICA PIER, 1940

"Hey, where you punks goin'?"

My friend Dick looked around and said, "Are you talkin' to me?"

"Yeah, I'm talkin' to you, punk." We turned to see who it was, and there were these two soldiers, pretty big guys, one was about six feet, weighing a couple hundred pounds. Dick said, "What's up?"

One of the soldiers taunted, "Your mama know you're out? I'm talking to you two punks."

"What do you mean, punks?" Dick hit him with a right and charged into him, and ten seconds later, he was laid out on the floor, cold. I'd never seen anything like this before in my life. The soldier had destroyed Dick in a matter of seconds.

Then he looked at me, and said, "You're next, punk." I put my hands up, and he hit me with a left hook to the jaw, which didn't hurt that much; but I was so scared I thought I was going to faint. Then he hit me with a right to the chest, which knocked me down. I wasn't hurt, yet I was so frightened, I couldn't get up. I was paralyzed with fear. He started talking trash to me a little bit, calling me a punk, telling me to get up and fight like a man—God, I was too scared to move, and it was just killing me!

Finally, after cussing me out a little more, he and his friend just walked away. A minute or so later, Dick came out of it, and God, he was really messed up. His jaw was broken and he had cuts all over his face. I didn't know how that guy could have done so much damage in such a short time. The first thing Dick asked me when he got up was, "Woods, did you get to hit him?"

"No, he wasted me too," was all I could say. I was so ashamed I couldn't look at him.

"Hell, that's a shame. I know you'da really hurt him."

"Yeah, I woulda, Dick," I mumbled. And all the time, I'm feeling worse and worse about myself as a human being. Later, I told myself that what just happened to me on the pier that night was never going to happen to me again, and you know what? It never did.

At that point in my life, I was going to a club called The Hollywood Boys' Club, and they had the speed bag there, and a heavy bag, and a ring where you could box, and man, I lived at that place. This was in the summer, and I went there from morning until night, and I punched that speed bag till I thought my hands were gonna fall off. And I lifted weights. I was fifteen at the time, but I got myself in tremendous shape; and to prove I wasn't a coward, I used to go to different high schools to find out who the toughest guy was there. Kids would ask me "What do want him for?"

And I'd say, "Well I love to fistfight, and I've come to kick his ass." And I'd usually find guys there that I could do that to, and I never lost. I fought guys that were sometimes stronger than me and bigger than me, and knew how to fight more than me, but they could never beat me because I had such a total desire to prove to the world that I was not a coward—and I thought, at that time, that that was the only way I could do it. So, that's been a sort of thing in my life, to prove that I'm not a coward. It took a long time to finally recognize what was happening with me, and that's mainly what this book is all about—this fear that governed my life, and left me so afraid the world would discover who I really was.

About a year and a half later, I went to Preston Reform School for a robbery, and I was there about thirteen months;

that was the beginning of my crime career. It was an institution where you fought practically every day, and where the officers didn't bother to break it up as long as the fight was good. I remember there was this one officer who used to sit at his desk with his feet up just watching the kids fighting. The only time he would break up a fight was when it got dull.

Preston was a big step in forming my life as a criminal and as an overall bad guy. Once I really learned how to fight, it changed my life. I felt invincible and I was out to take everything I could from everyone because I figured life owed me a living, and I was going to collect it.

V.W.
Los Angeles, Nov. 2005

Part One
THE GORILLA

CHAPTER 1

I was sitting in a shabby worn-out chair with my hands over my closed eyes, hands that had been broken so many times they resembled Virginia hams. I shifted my head slowly, opened my eyes and gazed at Sylvia lying naked on a pull-down bed. She was in her twenties, tall with long shapely legs and a slender upper body. She always looked elegant, even when she'd just woken up. I imagined her as a Peruvian goddess with her large bottom lip, those Chinese eyes and high cheekbones.

I looked around the small, dark apartment. Directly in front of me stood a rickety old dresser covered with cigarette burns. The top was littered with a woman's makeup, hairbrush, cold cream, rouge and eye shadow, and on a flattened brown paper bag lay a burnt spoon, an eye-dropper, a hypodermic needle and a stack of sheet music.

I picked up a shiny baritone saxophone and held it affectionately in my lap for a few minutes. Hunching over, I hooked up the neck strap. To warm the instrument, I blew gently through the mouthpiece without producing any sound. When I was ready, I tightened up my embouchure and the notes rolled out in sub-tones.

After a dozen choruses of "Stella," I carefully placed my horn on top of the case, stood up and stretched. When I turned around I was surprised to see Sylvia watching me. I looked at her body briefly, then went to the dresser and started preparing the heroin.

"Come on baby. Get dressed," I said.

"You were sounding so good, honey. Why don't we go somewhere where you can play tonight?"

"You know why. Don't start that shit."

"I just thought—"

"Look, I haven't been driving to Lynwood and back for over a week just for the scenery. Come on now, get dressed."

I had the jolt prepared.

"Give me your arm," I said. I deftly found her vein, then fixed myself. The strength of the jolt was so jarring I had to sit down.

"Are you alright?" she asked.

"I'm okay. Just get ready."

I got up slowly, went to the closet, and started taking the tools out and placing them on the bed; a small lead sledgehammer, a large brace and expansion bit, two crowbars, thirty feet of heavy rope, and a fishing knife. I put everything in a pillowcase, wrapped it carefully, then tied it together with a string.

"I'm ready."

"I guess you got your mind set on doing it tonight?"

"You got any other ways to come up with some money?"

"It's not like we're broke. We still got two spoons."

"Two spoons will barely get us through tonight and tomorrow. I don't know about you, but I sure as hell don't want to be climbing around on somebody's roof desperate and sick. Bring the outfit and stuff with you and let's get the hell out of here."

"Why do you want to take it with us?"

I just looked at her and shook my head. I opened the door and she followed me out. We got in the car and drove several miles without exchanging a single word. I could sense Sylvia's anger and fear, but there was nothing I could say to change anything, so I continued to drive in silence. We were almost there before I spoke again.

"Listen to me carefully. You're gonna pick me up as we planned it. Shouldn't be any longer than fifteen minutes, but in case I'm not out by then, don't panic. The safe is a cracker box, but I can't tell what might happen once I get inside. You don't have to hang around after you drop me off. Go have a cup of coffee or drive around for ten minutes, but be parked in the lot across the street exactly fifteen minutes after you drop me off. Are you still nervous?"

"A little," she replied.

A few minutes later I pulled into a vacant lot and parked. "That's the lumberyard, honey, and this is the exact place I want you to park the car."

The building was an old one-story wood structure in the center of the block. A five-foot chain link fence encircled it on all sides, and stacks of lumber lay alongside, providing good potential cover from the road.

"That window on the side, do you see it? That's where I'll be signaling you from. Park and keep your eye on that window. I can see out from there, too, so I won't leave the building until I see you start the car. It should take me about ten seconds to get out of there."

"What if something goes wrong?"

"You mean if the cops show?"

"Yeah."

"Go to the drive-in and wait."

"How long should I wait?"

"Just wait. It could take me all night, but I'll get there." I got out of the car and transferred the tools to the front seat.

"You drive," I said. " Just go around the block slowly. We'll see if anyone's out walking their dog."

I was psyching myself out now and didn't say anything. It was an easy burglary, but I had to get myself in the mood.

"When you turn down the alley, cut the lights and I'll be on my way. Don't turn the lights back on until you leave the alley. Slow down a little, hon, and whatever you do, don't put the brakes on. Just take your foot off the gas." The muscles in my stomach were tight and my mouth was already dry. She stopped the car. I picked up the pillowcase and stepped out.

"See you in fifteen minutes," I said, and was gone.

CHAPTER 2

I stood by the fence for a moment just to get the feel. I gently dropped the pillowcase on the other side, and then jumped quietly over the fence. In order to get to the roof, I had to scale a small shed, so I threw the pillowcase on top and then pulled myself up. A parapet wall offered me protection from one side of the street. Huddling close to it, I prepared the expansion bit and drill and put them together. I squatted down like a Russian dancer and counted out twelve steps from the front of the building. I took out a knife and cut a square of tarpaper out large enough to allow my body to enter. Now, with the bare wood exposed, I started in with the brace and bit, butting out two-inch holes in a circle. It took only a dozen holes to make an opening in the wood large enough for me to get through.

Shining the flashlight down the hole I had made, I saw that I had about three feet under the roof before reaching the rafters. It could not have been better. I moved the tools close to the opening and lowered myself in. I felt around with my foot until I found a rafter to stand on. Searching with my other foot, I found the next one to the right. Once I had planted my feet firmly on both rafters I eased myself into the attic.

I jabbed a hole in the ceiling with an ice pick I'd brought with me and got to my knees and peered down. I could see the office clearly from the light coming in from the window. I was about two feet from where I wanted to enter, so I made adjustments accordingly; I placed my left foot on the two-by-four, and, keeping my balance by putting my hands on the roof, came down hard with my right foot. With four stomps, I had a hole large enough to enter.

I lifted myself back out of the attic to get the tools. Taking the rope out of the pillowcase, I attached it to a pipe coming off the roof. I got back down into the attic, dropped the pillowcase and rope down the opening, and lowered myself into the office. I made a quick check around the room for any kind of hidden alarm system. It was clear. I gave the safe a thorough inspection. Everything was right, so I took out all the tools and placed them nearby. A glance at my watch revealed five minutes had passed. I knew that in a matter of minutes I would have that safe open. Perfect.

Every time I worked a safe, I thought of Red. He had given me the "safe game" in just twenty minutes one night a few years ago as he lay on his back and ate a sandwich. Red's attitude was that if the entry was done right, everything else was routine and you were as safe inside the building as you were in your own living room. It took me several jobs to accept that fact, but when I finally did, I never had to rush again.

"I want you to hit that safe as hard as you can with the cleaver, right there," Red said, pointing to the top left-hand corner of the safe. "Now, get out that little mechanic's crowbar and insert it into the hole."

As I did this, he picked up a two-foot-long pipe and handed it to me. "Put this over the crowbar and peel it back slowly. Get it in there good, so it doesn't slip off."

I peeled the top corner of the safe back about half an inch. "Get the hook part of the big crowbar in there and peel it back enough to allow the cleaver to get it. You got it? Good, now we're in. That front plate is connected by rivets that the cleaver will slice through like butter. Now, insert the meat cleaver and hit it with the lead hammer. It will pop them right down the line."

Red was right. With each blow, I could hear a rivet pop and see the front door plate coming off six inches at a time. When I got to the bottom of the safe, a sand-like substance started pouring out.

"What's this?" I asked.

"It's the fireproofing. Just keep hitting the rivets."

I had gone down one side from the top left corner around the bottom and halfway up the other side when he got up and told me to stop. "Here," he said, "Help me pull that front door plate off." As we did, fireproofing fell out at our feet.

"Kick that shit out of the way and brace yourself for an education on the finer points of safecracking." I quickly scraped and kicked the concrete-like material from the front of the door and waited.

"The safe is now open," Red said. It didn't look open to me, but I waited. "You see that bar there?" I nodded. "That's the door handle, but it won't open now, because this particular safe has an interlocking device. We have to disconnect a few things to release the handle. There's a bar on the bottom that runs the length of the door. You see it?" Red asked.

"Yes."

"And those metal horseshoe-like clamps that fit over it?"

"I see them."

"Reach down and take both of them off. Just lift them off." Red ordered. I did as he asked and then looked back at him.

"Well, what are you waiting for?" Red asked. "Turn the handle." The door opened. I stood there for a moment, amazed at how easy it was. That was almost four years ago.

Shortly afterward, I'd heard Red got busted for robbery. I went to see him in the county jail every week until he went to the joint. I was going in and out of jail at the time myself and we lost contact, but I'd never forget that it was Red who had shown me how to support my habit in style.

In ten minutes I had the safe open. It had been easy. I looked at my watch. I still had five minutes left. I started taking everything out of the safe, every envelope and every piece of paper. I sorted the money and put it off to one side, stacking it methodically. There was too much to fold and put in my pocket, so I put it all in the pillowcase, wrapping it neatly in place around my stomach. I loosened my belt a couple of notches so I had free movement and the money wouldn't fall out.

There were two doors, one of which had about eighteen inches of crawlspace, and I decided I'd rather go out the back door than climb the rope back up to the attic. I crawled under the door into the other office, which led to the dock with a big sliding door held closed by an iron pin and some Mickey Mouse alarm wiring. I turned around and reached for the wire in my pocket and there it was—another safe! I hadn't counted on this.

It was too heavy to lift, must have weighed two hundred and fifty pounds. If I could find a dolly I could wheel it right out. But why bother with it? I already had several thousand dollars. Even if I could get it home, I might have to take it out to the desert to open it. I'd have to rent a compressor to hook up an abrasive rubber wheel, and there was a good chance of getting busted on the way out when I'd already gotten what I came for. Besides, there probably wasn't any money in it anyway.

But what if there was big money there? How many times had I read about people overlooking thousand of dollars in the other safe? Okay, let's make a decision, do I settle for what I got? Can I get it out? What do I need? First off, a dolly, which they're sure to have, and a pair of bolt cutters to cut the chain on the back fence, because there's no way to pick it up and throw it over the fence. A lumberyard has got to have both. Do I go out and tell Sylvia? Or do I just work until I finish? Christ! She'll have a stroke if I hang around here another thirty minutes. OK, it's getting clearer. I'll rewire the back door, locate the bolt cutters and make the exit just like I was leaving. I'll carry the safe to the back door on the dolly, park it by the gate, cut the chain on the fence and go back to Sylvia. I'll fix, and get a cold lemonade at the drive-in, and when I get back, the safe will be sitting there waiting for me. Christ, do I need a cold lemonade. The biggy now is to locate the dolly and bolt cutters and make a smooth exit. If it isn't smooth, I can't come back.

I started looking for the dolly. It was not on the dock. I looked in the aisles past the bins filled with nails and, in the second aisle, I spotted a nice big heavy one. I could've put the entire building on it and carried it away.

Now I had to find the bolt cutters. There was no way to get the safe through that fence without cutting the chain. I continued searching the nail bins. I went to the other end of the dock used for shipping, but I couldn't find anything but a crowbar and a pair of pliers. I was getting nervous now. The desire to get this safe had taken over, and those goddamned bolt cutters were going to rank the whole play. I had searched every part of the dock, and no cutters.

What kind of fucking lumberyard is this, with no bolt cutters? How about the offices up front? That's where they're at, of course. I was obsessed now. I was either gonna take the safe with me or have a booking number in the county jail. I rushed back to the office, slid under the door and back into the other office. I crawled on my stomach to the front office and there, just inside the front door, was a beautiful pair of cutters with the price tag still on them.

I waited for a minute before I did anything. My street sense was working overtime. I decided to go to the other end of the counter and have a look outside before pulling the cutters off the wall. I made my way to the far counter on my stomach and was just about to look up when I heard a car pull in front of the building and stop.

"Sonofabitch! Who's parked out there?"

I was close enough to be able to hear two men talking. I waited. I couldn't distinguish what they were saying, but I could tell they were men. This is a strange place to park and be talking this time of night, I thought. I crawled carefully to the front window on my stomach and peeked out. I turned cold. There was a black-and-white parked right in front. I started to bolt for the rear door, but hesitated, and cautiously looked again.

They were just sitting there. Why weren't they out of the car making some kind of move to catch me? I waited ten seconds. Twenty seconds. I was on my mark if they opened the door. Nothing. They hadn't moved. I rose up one more time and watched the backs of their heads. I could almost hear them. They didn't even know I was there. They were too busy eating their fucking sandwiches. Those assholes! I continued to watch them, my panic suddenly gone. I knew I was safe. I prepared myself mentally for a long wait, when suddenly the radio came in loud and clear: "Adam 4, Adam 4, a 415 in progress at 815 Cherry Street."

By the time the radio had finished repeating the message, the cops were gone. I waited until there were no cars coming and it was clear. I took two quick steps, jerked the bolt cutters off the wall, and fell to the ground in back of the counter. I retraced the route I had come by, the adrenalin rushing through my body. It was almost better than being high. I knew I had it. It was just a matter of putting things together. I would have been a goddamned fool to have left that safe. Wasn't that my business? I liked that. I was too hooked to laugh, but I chuckled to myself and said in a whisper, "Isn't this my business, taking care of bid-ness? I said it half a dozen times, making up a little melody to it on the upbeat of the second "bid" and the syncopation sounded hip.

I quickly wired the back door and took the iron pin out, which was the only thing holding it shut. The safe didn't present a problem to get on the dolly, which I wheeled over to the door. I tried to balance the dolly and open it with one hand, but it was hard to open and made a screeching sound. I set it all the way down and used both hands to open the door. I picked up the dolly too quickly and the safe fell off. The light from the inside was shining and my nervousness reached a new high. Nevertheless, the determination, the obsession to get that safe overpowered the fear.

I got the safe back on the dolly, but the door wasn't wide enough. I pulled hard with one hand. It moved barely three inches. Not enough. But one more tug and I wheeled it through and set it down outside. I went back to the bolt cutters and then put all my weight on the door, and it shut. I lay flat on my stomach and waited for the moment. This was my jungle. I knew how to play the shadows. If anyone were to try and stop me, they couldn't. I had a powerful upper body. I could do a hundred chin-ups without stopping, go up the side of a building like a cat, and if it ever got to hand-to-hand, I could break your neck. Nothing but a bullet could catch me now.

There weren't any noises and that meant danger, so I quickly went to the fence, cut the chain, eased the chain through and walked out down the alley. Ten seconds later I was in the car with Sylvia.

"Jesus! You didn't signal me. You've had me crazy out here all this time. Did you have a hard time with it? What were the cops doing over there?"

"Trying to give me a stroke. I thought it was over. I was so close to them I could hear them talking. It's a good thing I didn't panic and try to make a Bogart exit. Can you imagine those assholes eating their lunch in front of my lumberyard?" I said, smiling at the thought. "We've got to get to a motel where I can stash you and the money."

"What do you mean, a motel? Why aren't we going home?"

"I left a safe back there in the yard and I'm going back to pick it up, but I've got to stash this money first. That way, if I get popped back there, we'll have the bail money and you'll be out to post it. I don't want to take the chance of getting caught and not being able to make bail. Don't worry, baby. The safe is lying on a dolly in the yard and I got the back gate open. All I gotta do is drive over and pick it up. But for Christ's sake, let's get to that drive-in on Vermont, so I can get a lemonade. I'm dying of thirst."

I suddenly felt tired. The constant strain of the evening had begun to show. The pressure was supposed to ease up after getting the money, but now it had started all over again. And at that moment, the only thing I wanted to do was get some heroin into my veins.

CHAPTER 3

Sylvia stopped in back of the drive-in and I got out. In a few minutes, I came back with two lemonades and a cup of black coffee and hopped back in the car, and we drove to a motel a few blocks away.

After registering, I got back in the car with the motel key and told Sylvia to pull around to room 108. I asked her for the stuff and the outfit, which she produced from her bra, all the while giving me a funny look.

"No lectures, please. I'm feeling icky. And I'm not gonna take a big jolt."

I always felt like I had to justify a jolt to Sylvia. She kept insisting I take a little less each time. According to her, I fixed too much and too often, but she was always there fixing with me, every time I did. I fixed her first and then myself. That was the way I kept the nag off me. I didn't wait around now to try to enjoy my high. It had supplied me with just what I needed to get the safe into the car.

I said goodbye to Sylvia, giving her instructions about what to do in case I was not back in an hour, and got into the car and drove back to the lumberyard.

I parked the car on the side of the street next to the alley, got out and walked straight to the yard. Instead of opening the gate, I pulled myself over the fence and took cover behind a tree. I didn't want to swing the gate open until the last possible minute, in case a car came by and someone spotted it. Once inside, I waited a second or two, tuning in to the feel of the neighborhood. In ten quick strides, I picked up the dolly with the safe. I didn't bring it up completely, but walked with it at a forty-five degree angle. When I got to the fence, I leaned one shoulder into it to push it open while still moving forward with the dolly. The gate fell back automatically. I walked the dolly ten feet to the tree and set it down where the branches would provide camouflage. In a matter of seconds, I reached the car and waited again for the feeling I needed to assure myself it was all right.

I took everything in at a glance, started the car, drove down the alley with the lights off and stopped just past the tree, leaving just enough room to allow me to move freely on the driver's side. I got out, walked around the back of the car, opened the trunk and, setting the dolly straight up, reached down with both hands, grabbed the safe, and lifted it to the bumper. I got under the safe, and with the help of my knee, bullied it into the trunk of the car. It dropped in with a crash, but fit snugly in there, tucked in for the night. I closed the trunk—another noise. I went straight to the drive-in and ordered another large lemonade and coffee to go.

Back at the motel, I knocked three times and heard Sylvia ask, "Who is it?"

"Hey, momma, we're in the money! We're in the money! Come on; let's get out of this fleabag. Let's go to the Digger, and see my man Ray Graziano. We'll stop and pick up my horn. It's still early. I'll just play a set and we'll go home."

"What about the safe? Is it in the car?"

"Yeah, it's cool though. Only you and I know it's there. I'll drop the dough off at the pad."

"Honey—"

"No, that's it. We're going there. I haven't played there in a couple of months."

"Alright, alright, if that's what you want."

I felt like my old self at the thought of playing at the Digger. There was always a good rhythm section there. It was Ray Graziano's gig. I loved Ray from the first night I met him. He was from Cleveland, self-taught, and had ears like an elephant. He was the sweetest guy in the world; everybody loved him.

I remember one night, I was in the audience, and he was playing a show tune at close to 300 bpm on the metronome. He was just killing everybody, and when he finished playing, I went up to him and told him how much his playing had moved me. I asked him: "What key were you playing that in?"

He held up three fingers of his left hand, and the middle finger of his right. "It starts on this note," he said, meaning F-sharp, which would have put the key in D. Ray was a total ear player. His dad got him a saxophone when he was about twelve, and he never had a lesson in his life, but boy, he could play any tune in any key at any tempo. I remember, when he was drunk some times, he'd get into a high note, and it would be a little off, but he'd stay on that note and fuck with it until it was finally back on pitch, and everybody would just be relieved! But God, he was a joy to play with and a really great guy.

Sylvia and I got there just before the last set was about to start. Ray was in the parking lot, smoking a joint. He didn't recognize me at first, but when he realized who it was, a look of horror came over his face.

"Man, Woods, what are you doing here?"

"I just came by to play a set."

"Woods, you can't stay here! The heat comes by all the time, and asks me where you are. They want to know everything about you. Don't even go in the club, man. Get in your car, and blow!"

"But Ray—"

At one in the afternoon the next day, I was in the carport looking at the safe. I came back to the apartment and Sylvia asked what happened.

"It looks like Fort Knox down there. I'll need a machine shop and eight machinists to open it. I'm gonna take an outside chance and ask them for the combination. I'll tell them I'll call them after they give me the combination and tell them where the safe is. Shit, I'd go for that myself. That fucking safe must be worth $500.00."

I sat quietly for a while, thinking, trying to put it together. There has to be a way to get into that safe without taking it to the desert. I grabbed a pencil and started making some notes. Sylvia came over and asked me what I was doing.

"Hand me the telephone." I got the number for the lumberyard and dialed. "Hello, this is Captain Murphy at the 77th Street Station. Is the owner there? No? What about the detectives I sent down there this morning?"

"No, sir," the voice at the other end replied, "They were here but they left over an hour ago."

"Damn! They never do anything right," I said. "I told them to check with me every two hours while they were on that case. You see, we had a break this morning and there's a very good chance that we can make an arrest, maybe even today with some luck. We've already recovered the safe. It was broken into, but they didn't wear gloves. We can tell by the smeared prints. Now, as soon as we can get into the door of the safe and get some good prints we'll be able to find out who it was. This is obviously the work of some ex-convicts working in that district. You be sure and tell my men to call me at once because I need the combination of that safe to get the prints. Is it possible to contact the owner for the combination?"

"I have the combination, Captain."

"Oh, good. Sergeant, hand me that pencil," I said this looking at Sylvia with my eyes wide and a sly smile on my face. She handed me the pencil with a look of disbelief.

"Thank you, Sergeant," I said taking the pencil, "Alright, young man, I have my pencil ready."

"Yes, Captain. It's 32R, 46L, 16R, 31L, but you have to twirl it around zero twice before you start. That's the way I always do it."

"Is that it?"

"Yes, Captain, that's all there is."

"Well, let me see if I've written the numbers down correctly, you said, 32R, 46L, 16R, 31L, and twirl around to zero twice. Thank you, you've been most helpful. I have the lab man waiting to take the prints. Oh, yes. I won't need to hear from the detectives now that I have the combination, and thank you again, young man."

"You're welcome, Captain."

"Goodbye."

I gave Sylvia a sly look. She just shook her head, and said, "That, my love, was as smooth as a Charlie Parker solo."

CHAPTER 4

The take from both safes was a little over eight thousand dollars. I was thinking maybe I would sell the safe, but I had too much money to bother with it, so I dumped it in the Los Angeles River, but not before locking it back up. I wanted some square john to find it and report it to the police. I would have given anything to see their faces when they opened it up and found it empty.

Now the problem I faced was how to use the money I had acquired to get off drugs and hook up my music. I had only a couple of jolts left, and I wasn't going to go cold turkey. I had tried that before and hadn't made it. If I could get some Dolophine I could ease into it. Sylvia was going to expect me to quit now that we had some money to lay back on. But what would happen if I couldn't do it? I always felt I had the strength to do anything. Anything! Wasn't it a year ago that I had given it all I had? When I came out of the bathroom after having just fixed, the outfit still in my hand, saying with real conviction, "That was my last jolt"? With that, I had broken the outfit and flushed two spoons of stuff down the toilet.

It lasted three days, and in those three days I thought I was going to die. It wasn't so much the physical pain; I could almost make that if that was all there was to deal with. It was the accumulation of the physical and mental pain that was the killer. Being on the natural was what was so unbearable. It was almost worth anything not to have to live a Sears & Roebuck existence.

Now with some money, I could take my time kicking. Kicking in a nice pad was still kicking, but it was a lot easier. With my newfound wealth I decided to make one last buy, an ounce or two, and then go to "dollies" until I was clean.

"I'm going downtown and see if I can find some "dollies," I said.

"And if you don't find them?"

"They're always downtown. I'll find 'em."

I could tell Sylvia wasn't fooled. I knew she knew I had no intention of buying anything but heroin, but she didn't say anything.

I fixed her and myself and took a thousand dollars from the stash. As I walked to the carport, I made a mental note to move soon. We were living in a trashy part of North Hollywood, but there hadn't been any heat since we moved there. I liked the fact that the neighbors never asked questions or talked to one another.

I got downtown and parked in a lot a few blocks away from Second and Broadway, the dope capital of Los Angeles. There were mostly bag hustlers hanging out by the juice stand, but they couldn't score an ounce, so I didn't even call them over. I walked down to Third Street, window shopping. I was in no hurry. Someone would eventually show me who I would be able to make a connection with. While I was looking at a radio in one of the shops, I spotted Chuey on the other side of the street. I gave a whistle and motioned for him to come over. I raised my head up, but my eyes stayed on the same level. I put one hand out in front of me, palm up, a quick gesture that said, "What's happening?"

I knew Chuey from jail. He was a tall Mexican drug addict with a quick sense of humor. I had never heard anything bad about him, but I couldn't be sure about anyone who used dope. Chuey walked across the street to where I was waiting.

"Let's take a walk. You doing any good?" I asked.

"Like what?"

"On the smack side."

"How much?"

"A couple of pieces?"

"When do you want them?"

"Right now."

"I got to make a call first."

"Have you used any of it? I don't want talcum powder."

"It's alright. It holds ya a long time."

"What color?"

"Brown."

"Okay. Make the call. If you hook it up, I'll throw you out with a spoon."

"That's hip."

Chuey went into the drug store to make the call and I followed him. I browsed and faked around until he had completed the call. I walked out as he followed a few steps behind me.

"It's alright. He said I can do it anytime before five o'clock. He shuts down at five and wouldn't sell a cap to his mommy after that."

"How much?"

"Two and a quarter an ounce."

"You sure it's good?"

"It's not bad. It'll hold ya. I can put it together in a half hour with no hang-ups."

"Alright. I'll give you five bills. You can have half a yard for putting it together."

We walked to the parking lot where I was parked. I sat in the car and brought out five one hundred dollar bills and a pencil and handed them both to Chuey. "Here, write your number down."

Chuey wrote it down, handed it back to me and said, "What did you do, rob a bank?"

"No, my sick aunt finally died and left me some dough."

"You fucker." Chuey chuckled and walked off. "I'll see you in a half hour."

"Right here. I'm going to walk around for a few minutes, but I'll be back here in half an hour."

"See ya." Chuey disappeared around the corner.

I had lots of money now. I wouldn't have parted so easily with that much money a week ago when I was broke. I didn't like the vibes in the last few minutes of the transaction, though. Chuey's attitude wasn't quite natural. After about ten minutes I stopped by a restaurant and decided to call the number Chuey gave me.

"Hello. Is Chuey around?"

"You must have the wrong number. No one by that name lives here."

I dropped the receiver and was out of the phone booth quick. I ran down First Street to Broadway and then on to Second. I was in the thick of it now. There were a few guys standing by the juice bar.

"You seen Chuey around?"

The two guys gave me half a smile and the first one said, "You didn't give him any bread, did you?"

"Why?"

"Where you been, Woody? He's been burnin' people down here for a month. Mostly boot and shoe dope fiends."

"You know where I can find him?"

"He's got an old lady lives over near Sunset and Western,

and he hangs around the sandwich joint."

"The one on Western above Sunset?"

"Yeah, that's the spot."

"Look, I'm going to be gone for a little while. Can you hook up a piece when I get back?"

"I can do it. You should have seen me first."

"Is there any chance he'll come back here? I don't mean today. Say a week, two weeks, a month?"

"Yeah, he'll be back. I just can't figure him burnin' you. Maybe he didn't. Like I said, he's been burnin' dope fiends and punks. But you, you're a different story."

"You going to be around?"

"I'll be here. If I'm not, I'll be right back."

"All right."

"Thanks. I'll see you in an hour or so."

I walked back to the parking lot as fast as I could without looking conspicuous. Before I got into the car I opened the trunk and took out a hunting knife which I always carried there. I put it in my waistband and got into the car, paid the parking lot attendant and drove off. In a few minutes I was in Hollywood. I parked on Sunset, got out and walked around the corner. I strolled into the restaurant and saw Chuey sitting in a corner booth, loaded. I took in everything in one glance. There was a counter man and a middle-aged waitress. One guy was sitting with Chuey. No threat there. Two more people were in the place, no partners of Chuey. I walked straight to him and said, "Hey, Chuey, what's going on?"

Chuey almost swallowed his coffee cup but was smart enough to know his only chance was to keep his head.

"Did you give up the money yet?" I asked. I knew Chuey was stalling for time. "I'm sick, Chuey, and those greasy stoves are killing me. Let's wait outside."

"If you want to, it's cool," he replied.

I faked at being sick knowing Chuey would try to run when we hit the front door. I stayed close to him while he paid the check, just in case he tried to bolt out the back door through the kitchen. When Chuey turned around I looked in his eyes, and wondered, how could I have missed it? It was all there. The weakness and fear showed on his face like a road map.

I walked out first with my back to him, then reached inside my shirt and eased the knife out. Without giving Chuey a chance, I grabbed him by the shirt with my left hand, shook him like a rag doll and made like I was slashing him across the chest with it. Once, twice, three times. The knife cut his shirt open in a zigzag pattern, scattering buttons onto the pavement. Chuey screamed like a woman. Still holding him with my left hand, I pulled hard and threw him to the ground. He grabbed his chest to see if he was cut, and I kicked him in the head. I reached down and quickly snatched my money from his wallet.

I ran around the corner and got into my car. I started the car quickly, pulled out of the way of an oncoming car and was gone before anyone knew what happened.

CHAPTER 5

I drove straight back to Second and Broadway and parked. I was beginning to get sick. There was dope at home, but I didn't want to go back to North Hollywood.

I got out of my car and walked down Broadway. I would often get overly sensitive to people when I was sick. I used to look at the poor people walking down Broadway, people I knew would live there and be poor until the day they died. My heart would fill up with pity for these people. I wanted to rush up to them, put my arms around them and tell them not to stay there; to leave Broadway and go some other place in the world, any place but there. Funny how I never felt these emotions when I was fixed, I never noticed people or the way they really looked, I never looked into their eyes. It frightened me whenever I thought of coming down. I didn't want to deal with any emotions, good or bad.

I got to the juice stand and spotted one of the two guys I had talked to earlier. I knew one of them vaguely and asked, "Where do I know you from?"

"I used to deal around the Digger when you were playing there a couple years ago."

"You still got the bag?"

"I got it."

"What are you dealing?"

"Anything from quarters on up."

"How long does it take to do it?"

"Five minutes from here."

"What's the stuff like?"

"It's good."

"How good?"

"Real good."

"Color?"

"Brown."

"Dark or light?"

"Dark."

"I won't give the dough up in front. I'll have to go with you."

"That's alright with me. Where are you parked?"

"In the parking lot on First and Hill."

"Alright, go to your car and I'll follow."

"I just don't want anyone seeing us leave together. The heat will roast two dope fiends faster than they would one walking by himself."

"You're right. Let's go."

We left the juice stand, with me twenty or thirty yards in

front.

"What's your name?"

"Lee."

"I guess I should know who I'll have to fuck up if anything funny happens, "I said, half joking.

"Yeah okay. Drive down First Street over the bridge. I'll get the stuff and you can wait with the bread. When I show with the stuff, you can pay me. My cousin's got the bag. I deal with her and she'll trust me."

We went over the bridge, down four blocks and turned left.

"You want to wait at that drive-in? I'll be five minutes."

"What's the price?"

"Two and a half."

"You sure it's dark brown and good?"

"It's good."

I drove into the drive-in and parked, and Lee got out.

"I'll be five minutes, no longer."

I felt secure. If Lee was going to burn me, he would have wanted front money. In about five minutes Lee showed up and got in the car. I pulled out five hundred dollars and gave them to him. He handed me two loose condoms. I held them in my hands and bounced them up and down a little.

"It's a good count. You know anywhere we can fix? I'm spreading."

"Yeah, we could do it up at my cousin's house."

"Well, why in the fuck did you make me wait at the drive-in?"

"She doesn't like me to bring anyone around. Have you got an outfit?"

"I got that with me."

"Take a right on that street," he pointed, "and it's the third house from the corner."

I started the car, made a right and stopped at the third house. We both got out and walked around to the back of the house where there was another house about a quarter the size of the one in front. Lee knocked twice and the blind came up.

"It's alright."

A woman opened the door.

"This is a good friend of mine," Lee said as we walked through the door.

"You could have fooled me. He looks more like the heat than the heat."

"I've had a hard time scoring because of that," I said.

"Yeah. You sure don't look like a dope fiend. What do you want?"

"We just want to use the pad for a few minutes."

"Christ, Lee, I told you I didn't want a shooting gallery in my house."

"Well, I wouldn't bring just anybody over here. This is a real good friend of mine."

"Go on, but give me some air. I don't like it. It's inviting trouble."

"We won't be but a minute and I won't ask you again."

When I heard the okay, I pulled out one of the ounces from my pants pocket and started to untie the rubber. Lee went in the kitchen and got a glass of water.

"I'm spreading, Lee. Take as much as you want. Just don't be such a pig that you over-jolt."

It didn't take long. I knew right where to go. I handed the eyedropper with the spike on it to Lee and motioned with my hand toward the stuff. I took more than I usually did and finished up quick. I took the glass back to the kitchen and washed out the outfit and came back in wiping my arm until the blood was gone. We both stood up, thanked Lee's cousin and left. As we drove off, Lee's head was on his chest. I took one look at him and didn't like what I saw.

"Come on, Lee, straighten your ass out. You're going to put us in the growler with that nod shit of yours."

Lee straightened up at once. "Yeah, alright. I'm sorry. That was some good shit."

"Can I drop you someplace? I don't want to go downtown with that shit in the car."

"You can drop me on the other side of the bridge in that little bar. I'll have a few beers and ride this motherfucker out."

I pulled up on the other side of the street and stopped.

"Where do I reach you if I want to do it again?"

"I'll be at the market, same place you saw me today."

"Do you always take people to your cousin's house?"

"No."

"How many trips do you make over there in a day?"

"I don't make any. I plant in town and sell it from there. You're the only one I've sold an ounce to. I do about twenty balloons a day. It keeps me going. Don't worry. Her joint ain't hot. Is that what you were getting at?"

"Well, connections don't last long. Especially taking people to the pad."

"Well, the only reason I took you is that I've been hearing about you for a long time and it's all been good. I knew there wasn't any risk with you."

"Man, it's your business. I'm not trying to tell you how to run things. Go on, get out of here. I got to get home or my old lady will think I'm in the bucket."

"Drop by. I'll do it for you anytime."

"Alright, later."

I drove off with a secure feeling. I had two ounces of drugs and a pocketful of money at home. Maybe I would give kicking a try when the two pieces were gone. I made a mental note to see my grandmother and leave her some money. I always made sure I took care of her whenever I had some extra dough in my pockets. It was the least I could do considering all she had done for me when I was little.

I started thinking about the times with her when I was five years old, which were some of the happiest moments of my life. She and my mother weren't living together at that time; she was renting a little room on Maple Street in downtown Los Angeles. Sometimes, she would take me for the weekend, and when we'd get to her house, she would always have a big gallon of apple cider there because she knew how much I liked it. We would play checkers, and she would turn on the radio and play classical music, and hum along to me as we played. I used to be in such ecstasy when I was with her then.

Eventually, she and my mother got a one-bedroom apartment together in Hollywood, and that's when she really became a strong influence on my life. My mother was a piano player who played in these shitkicker bars; she was gone every night, and slept most of the day. So, my grandmother at that time went to work in a millinery store, and on Saturday nights when they both had to work, my mom would drop me off at the Apollo Theater on Hollywood Boulevard for the afternoon. After the movie, my grandmother would pick me up, and she would always buy me knackwurst and cream cheese and cream soda, and we'd go home after the movie and eat dinner together.

Some mornings, when she didn't have to go to work until ten o'clock, she'd take me with her to the playground at the junior high school a couple of blocks from our house. She taught me how to do a kip on the horizontal bar, and then got me doing chin-ups, and she'd give me a little reward when I could do one more, and I used to just really try to get one more every time I did 'em until I got up to twenty, and she would give me a nickel or a dime or whatever she could afford, and it spurred me on. I just wanted to do so much for her, because I loved her so dearly.

She took me all sorts of places and always introduced me to everyone. I had never known my father, and my mother had died when I was young, so she was my family. Since we were poor, she would have to save for months to go to the theatre. We would take the streetcar to the Shrine Auditorium where we would hear music, great music, the masters. She would explain to me in her uneducated way what the music meant to her. She could communicate to me and, more than the words, I understood the feeling behind what she said. She was surely the main influence in my life, the one who had formed my heart.

She had a certain type of nobility about her, the way she talked, the way she walked. When she posed for a picture, she would always bring her instep up, or she would tilt her right foot, which was the style in those days, and lean at a forty-five degree angle. She was so elegant when I was with her, and by being with her, I felt elegant myself.

I felt a difference with her I never felt with anyone else, not even my mother. I loved my mother too, but she was mostly unavailable due to her alcoholism. Sometimes, she and my grandmother would have fights over what each thought was best for me. But my grandmother always accepted that it was my mother's decision that stood. I don't know how she managed to overrule my grandmother, and her decisions were not always the right ones. But she gave me a piece of my heart, too, that I couldn't have gotten from any other mother, which was so much different from my grandmother's.

CHAPTER 6

All of a sudden, I saw a flashing red light glaring in my rearview mirror. I had been lost in my thoughts when the black and white had gotten behind me, but I couldn't imagine why they were hassling me. I pulled over to the right and stopped. My mind was racing. It had to be routine. I didn't go through any lights, or speed. Should I try to stash the stuff under the seat? I had it in my right hand, but decided against making a move, so I just sat there and waited for the cop to get out.

He was about twenty-three, had a short crewcut and his shoes were spit-shined, probably done by a trustee in a sub-station. He looked like he had just graduated from the academy. He approached the car stiffly, apprehensively.

"May I see your driver's license and registration slip?"

"Sure can. What did I do, Officer?" I was trying to act very innocent and clean cut.

"You don't have any brake lights."

"Well, it's my wife's car and she just uses it to take the children to school. My car's in the shop. When you have one of those Jags they're in the shop more than they're on the road."

I was sticking every bit of my personality to this asshole and still wasn't reaching him. I handed him the registration slip and my driver's license. The officer then walked back and stood silently four feet from the door in a post arms stance. I started to get out of the car to establish some kind of communication, but the cop said, "Just stay there, Mr. Woodward."

I was in a neighborhood where they would run a make on grandma getting a jaywalking ticket. My mouth was dry. The cop was watching me like a hawk watching a rabbit. All I could do was sit there and hope they weren't running a make on my record. I didn't have any tickets out, but if my make sheet came back, it was all over. I waited.

Finally the other cop got out of the car and walked toward my car. When he got to the other officer, he stopped and whispered something. I still had both ounces in my hand, waiting to make a move. Fortunately, I had large hands and could hold the two ounces without their being noticed. The first cop walked toward the car and said, "Would you get out, Mr. Woodward."

As I did, he told me to stand off to one side of the car. The other cop had his hand on his holster. The first cop started shaking down the car. I had my hands by my side, but the other cop was watching me, so I couldn't make a play. Just then, some low riders in a Chevy came speeding down the street and slammed on the brakes when they saw the black and white. The cop watching me turned when he heard the screech of the brake, and that was all I needed. I flicked the stuff with my wrist in one quick movement, and it landed close by the curb where it was dark. I knew I was going to jail but at least now it wouldn't be for possession. After a few minutes, the cop finished his investigation of the car, walked over to me and spoke in a formal attitude, "You want to roll up your sleeves?" He acted offended that he hadn't found anything in the car. I rolled up my sleeves, and the cop shined his flashlight on my arms and then in my eyes. That was all I needed. Then came the handcuffs. I took a few short steps toward the other officer, but not deliberate steps. I merely wanted to pull the other officer away from the vicinity of the stuff. "May I talk to you a minute?"

The cop who just examined me for marks followed me, which was what I wanted. "What do you want?"

"Well, I've been using for a while, but in the last month I've been clean. I haven't had a fix in a month and I'm trying to quit. Why don't you guys give me a break? If you'd have caught me a month ago you would have been doing me a favor putting me in jail, but not now. I'm not hooked and I'm working on a job. I haven't had a fix in thirty-four days. All these are old marks. I've been working at a dairy in South Gate. You could call my boss."

The officer who first looked at my arms said, "Come on, don't bullshit me. Your eyes are pinned. You're loaded right now."

"No, I'm not. I just got through working twelve hours and I'm tired. I've been working ten to twelve hours a day for the past month. Sure, I'm an addict, but I've been off the stuff for over a month now. My wife had a baby on the eighth of last month, and I haven't had a fix since. If you take me to jail for marks, the only ones who are going to be hurt by it are my wife and kid. Come on, man, give me a break. I'm really trying to straighten out my life. If you call my boss he'll tell you I've been working every day and staying home every night." I knew he wouldn't call, but I tried to get all the mileage I could out of the story. "My boss is my wife's brother and when I started working for him he told me he'd give me a chance if I stopped using, and when I saw my baby in the hospital I knew I couldn't go on leading the kind of life I had been living. I talked to my brother-in-law the same night and asked him to give me a chance at an honest job. He told me if I was really serious he'd try it out, and he did. All I'm asking you guys for is a chance. I know I still have some marks on my arm from before, and you guys could take me downtown if you wanted to and make the case stick, but I'm really trying to make it." I was giving them my best material. If they took me to jail, I could forget about the two ounces by the curb.

"Come on, your eyes are like pins. You've fixed in the last two hours."

"My eyes are always pinned whether I'm fixed or straight. I'll make a deal with you. You take me to hospital and I'll take a urine test and pay for it. If it comes out positive, I'll go to jail gladly."

I had no compunction telling them anything if it would work and it was double sweet when it did. If I could have put a story on them before they ran the make on me, I would have had a chance, but in this goddamned neighborhood they ran the make first and listened to stories later.

Up until this point there had only been one cop asking the questions. The cop who was driving hadn't said anything but had been hanging onto each word. I could tell it was coming, I could just feel it. Finally, the quiet one walked over to me and said, "You want to help yourself? Give us your connection."

"I told you I haven't used any drugs in over thirty days and connections move around; they don't stay in one place long. You guys know that."

"I know if you needed some dope in this city you'd be able to get it, so you take a few minutes to figure out where to send us and if you can't, we'll take a trip to the glass house."

While he was saying this he looked right at me. I was angry at myself for talking to them in the first place. What I felt now went beyond contempt—it was total hatred.

The cop was still looking at me. "Were you able to remember anyone?"

I looked at the cop's name plate and saw the name McNally. "Yes, I have, as a matter of fact. Well, you guys got me, that's for sure. I guess I'll have to tell you everything. You see, I was connecting from a big fatass bitch in East LA called mommy McNally and she had a fruity son on the force..."

CHAPTER 7

The jail was always the same. The cops came and went but the jail remained the same. Misery seemed to seep out of the walls. For some it was the end of the line, and some just passed through, but the misery always hung in the air like the ever-present scent of cockroach spray and strong disinfectant.

I was tired and picked out a lower bunk in the corner of the jail. At least I wasn't sick and kicking, that was something to be thankful for. I rolled out the pancake-thin mattress and lay down.

The lions were roaring and huge, but the elephants were even bigger. Grandmother handed me peanuts to feed the elephants, but she wouldn't let me feed the lions, which seemed very silly to me—they needed food, too. She was wearing a large picture hat. She was a small woman, but there was a power about her that made her appear larger. From her years in the circus, she had developed a stately walk that commanded respect. She had a gentle intensity, a combination of spirituality and the worldliness of circus life. She had overly large blue eyes, which I inherited as well. I was the light of her

*life and had been from the moment I was born. Her husband
had died in a trapeze accident and she had never remarried.*

*Grandmother always got free tickets to the circus and knew
almost everyone there. I especially liked the clowns, and she
introduced me to all of them. Sometimes she would talk circus
talk, which I didn't understand but then she would very
carefully explain what each word meant.*

*She led me out of the big tent, out in the back to the
smaller tents, the ones used for dressing rooms. It started to
rain, lightly at first, but in a matter of seconds it was pouring.
She took my hand and we started back to the Big Top. The
animals were nervous and excited. The wind came up out of
nowhere, rattling the tents so violently it appeared they were
going to collapse. People were coming out of the Big Top and
running to get out in the open. The lions were roaring and the
lightning struck so close the thunder hurt my ears. By now the
circus was a mob, and we became separated. I was pushed and
shoved and kicked, but finally managed to get under one of the
animal cages, where I stayed for what seemed like hours.
When it was over, I started looking for her. At first I just
looked, not saying anything. I walked over all the circus
grounds but she was nowhere to be found. I was crying. In
between sobs, with the tears running down my cheeks, I was
screaming, "Idamommy, Idamommy, Idamommy—"*

"The cop wants you up front."

"What?"

"The cop said to roll 'em up."

"Alright, thanks."

I couldn't shake the nightmare. I stood up, but didn't move.
I just stood there.

The cop brought me out of it.

"Alright, asshole. I ain't calling you again."

I quickly rolled up my mattress and blankets and walked
briskly to the gate to be released. My grandmother was strong
in my mind; I had to remember to call her.

As I reached the last door and was released, I saw Sylvia
waiting for me. I wondered if she'd brought along some dope.

My rest was over. I was back in the jungle, on my mark when I hit the door.

"Did Carl do it?"

"Yes, but I had to put up half."

"Half?"

"That's the only way he'd take you out and the bail was $5,000."

"For what?"

"They filed driving under the influence and marks."

"Those rotten fuckers."

"You must have gotten smart with them."

"No more than usual."

"Did you give them your 'recommended the penitentiary' line?"

"Of course. You mean Carl made you come up with $2,500?"

"He did."

"Well that fuckin' dough is iced for six months. We'll just have to replace it. By the way, what time is it?"

"Four-thirty."

"Wow. Come on. We've got to catch a cab." We walked out on the street.

"Aren't we going to get the car out of the impound?"

"We'll get it later. Right now I've got to get to first and Los Angeles Streets and see about two ounces I had to plant there."

Just then a cab drove by and I hailed it down.

It was only a few blocks but every minute meant something now. When we took a right on Los Angeles, I saw a street cleaning machine coming my way and my heart sped up. I looked out the window and checked the street. It was clean as a whistle. We got to First Street and I could see that the street cleaner had already been there.

"What's wrong?"

"We just lost two ounces to the City. I had to throw it by the curb. If you'd have been twenty minutes sooner."

"I got there as fast as I could."

"It's not your fault. It's been a bad day."

"Where to now?" the cabbie asked.

"Take us to the impound garage over on Fig."

The cab pulled a U-turn and headed back. I didn't say a word until we got to the police garage. "Give me some dough."

I paid the driver with a dollar tip. It took about half an hour to get the car. I asked Sylvia if the stuff was home with the outfit. She nodded. I didn't say another thing on the way home. She sensed my mood and didn't say anything either. I was sick and just had enough juice left to not show it at the garage.

We drove straight home. After being in the cage all night, the place actually looked good to me. My horn was there and I knew there was stuff, so the overall picture wasn't that bad. And there was still money left. I went straight to the bathroom and told Sylvia to get the stuff, which she had stashed in the stove. I put in almost a full spoon; the week before it had only been a half.

Sylvia watched with dull eyes but didn't say anything as I fixed. She watched me pull the needle out of my arm and after a few seconds she said, "Honey, what is it about the stuff that makes us keep coming back?"

At that precise moment the heroin hit me. I smiled with my eyes, "It's that feeling, right there."

CHAPTER 8

Sundays were bad days for drug addicts. The connections went underground and weren't standing on the corners. All the stores were closed, which left very little to steal, so if you didn't have your money or connection together, you were in trouble.

I had just enough dope to get Sylvia and myself going. Hopefully, I wouldn't have a problem with Lee's cousin, but there was always that chance. There was always so much at stake every day—a stopped-up needle, a lost phone number, someone not being on time—simple things like that could mean disaster.

I dressed quickly with one thought, one purpose. "Shall I go with you?" she asked.

"No, I'm only going to be a little while," I replied. I felt confident I could handle any situation by myself and didn't like to take her with me because of the responsibility.

"Where do you have to go?"

"A few blocks into the east side. I'll only be a half hour, maybe forty minutes. No longer."

I put my arm around her on the way out, an affectionate gesture one would bestow on a sister. Sex was a thing of the past. I hated the thought of coming. It was such a chore, I didn't like the feeling anymore. Most of the time I didn't think of it. Sylvia had accepted my lack of interest and didn't take it personally because she understood it was the heroin, not her; nevertheless, it was no doubt frustrating for her.

I stopped in front of the market for my usual breakfast, a quart of milk and two or three candy bars. As I finished the first one, I saw two narcs driving in the opposite direction. I turned my head quickly. They knew me well. If they saw me, I was going to jail. I couldn't outrun them in the car, but I could get away on foot.

The goddamned money had changed my style. If I'd been broke and couldn't make bail, I would have been gone by now. There was nothing I wouldn't do to keep from kicking in jail. Running over fences, through houses of people I didn't know, in and out of stores, right through traffic at full speed, into and over pedestrians, whatever it took to get away. The command "Stop or we'll shoot" never even slowed me down. There was no chance I wouldn't take. But now it was different.

O'Rourke was the first one out of the car. He told me to put my hands on the steering wheel. I hated O'Rourke more than any other cop because he was a bully who picked his shots. O'Rourke would beat you up when you were handcuffed, kick you, scratch you, bite you, step on you or even fight you head up if he had a winner. He'd make a dope fiend whore cop his joint and then take her to jail anyway.

"Alright, Woody, out of that car and keep your hands in sight." O'Rourke had his gun out.

I moved very slowly. I knew if I gave O'Rourke the slightest reason to shoot me he would.

As I got out of the car, O'Rourke grabbed my arm and pushed me up against the car hard. I pulled my arm away viciously. O'Rourke shook me down hoping to find a gun. Not finding one, he then more meticulously looked for drugs or an outfit, something he could charge me with.

"Everything out of your pockets and put it all on the hood."

I produced five hundred-dollar bills, a pack of cigarettes and my wallet, and placed everything on the hood. I knew now I should have run. Both cops were forty pounds overweight and couldn't have lasted two blocks. I would have blown the car, but that was better than having to go for another bail.

"Where did you get all this money, Woody?"

"Why, is there a law against it?"

"I suppose you got it working," he said sarcastically.

"Who are you, the fucking IRS?"

"Turn around, you sonofabitch." He pulled out his handcuffs and put them on me and locked them down as tight as they would go. He grabbed me by the arms and tried to throw me into the car.

"Watch your fuckin' hands, you pig bastard."

"I'll watch my hands, you sonofabitch. I got a little something for you when we get downtown."

"What the fuck do you mean 'a little something'?" I asked.

"You'll see when we get downtown," O'Rourke replied.

I was infuriated, but the hate I felt inside made me extremely calm. Hate was my obsession; I was consumed by it.

Nothing else mattered. I could kill O'Rourke easily. I could kill him in the police station in front of a hundred witnesses. The consequences were of no importance, only satisfying the hate.

I looked into O'Rourke's eyes, and we glared at each other for nearly a full minute. I was the first to speak. "Let me tell you something so you know where I'm coming from. If you handcuff me and fuck me up when we get downtown, don't do a half-assed job, take it all the way because if I can still use my index finger to pull the trigger, I'll get the biggest fucking shotgun in the world and blow your goddamned brains all over the street. That's a motherfuckin' promise, O'Rourke."

"You're nothing but a *punk,* Woody, like all the rest of the drug addicts. You'd sell your own mother for a fix." O'Rourke knew what the word "punk" meant: a weak, unprincipled bastard who would let someone fuck him in the ass for a pack of cigarettes. He also knew the effect it would have on me so he accented the word.

"You want to get it on head up, you and me in the cell together? We'll see enough who the punk is."

O'Rourke said to the other cop, "Let's go. Paul. Let's get this asshole downtown and booked for marks and driving under the influence."

I didn't say a word on the way to jail. When we got in the booking office, O'Rourke took off my handcuffs and started to leave. "Are you leaving, O'Rourke?" I asked.

O'Rourke just glared at me and said, "I'll make it a point to see you."

I smiled.

CHAPTER 9

Sylvia got there a half hour after I called her. Same procedure as the night before: signing bail papers, going to the police garage for the car. The hassle with O'Rourke and the jail had me drained, and I could feel the sickness coming on. But after I got to the car I felt more secure.

"How far is it, honey?"

"Not far. Maybe five minutes."

"Order a hamburger or something while I'm gone."

"Are you kidding?"

"Alright, I'll be right back. Give me some dough."

"How much?"

"Five hundred."

"We only got tens and twenties left."

"Well, count it out for Christ's sake."

When she got to four-fifty, I said, "That will do. I'll be as fast as I can."

I counted out the money and gave Lee an extra twenty. "Here's a double saw for being a sweetheart."

"Thanks, Woody."

I turned and walked away. As I approached Sylvia, I extended my palm horizontally and moved it back and forth across my chest. This was the "George" sign, which meant everything was taken care of.

"He'll be here in a minute with the stuff. I'm going to try and fix that fucking brake light. Sit behind the wheel and when I tell you to step on the brakes, step on them."

"Okay."

I got under the car. "Okay."

She stepped on the brake. I connected the loose wire, got out from underneath the car and walked around to the rear.

"Okay, honey, hit the brakes again." She did and the lights went on.

"Man, that's a scream. A wire comes off and I'm down a

thousand potatoes for openers, not counting the lawyers. But it could have been worse." Just then Lee walked up.

"Hey, hey. Get in the car. This is my old lady. Sylvia, Lee."

"Hi."

Lee handed me the stuff. I didn't inspect it this time. I knew I was dealing with people. "Thanks, Lee. We're going to blow."

"I understand. I'll see you around the market."

"Cool. You know, I wouldn't have come out here by myself, but I didn't know where to find you."

"That's cool. I told my cousin and she said you can drop by anytime."

"Has she got a number?"

"She won't talk on the phone, hasn't even got one. She has a thing against phones."

"Okay, Lee, if I want to do it I'll stop by later."

I didn't get sick very often but when I did, I got horny. Sex was the last thing on my mind when I had heroin in my veins, but let me go six hours without it and everything with hair on it reminded me of pussy. I put my hand on Sylvia's thigh and moved it gently up to her crotch. Christ! I had forgotten what that was like. She moved her legs apart slowly, and I ran my hand down her leg and then back up under her dress until I had my hand right on it.

"If you aren't going to take care of business, don't start nothing."

"Just call me Business Jones."

"Well, Mr. Jones, can you hold out on fixing while we make love?"

"I can make it. It makes all the difference in the world when we know we got it. Christ! I might even be able to hold off in the morning, too."

"Well, you don't have to lose your head."

In spite of our sickness we were both feeling good. I laughed and said, "Am I your candy man?"

As we drove down the street I hummed a Bird tune and then got carried away improvising on the changes. I stopped and looked at Sylvia. She seemed more secure now and smiled and said, "Hurry."

I started scatting again and even put my arm around her. "Hey, girl, you feel pretty good."

"How would you know? —C'mon, I'm sorry."

Sylvia looked at me laughingly. It was good to laugh. Whether you're hooked in China, New York City or Los Angeles, heroin is a cinch to do three things: it will take your sense of humor away and make it impossible to laugh, soon after that the sex goes; and then comes the one advantage of heroin—as long as you're using, you'll never catch a cold.

We drove up into the carport and parked. Sylvia was about to get out, but I stopped her with my hand on her shoulder. I turned her around gently and kissed her. It was not one of my usual kisses. I ran my tongue over her teeth and around her gums. She opened her mouth wide, and put her hand between my legs.

"My word! What do we have here?"

"Christmas, my love."

"Yeah, once a year."

"You ought to be on TV with your witty ass. Come on, let's go upstairs."

When we reached the apartment, I went straight to the bathroom.

"What are you going to do?"

"I'm going to the bathroom."

"For what?"

"Look, I'm going to take just a small one to get these chills off me."

"Can't you wait for a few minutes?"

"Listen, if there's one thing I'm hip to, it's my capacity. Now, if I just take a small jolt it'll take the chills off me and keep me from throwing up. I know how much to take."

"Do what you want. Fix the whole fucking bag. I don't give a damn what you do."

I shut the door and started preparing the stuff. While I was drawing it up, I said, "Sylvia, come on."

She came into the bathroom holding her left bicep with her right arm. It was faster than using a tie. I hit her fast. She walked away slowly into the other room and lay down on the bed.

I wiped the back of the spoon off and dipped it into the rubber. I got too much in the spoon and was about to put some back, but instead I dipped it again, putting still more in. I drew it all up. There was so much it went up the pacifier. I tied the handkerchief around my arm, and the needle found its way in with a couple of gentle taps from my index finger. The whole room came up before me and I experienced a wave of nausea I couldn't control. There was barely enough time to raise the toilet seat. The candy bars and milk I had that morning were on their way to Long Beach. My head was throbbing, but everything felt good. On the whole, everything seemed to be all right. I would cool out Sylvia. The beefs could be straightened out with some dough.

Maybe I'll get into playing again, I thought. I've got those short stories I can get into, and in a few hours if I feel like another fix, I got it all here. Yeah. I'll get everything straightened out. I've just got to take it easy.

"You alright?" Sylvia asked from the living room.

"I'll be right out."

"What are you going to do now, lover man?" she asked sarcastically.

"What do you mean?"

"You know what I mean. That Valentino shit you were talking in the car. Asking me if you were my candy man."

"Honey, I'm sorry. I guess I took more than I should have. Would you like some head?"

"I would like some rod, have you got one of those? Maybe you could rent one. That's it, rent one. It would be the only way you'll get one. Or maybe I'll rent one. That seems to be the only possibility."

"I told you I just took too much."

"You couldn't wait another half hour. You've got my fucking pants wet half the time and you can't wait to make a pig of yourself. That's all you think about, anyway—yourself. You could give a fuck about taking care of me. Do I want some head? That's a joke. If you weren't serious, why did you start playing around with me in the car? You know what heroin has done to you? I'll tell you—"

"I'm not interested in hearing your point of view. I know what it's done."

"Well, just answer me one question—"

"God dammit, Sylvia, shut up. We've had a bitch of a day but we finally got fixed. Can't you just relax instead of grinding me out?"

"Just answer me one question before you start reading those wonderful books of yours."

"I don't want to fucking bother with questions now. Have you got it?"

"One question and I'll shut up."

"For Christ's sake what? What is it?"

"What do you have me around for?"

"Get off it, for Christ's sake."

"I just want to know."

"I don't want to talk about it now." I lay down, picked up a worn copy of Dostoevsky's short stories and started to read, but I was thinking about her question. Deep down inside I knew I couldn't answer it.

CHAPTER 10

"What time do you see the attorney?
"Four-thirty. He's in court today."
"Don't you think you should get ready? Maybe get dressed

up a little bit?"

I went into the bathroom and fixed. When I came out I got my clothes out of the closet. My only blue suit and my white shirt needed pressing.

"For Christ's sake, shave. You look like Pete the Tramp."

"You don't think I can get by?" I ran my hand over my face.

Sylvia shook her head.

I walked back to the bathroom reluctantly, shaved, came out and finished dressing. I knew I looked bad. I had a lost look, and my eyes were a dead giveaway.

"I'll be back in a couple of hours."

"You want me to go with you?"

"No. Clean up the house. It looks like Fifth Street."

"You don't make it any better the way you throw your clothes around."

"Later."

I walked down the corridor wondering how I had wound up in an apartment like this. The carport was littered with tin cans, bottles, and papers. There was no relief in the car. It was a continuation of the apartment, shit all over. What a fucking existence, and hardly any money left. I hated having to go downtown. It was so crowded, and crawling with cops.

The attorney's office was on Hill Street. I parked in the Pershing Garage and took the elevator to the eighth floor. I registered with the secretary and waited my turn. I heard my name and turned around slowly. It was Jimmy James, the set-up man. Jimmy could set up jobs, but didn't have the balls to pull them off. He was an Okie, but a damn hip one. He could wear bib overalls and sound like he had just driven in from the open range that day, or he could put on a businessman's suit and play a role so straight you'd think he was a bank president.

"What you doin' here?"

"I'm trying to fix a case for a friend of mine."

"Can you?"

"You can fix anything with Herman Royce if your money's

right."

"Is he expensive?"

"Yeah. He's high but if he tells you he can do, he can. And he won't bullshit you. He's a good man to have in your corner."

"What are you doing now?" Jimmy asked.

"I don't have anything going that's going to make me a millionaire."

"How would you like to make some money?"

"What have you got?"

"I got a robbery that's almost ripe and the money is big."

"How big?"

"Ten grand, your end."

"When can we get together?"

"Why don't you come out tonight and meet a couple of guys."

"What time?"

"About nine. There's a bar on Paramount just as you get off the freeway called The Hucksters. I call it my office, that's where I work out of."

"Alright. I'll be there."

"Mr. Woodward," the secretary said.

"Yes?"

"You can go right in."

"Thank you."

As I got up, I told Jimmy, "I'll see you at nine."

I walked into the plush office. The door must have been fifteen feet high. There was a beige chaise lounge covering the entire width of the room and a chrome and glass coffee table. All the fixtures were chrome, even the wastepaper basket. The wall-to-wall carpet was a beautiful rust color and a good two inches thick.

"Sit down, Mr. Woodward. This is the first time you've been up here, isn't it?"

"Yes, it is."

"I was in the Richfield Building for years."

"I'm familiar with the Richfield Building."

"I moved here two months ago and I really like it. It's very comfortable to work in. And now, what can I do for you?"

"Well, I have two cases of driving under the influence and I don't want to go to jail on either."

"Nobody wants to go to jail and that's what I'm here for. There are some cases beyond my control; however, driving under the influence isn't one of them. Who are the arresting officers?"

"I got stopped by a squad car on one and O'Rourke, a narc, got me on the other one."

"That's no problem."

"What about O'Rourke? He hates my guts."

"Just come up with $3,500 for each case and don't worry about it."

"I don't want a jail sentence."

"I know. The cases will be dismissed."

"Well, you're my man. How about giving you a three thousand retainer and the rest in full before I go to court?"

"That's fine, Mr. Woodward. When is your court appearance?"

"The eighth of next month."

"Good, you can leave the retainer with my secretary. She'll give you a receipt and I'll see you on the eighth."

I thanked Royce, and walked out thinking my two cases probably wouldn't pay for the door I just walked through.

Jimmy Jones was still outside and asked, "How'd you like him?"

"He's direct. Seven thousand dollars direct. I got two hundred and fifty left after the retainer."

"Well, if he gets the job done—"

"Yeah, you're right. That's all that counts. Look, I'll see you tonight. I'd like to start working on that seven grand."

I walked to the car feeling a lot better than when I had left the house. The drive home wasn't nearly as boring as I thought it would be. There was hope in my life now.

I drove into the funky carport, parked and went upstairs. I tapped a dope fiend code on the door and Sylvia let me in.

CHAPTER 11

The house was torn apart. The mattress had been pulled off the box springs and was in the center of the room, and all the drawers had been emptied on the floor.

"What happened? Where's my horn?"

"They got everything."

"Who the fuck is 'they'?"

"I don't know, honey. I went to the market, and when I came back I found the house like this."

"How long ago?"

"Twenty minutes, maybe a half hour."

I inspected the windows. "They didn't come in through the windows. They knew what they were looking for. Did they get the dope?"

"Everything. I had the outfit stashed outside with two balloons, but they got everything else."

"Give me the outfit and the stuff."

"What are you going to do?"

"What would you like me to do, call City Hall? I'm going to fix first and then think about it. Someone who knew us did this, it had to be. Come on, get the works."

I went into the bathroom and in a minute or so I came out, very loaded. I sat down in the middle of the room with my head in one hand. Without looking up I said, "I didn't tell anyone, not anyone, that we lived here. Have you?"

"No."

"Think! This isn't the work of some dumb kids. They came right through the front door with a 'loid,' and no professional burglar is going to give this joint a second glance. Come on, God dammit, think! Who have you told? Who has seen you come in? Anyone? Anyone at all?"

She had a pensive look on her face.

"Well?"

"A week ago Mary gave me a ride home."

"Mary? Mary who?"

"Freddie's old lady."

"Freddie Cole?"

"Yes."

"That's fuckin' wonderful. You let Freddie Cole's old lady drive you home. You got any idea what kind of character Freddie Cole's got?" There was a pause. "God dammit, answer me. You know what kind of fuckin' punk he is, not to even mention his old lady who'd turn a trick with a donkey? He'd rip off his grandmother. Christ, Sylvia, how could you let that scumbag know where we live? Goddamn you!"

"Well, I—"

"Don't say a fuckin' word. Don't try to clean it up. You can't. You remember, goddamn you! You remember every fuckin' word you spoke to that bitch, and no bullshit! No ad libbing to make yourself look good. I want the fucking truth out of you. Where did you run into her?"

"In the market."

"Did you talk to her while you were in the market?"

"Casually."

"Casually, my fucking ass! What do you mean, casually?"

"Please, honey, don't yell. You've got me crazy. I can't remember a thing if you're going to scream at me."

I looked at her hard. "I know the first words out of that cunt's mouth were, 'How are you doing?' I want to know what you said to that."

"I said we were doing alright."

"That was the first bad move. You had to floorshow for that case of arrested intelligence. I know she asked you if you were still using. I know that subzero-IQ motherfucker asked you that, didn't she? Didn't she?"

"Yes."

"And what did you tell her?"

"I said we were getting ready to clean up and—"

"Don't give me that weak shit, Sylvia. I don't want to hear that rainwater stuff. What did you tell her about our using?"

Sylvia started to cry. She was looking at me with tears running down her cheeks. Finally, I lowered my eyes, walked over to her and put my arms around her. I knew she had said too much to Freddie's woman, but to pursue it further would only make her feel worse. I had accomplished what I had set out to do, to get to the truth of the matter. There was a feeling of hopelessness in both of us as we stood with our arms around one another.

"How much money do you have?"

"Just a couple of dollars. I took twenty to go shopping and spent all of it but a couple of bucks."

"I got about two hundred and fifty. I gave everything else to the attorney."

"I forgot to tell you. The manager was by for the rent. I didn't know if we were going to move, so I didn't pay him. I told him you were working and you'd talk to him when you came home."

I experienced another wave of panic. "I'll talk to him in the morning. Right now I'm going to sleep."

I lifted the mattress back onto the box springs. I didn't bother to straighten up the house but took off my clothes and lit a cigarette. I walked to the window.

"They must live around here. Did she buy lots of groceries, or did it look like she just stopped in for a pack of cigarettes or a soda, something like that?"

"She had two big bags."

"Then she lives in the vicinity. Can you remember what kind of car?"

"A blue Ford, old and beat up."

"Did she mention anything about where she lived?"

"No."

"Was she using?"

"I think so."

"Did you invite her up?"

"No."

"Did she see what apartment you went to?"

"There's a possibility of that."

"Just what did you say when you got ready to leave?"

"I told her we were going to be moving soon."

"I want you to know one thing, babe, that we're into the scurviest type of existence we could be in and I don't know how I got here, but I'm here, living it. You're in it with me and if you're going to be with me, you're going to have to adopt the same kind of principles I've got. The scum of the world use heroin and you don't develop character while you're using it. Sometimes I got to hold onto both balls to keep from making a concession to the scum, but I don't. In case you've forgotten it, the rules are: name, age and a 'not guilty' statement to all coppers. And you never bring those fuckin' garbage cans home, and for Christ's sake, don't ever volunteer any information to anyone. Can you handle that?"

She nodded her head up and down slowly.

CHAPTER 12

A loud bang at the door awakened me out of my twilight sleep. "Who is it?" I asked.

"The manager," came the reply from the other side of the door.

"Can you come back a little later? We're sleeping."

"I've been here once already."

The voice had a sarcastic edge to it, and I was in no mood to deal with a manager who was going to dog me for the rent. I didn't want to deal with him at all, but there was an outside chance he would call the cops if I didn't answer. I had kept him at arm's length ever since we'd moved into the apartment, usually telling Sylvia to pay the rent because I knew I couldn't take too much from the guy.

I got up slowly, and before I reached the door there was another knock, this one louder than the first. I made an effort to control myself, but was furious when I finally opened the door.

"The rent was due yesterday."

"I know. I'll get my check tomorrow and cash it on my lunch hour."

"The rent has got to be paid on time. I am not running a charity house here. I expect the rent to be paid on time."

At this point, he put his head in the door and said, "And you've got to clean up here if you want to stay. I don't want tenants who run the place down."

"Look, my lady's been sick, that's why the apartment is in such a mess."

"There's no excuse for any apartment to look this way."

"I told you, my lady's been sick."

"You call that a lady?"

He shouldn't have said that. He could have said almost anything but that. One right hand and it was over. I looked at him lying on the floor and wondered what to do. I didn't take too long making up my mind.

"Get your make-up and what clothes you can carry right now. Leave everything else. I'll stay here with him while you take your things to the car."

"What are you going to do to him?"

"I'll just make sure he stays here until we leave. Come on now, and hurry."

Sylvia didn't know where to start. I could see she couldn't get it together and said, "Honey, take it easy, get the pillowcase from the bed and put all your make-up in it. When you finish with that, fill up the other pillowcase with your clothes, okay?"

She finally got it in gear, filling both pillowcases, but then stood there confused.

"Come on, honey, take it all to the car and come right back for another load." She left, struggling with both pillowcases.

I sensed that this scene had taken too long and as Sylvia came through the door again, I pulled her to one side and whispered, "I'll meet you at the market. Drive straight there, right now."

"What about the rest of the things?"

"Leave them."

She left. I hesitated a minute. I knew the manager was going to call the cops but I really didn't care. I picked him up by the shirt and sat him in the chair. "You can do what you want about what happened here or you can forget it. In any event, it's going to cost you more than it's worth and after all, it is my word against yours."

"You hit me hard."

"You shouldn't have made that creepy crack about my old lady. You had no reason to say anything like that."

"You held me here against my will."

"Well, you just go ahead and prove that."

I walked out of the door. When I got to the street, I ran the two blocks to where Sylvia was waiting. She was excited and asked me what happened.

"Don't worry about it. It's over with. We've been threatening to move for two months, so now we've moved."

"You think he'll call the man?"

"Who cares? We got more important things to worry about now. He's the least of my worries."

She didn't have to ask where I was going. She knew.

We drove over the bridge to Fourth Street and I thought of all the bad luck we'd had since I took that safe off. Less than a week ago I thought my troubles were over. Now it seemed as though they were just beginning.

"I'll be right back." I said as I parked at the drive-in.

As I got out of the car, I saw Lee talking to two narcs in

front of his cousin's house. I ducked into the drive-in and watched for a minute. Lee had his hands in back of him, and now I could see that he was handcuffed. I went to the car and told Sylvia to come into the restaurant. We sat by the window as I filled her in on what was happening.

"If they have Lee, why are we waiting?" Sylvia asked.

"It doesn't look right. I want to see what they do."

We drank coffee and waited. In a few minutes another car appeared and stopped in front of Lee and the two narcs. I recognized one of the men who appeared as a narc. "It's getting interesting."

Lee got into the car with the two cops, and they drove up the street forty feet or so and parked. The two narcs walked down the driveway to Lee's cousin's house and a few minutes later reappeared with Lee's cousin handcuffed.

"You see that?"

"Is that Lee's cousin?"

"That's her. That rat bastard set her up."

"You don't know that."

"I know it just as much as I know I am sitting here having a cup of coffee. They probably nailed him downtown with something and to get off the hook he gave her up. Why else would he be sitting in the car with two narcs and then have the other two cops go into the house and nail her? Come on. It can't be any more clear than that. And there they go straight to the growler. They're leaving her and the other two cops behind to gaffle anybody who shows trying to score. I'll bet eight to five he won't even get booked. He'll be on the streets tonight, probably right on Second and Broadway."

"I don't think he'd set up his own cousin, honey."

"Goddamn! Sometimes you are so fucking dumb it's staggering! Come on, let's get out of here. I'm feeling bad."

We got in the car, drove to Second and Broadway and parked in a lot two blocks away. I got out and left Sylvia in the car.

"I'll do it as fast as I can."

"What are you going to get?"

"Whatever's available."

I walked through the market on the Hill Street side, bought some fruit, and casually walked over to Broadway. There wasn't anyone around so I walked down Broadway a block south to Third, and then turned around and came back. I hadn't gone twenty yards when I spotted Carl, a guy I'd known for five years. If Carl didn't have something, he would know who did. Like all drug addicts, Carl was always in and out of jail. He wasn't into any heavy action, but he had had at least fifty petty thefts. He fought so many cases it was a toss-up as to who got the most money, the lawyers or the connection.

"My main man, what are you doin' down here with the peasants? I heard you were uptown."

"Now who told you that lie? Can you do it, Carl?"

"What are you looking for?"

"A piece."

"Can't do that until tomorrow morning."

"How about a couple of spoons."

"I got those at the room."

"Carl, I love you. Can me and my woman fix up there?"

"Sure."

"You still live at the same place?"

"Yeah."

"I'll go get my old lady and meet you in ten minutes."

"You got it."

Carl didn't live far. I picked up Sylvia and we walked the two blocks. When we got there, Carl had everything ready for us.

"I saw Jessie on the way over. He said if you want to do it in the morning to be at the phone booth on Brooklyn and Soto, that taco stand."

"Damn, why there? That's wall-to-wall Mexicans."

"That's what he said. I guess he cops close by."

"What time?"

"Eleven thirty."

"How much for two spoons?"

"Just what I paid. Fifty dollars."

I handed him the fifty. "Thanks. I have to be in Orange County at nine, so I'm going to scoot, Carl. I'll see Jessie in the morning and I'll drop you off a spoon when I score. Will you be home?"

"I'll show you where to put it."

We walked outside and Carl showed us a place in the laundry room where I could stash the dope. We left Carl's and were on the move again.

"We have to rent a motel somewhere close to Brooklyn and Soto."

"How are we going to make a buy?" Sylvia asked. "We aren't going to have the two-fifty."

"It'll be alright. I'm going to drop you off at the motel and hit Jimmy up for a couple of bills."

"Will he give it to you?"

"If he's got it he will. If not, I'll worry about it when I get back."

CHAPTER 13

The bar looked like a shit-kicker joint. A large neon sign over the entrance flickered on and off. There was no door, only an archway under which I could see Jimmy talking to a large man wearing a cowboy shirt and hat. I parked and approached the two. They appeared to be talking business, so I walked toward them slowly to allow them time to see me and guard their conversation if it was personal. Jimmy saw me first.

"Hey, ol' thing, you made it. This is Roy, Woody."

"Glad to meet you.'

It was relaxed and I liked the feel of things. Suddenly, a guy came rushing out of the bar on a dead run past the three of us, almost knocking me down. We all turned and watched him run into the parking lot and dive underneath a car. In a matter of seconds, he reappeared with a package in his hands. As he walked toward us, he unwrapped the package revealing a gun. He walked by us and back into the bar.

Jimmy said, "That's Stan. Come on, let's see what's happening.'

"Who's Stan?"

"The guy I was going to introduce you to."

We all followed him. As we walked in, all the customers were moving away from the bar. Stan was standing in back of two guys.

"Turn around slow, you two punks, and keep your hands in view."

He put the gun to the back of one guy's head. Slowly, they both turned around, scared. He cracked the guy on his left across the eyes. The blood started slowly, but in seconds it was gushing. The guy on his right was tense but he didn't know what kind of move to make. His eyes were wide and fear was on his face. His body was taut as he started to rise. Stan put the gun to his head.

"Easy punk. Slow and easy."

He pushed the gun right into the guy's face so hard it made him turn away. Stan then hit him with a brutal left hook. As he went down, Stan hit him on the top of the head with the gun and it accidentally went off. He showed no concern, but switched the gun to his left hand and with his right hand, hit the first guy in the mouth. He went crashing off the stool and into the table. They were both on the ground now. Stan walked back to the second man and kicked him in the ribs twice. The second kick rolled him over and although he didn't have any control, he instinctively put his hands out in front of his face for protection.

"You punks want to tell me you're not going to pay me? Hey, wake up, fellas. I'm waiting for you to tell me you're not going to pay me. Come on, sweeties, wake up and tell me something. Tell me what you said a few minutes ago."

He reached down and grabbed the first guy by the shirt and pulled hard. He pulled him up to where they were face to face. They were still on quiet street and didn't hear anything he was saying, so he dropped the guy he had by the shirt and sat at the nearest table. He laid the gun on the table and waited. No one had made a move to leave and no one had said anything. I was impressed by the way this guy had completely taken over. He sat there watching them for what seemed to be the longest minute in the world. Finally, one of them moved. Stan picked up the gun, walked over and stood there looking down at them.

"You guys got anything to say?"

"I don't have anything to say, Stan. I'd like to forget it. It's over with. I'll pay you right now and we'll leave it there."

"What about you, sweetie?" he said to the other guy. "What do you say, sweetie? You got my dough?"

"I got it right here. I'm not looking for any trouble."

"Put it on the table."

They both got up and walked very slowly toward the table where Stan had been sitting. They took out their money and started counting hundred dollar bills. When they finished they looked at Stan and then down at the money. Stan knew they wouldn't make a mistake counting it, so he scooped it up and put it in his pocket.

"You guys are finished here. I don't want to see you around again. You got it?"

They both nodded.

Stan looked over to the bartender, who hadn't moved. "I don't know what that bullet did, Walter, but I'll square it up, okay?"

"Okay, Stan."

Stan turned and walked out. Jimmy and I followed.

"What the fuck happened, Stan?" Jimmy asked.

"Just a couple of jerks thinking they could get away with

something."

"Well, ya didn't give 'em any air."

"Oh, this is my friend, Woody."

"Glad to meet you, Woody. What's up?"

"I brought Woody out to meet you. He's the guy I was telling you about."

"Oh yeah? Well, let's go over to my house. We'll talk. Come on, we'll go in my car."

We walked to a new Pontiac and got in.

CHAPTER 14

"Jimmy tells me you're an all around man," Stan said.

"I do what it takes."

"How do you feel about robbery?"

"If the money's right I could feel good about it."

"I got one now I've been watching for a couple of months, but I won't have the time to show it to you for another week. It's simple. Just one guy on his way home from work. He wears a ten karat diamond which I can fence in a day for fifty grand minimum.'

"When can we get to it?"

"I'll be out of town for a week, but if you call me a week from tomorrow we'll meet and I'll give you all the details. You doing anything tonight, right now?"

"No, I'm free."

"I got to see a girl close by; it won't take but a minute. Jimmy, did you get the ID made?" Stan asked.

"It's in my pocket."

"What about the checks from the electric shop?"

"I'll have them tonight.'

"Then you can roll it tomorrow. Did you pick up the money from Dorothy?"

Jimmy handed Stan an envelope and said, "Twenty-eight hundred."

"You count it?" Stan asked.

"It's all there," Jimmy said.

These guys were definitely into action. Stan hadn't stopped talking since they got into the car. It was all about making money.

We parked in front of an apartment, got out and walked through an archway past a swimming pool. The apartment had an air of respectability. Jimmy knocked and announced himself. The door opened and revealed a small girl with large Egyptian eyes. The eyes had the look of someone who had suffered for thousands of years, probably Italian or Jewish. She had a full bottom lip, the key to her sensual face, I thought. Small upper body, large from the waist down, but not overweight. When she said, "come in," her face lit up with sincerity. I wondered what a real person like her was doing with these creeps.

Jimmy introduced me to Helen; then, without hesitation, Stan took over the conversation. "I hear it went good," he said.

"Well, I was nervous as hell, but it went just like you said it would." She picked up her purse from the dining room table and produced a handful of hundred dollar bills. She handed Stan twenty of them. They talked for a few more minutes before Stan said he had some business to take care of and got up to leave. By the time we reached the car, my curiosity was driving me crazy, but I didn't say anything.

Stan had a full stealing calendar, three or four jobs every day with robberies and burglaries squeezed in. He probably needed that kind of action to prove something. He kept talking to Jimmy incessantly, telling him what to do, names, dates, people to see, things to pick up. How Jimmy remembered it all was a mystery, but he seemed to be on top of it.

Stan had ignored me until he stopped the car by the club. "I'll expect your call next Thursday morning. We'll get it put together right away. Nice meeting you." He turned to Jimmy. "Can you do it all tonight, Jimmy?" he asked.

Jimmy nodded.

"Good. Pick me up at 8:30. That will give us forty-five minutes to get to the airport." We both got out of the car and Stan took off like a hot rodder.

"That guy's an experience. Is he always in that much of a hurry?"

"From the time he gets up, and he doesn't sleep much," Jimmy answered.

"I saw a lot of hundred dollar bills tonight, so he must be doing something right."

"He is," Jimmy replied. "He has the sweetest forgery racket in the world."

I wouldn't ask Stan about his business, but it was different with Jimmy. All I had to say was, "Oh, yeah?" and Jimmy opened up.

"He fronts the entire set-up himself. He does everything but cash the checks."

"What does he do?"

"Well, he starts off with a burglary on some small business. A business with no more than two phones. He's a master burglar and he gets in and out without being detected. He takes one check that already has a signature and reproduces the signature on the blank check using the check protection while he's in the office to fill in the amount."

"How much does he go for?"

"He keeps it around four grand. Before he pulls the burglary he checks with the bank and sees how much dough they have. The next day he drives in with a telephone repairman's uniform on and tells them they are having trouble in the area with some wiring and that if they will take the phones off the hook for an hour he can make necessary repairs. If they don't, he tells them he'll have to shut off the phones all day. They always comply. He then makes a call to his passer, right from the joint. Whoever is passing the check waltzes right into the bank. If it's a guy, front him a new suit, a briefcase and a homburg hat. If they do call they get a busy signal. The guy looks so impressive with that homburg and a copy of the Wall Street Journal under his arm, they hate to keep him waiting, so they go to the files and check the signature, which matches perfectly. Stan fakes a repairman for an hour and then splits."

"That's a sweetheart."

"Yeah, and he's branching out, that's what we're going to Sacramento for tomorrow."

"What about ID?"

"He's got his own duplicating machine. It's as good as the one the DMV uses in Sacramento. We correspond the ID to the neighborhood."

"Did he think all this up?"

"Yeah, he is a jerk in a lot of respects, but a mastermind in crime. I got some things I got to do before tomorrow morning."

"You're as bad as he is, Jimmy."

All along I had been trying to figure out a way to put the touch on Jimmy. I didn't want to look bad, but I was going to need to have some money for the morning. Jimmy was so rushed I hadn't had time to warm up to it, so I just blurted it out, "Jimmy, could you lay a hundred on me for a couple of days?"

"Sure, man." He reached in his pocket and handed me a crisp one-hundred-dollar bill. "I got to get moving. Call Stan and we'll get together."

"Thanks, Jimmy. I'll give it to you next week."

He was gone. That wasn't hard. Maybe I should have asked him for two. This was going to leave me twenty-five dollars after the buy.

I thought of the dope I had left and wondered if I could talk Sylvia into using it tonight. I rushed home with that in my mind.

She was still awake when I came in, which was unusual for her.

"How are you feeling?" I asked.

"I don't know. I feel strange. I think it's worn off. How about you?"

"It didn't hold me either. Do you want to do what we have now? I borrowed a hundred from Jimmy which brings our bankroll to two fifty-five."

Sylvia asked me "What happened when you saw Jimmy?"

"They have hundred-dollar bills coming out of all their pockets. I'm going to make some money with them."

CHAPTER 15

"Wake up, it's eleven-thirty."

"Oh, shit! How did we oversleep?"

"Come on, Sylvia, we got to get there in ten minutes."

"Are we staying here tonight?"

"No, take everything. We'll figure it out later." We got into the car, which was like an oven and didn't help the way we were feeling. We both kept the sickness to ourselves. One of the characteristics of a stand-up dope fiend is never to complain about the sickness. My philosophy was if you cry when you're sick, you'll give it up at the police station.

We pulled up to a taco stand on Brooklyn. "That's where

we get the call," I said.

"A great place to score. Why didn't you have him meet us at a substation?"

"Wait here, I'll go stand by for the call."

Five minutes later, Jessie walked into the taco stand where we were having coffee. I got up and walked outside to talk to him.

"How you doing, Jessie?"

"I'm alright."

"How long will it take? We're sick."

"About ten minutes, but I can't take you with me."

"You got anything at all with you?"

"No, I fixed what I had when I got up."

"Have you talked to him?"

"Right after I talked to you. He said to come over."

"Well, how are you going to get there?"

"You want me to take the streetcar?"

"Alright, take my car. But for Christ's sake, take it easy. Get back as soon as you can."

I counted out my money—two hundred fifty dollars. "That's the whole BR, baby. If anything happens to you, we're in trouble."

Jessie assured me that everything was cool. I handed him the keys and the money. "Don't jerk around. Get back here."

"Well, let me get on the road." Jessie drove off.

It was 11:30 am. We hadn't had any dope yet and we were both starting to get sick. It was the middle of July and already hot. We looked out of place in the predominantly Mexican neighborhood. If we got stopped in this part of town, we would definitely go to jail.

We tried to drink some more coffee, but neither of us could get it down, so we sat and pretended to drink. We waited. I started to feel it now, the helplessness of the situation should Jessie not come back. I felt it in my bones. I got that sick feeling in my stomach, and a sixth sense was telling me I had made a big mistake. I was wondering what I would do if Jessie didn't come back. Christ! No money, no car, and sick. That was a hard place to come back from. But it wasn't over with yet.

Another half hour went by. I looked at my watch for the thirty-second time. Jessie had been gone an hour and ten minutes. Sylvia looked at me with a bitter look.

The counterman was starting to look at us suspiciously. He had seen us talking to Jessie and he knew something was happening, but he didn't know what. It was unusual for two patties to be sitting in a Mexican taco stand for over an hour. I decided to make a move.

"Come on, Sylvia. Let's go sit at the bus stop."

We crossed the street and stood at the bus stop. We had to keep watching the taco stand. From where we were standing, the sun was shining brightly and directly into our eyes. It would have been bad enough if we weren't sick, but it was maddening in our current condition.

I knew now that all was lost. I had either gotten burned or Jessie had gotten busted, and it didn't make any difference which one. The cigarettes tasted awful. Sylvia and I were both getting weak. It was becoming increasingly difficult to pretend we had any business in this neighborhood but there was nothing to do but stick it out. We had to face it to the end. We waited for four hours. By now I knew it was hopeless and said, "Come on, we're going."

I had been working out a plan since Jessie left. If you're a drug addict there's going to come a time when you're going to have to go for broke or go steal your mommy's TV set. I couldn't steal my mommy's TV set, so I was left with only one choice. My plan had become a little more refined as I walked the last few blocks. I saw a hardware store and went in and bought two alligator clips to wire a car with.

"Baby, do you believe in me?"

"Sure, what do you mean? What are you going to do?"

"Just do you believe in me?"

"Yeah, sure."

"Okay, I want you to take the bus to your mother's house. Wait for me there. I don't know how long I'll be, but I'll do it just as soon as I can. Now will you do that?"

"But what are you going to do?"

"Don't worry. It may take a few hours, but I'll put it together. Hey, here comes the bus. Go on now. Don't worry, okay? Get on the bus."

The bus pulled up and Sylvia got on reluctantly. I waved goodbye as the bus drove off, and stood there for a few seconds watching it get smaller and finally disappear.

There was a parking lot thirty feet down the street. It had a four-foot brick wall along the alley. A parking attendant sat in the front to collect the money. I walked down the alley with my eyes on him. When he wasn't looking, I jumped the brick wall and hid behind the rear of a car. I reached underneath the tail light, grabbed the wires, and pulled with everything I had. I watched the attendant and jumped back over the wall. I walked down the alley, stripping the wires with my fingernails, and then attached them to the alligator clips.

There was a supermarket two blocks down the alley with a big parking lot. I made it at a fairly fast clip. I needed a small screwdriver, so I boosted one out of the market. I was now ready for the car.

One pass through the parking lot and I had the car. I drove straight through to Fifth and Los Angeles. As I stepped out, I saw J.B. about to get into a new Cad. J.B. loved to talk, but wasn't sick and had lots of money. I had known him for years. He had always dealt drugs and never been caught. He was the big man, but didn't sell less than a thousand dollar buy, and not to very many people. He saw me and smiled.

"Where you been? I haven't seen you in months."

"What are you doing down here with your uptown ass?" I asked.

"I bought a tailor shop around the corner."

"You still doing alright?"

"Oh, yeah."

"I'll be together an hour from now. Can I call and make arrangements?"

"You know it takes a big one."

"I know."

J.B. wrote his number down on a card and handed it to me. "Remember the number and throw it away. I see very few people, Woody. I only take care of people I have known for a long time."

"I understand. I'm in a rush right now, but I'll call you in an hour for sure."

"Are you still playing?"

"Now and then. You know how that goes." If I didn't do something quick, I was going to run out of energy. "J.B., I'll call you in an hour."

I walked around the corner to the Five Star Pawn Shop, and saw the owner, Sid. "Hi, Sid. Can I talk to you a minute?"

"Sure, what's up?"

"A girlfriend of my old lady's has been having a hard time with some jerk who lives in her apartment and I need some kind of gun to put a little scare into him. I'll give you twenty-five to use it and I'll bring it back tomorrow." The story was so weak I couldn't tell it with conviction.

Sid shook his head. "You're good, kid, real good. That's the biggest horseshit story I ever heard. I can't let you have a gun. Are you nuts? What the hell you want a gun for?"

I was starting to get desperate, but was trying not to show it. "I really need it for what I told you."

"You've been coming in here for two years putting that horn of yours in hock, and I know if someone was giving you any trouble you wouldn't need a gun to put them in line. But if you really got to have a gun for scare, I can let you have a pellet gun."

"Pellet gun!"

"It looks like a .45 automatic. Just like a .45. You can't tell the difference. And if you need it for what you say, I can let you have it for thirty bucks."

"Let me see it."

Sid brought the gun out from under the counter where it had been on display and handed it to me.

"Christ, it looks just like a .45 automatic."

"If you don't have to shoot it, no one will ever know it ain't."

"Sid, can you run a tab on this for a few days?"

Pawnbrokers aren't the most sympathetic people in the world but somehow Sid said yes.

"Put it in a bag, Sid."

"You want some pellets?"

"Don't be funny, Sid. Just put it in a bag."

I stopped before I walked out the door and pretended I was looking at the window display. I wanted to make sure there weren't any narcs or beat cops around who would roust me since they were famous for hanging around pawnshops, but it was clear both ways. I said goodbye to Sid and hurried around the corner to the car.

I drove through Hollywood and parked in a Safeway parking lot. There was a phone booth in front of the market so I called J.B. and set up a buy a half hour away.

I walked into the market calmly or at least made it appear that way. One glance and I knew where everyone was. I had already located the manager. As I was walking down the aisles wheeling the basket, I saw something I hadn't counted on—a cop, one of those mini-cops who work in supermarkets for minimum wage. He carried a gun but only for show. It was just a part of the uniform. It didn't impress me but it did change the game plan.

I walked toward him with my head down like I was thinking of what to buy. When I got within several feet of him, I pulled out the gun and held it right at his stomach. I put the other hand over the gun to keep it from being seen. The mini-cop saw it as I said, "Put your eyes down and don't go for nothing or I'll blow you away."

He did as he was told. I moved to his side and took his gun. I put both guns in my waistband and my hand in front of my stomach to give the impression I could get to the gun before the mini-cop could make any move. I said in a quiet voice, "Call the manager over here and make it sound good or you're going to the clouds."

The mini-cop was scared. Most of the duty here involved arresting shoplifters. He had never been in a robbery before. He said, "Hal, will you come here for a minute?"

Hal walked over with a Jack Armstrong look on his face thinking there was some kind of minor complaint he could settle. When he got close enough, I raised my shirt for him to see the two guns.

"You see what's happening, Hal? Shut up and put your eyes down. I want you to listen to me because I'm only going to say it once. If you act natural it will be all right and no one will get killed, but if you try and be Dick Tracy, I'll shoot both of you assholes quick. Now, I want you to walk to the check stand and get a big bag. Go to the safe and put all the paper money in it. No silver. Get the bottom compartment, too. You got it? Yes? When you've taken all the money, bring it over here to me. Now get going."

Hal moved out. He stopped by the check stand and picked up a big shopping bag and proceeded to the safe. He got down on one knee and started putting money in it without looking up. I was talking to the mini-cop and making it look natural but was still watching Hal. No one in the market was aware anything was going on. Hal emptied the bottom compartment and started on the top. I continued talking to the cop while I watched everyone in the market. A girl checker was looking at Hal taking the money out of the safe. She first looked at the mini-cop and then at me. She knew. It had been too smooth. Something had to go wrong. I pulled up my shirt so she could see the guns, and motioned to her with my index finger to come over. She stopped in the middle of ringing up a sale and walked over in a trance, her eyes bulging in fear. I told her, "If you don't get excited, everything will be alright. If you do, I'll shoot the whole market up. Do you understand?"

She nodded. Hal finished with the safe and approached with the money. He handed it to me and I took it smoothly. "Alright, all three of you walk straight to the back. Get going."

They moved off like robots. The lady the clerk had been waiting on walked past me and said in a loud voice, "Are you going to wait on me?"

I told her quietly, "They'll be right back, honey. Just be patient. They'll be right back."

The trio continued walking. The woman mumbled to herself and started following them, asking where they were going. They did not look back and I walked out of the market. I got to the car without running and drove away unobserved.

Passing a gas station a mile away I saw a "For Sale" sign on a nice-looking Chrysler. I parked around the corner, stuffed my pockets with money and walked back to the station. In five minutes I was driving off in my new car. I still had ten minutes to go when I arrived at J.B.'s house. J.B. let me fix there, and I called Sylvia to tell her it was all right. She wanted to know everything, but I only told her that she would be well in ten minutes.

In less than ten minutes I was in front of Sylvia's mother's house. I left the guns and money in the car but took the open ounce and outfit with me. As I approached the house I thought, this is going to be more difficult than robbing the supermarket. It was always so tense there. Her mother refused to believe her daughter was using drugs. To her, Sylvia was still her little girl. If she saw Sylvia with a needle in her arm she'd convince herself it was a vitamin shot. I knew she hated me and held me responsible for what her daughter had become, but there was nothing I could do to change the fact. As I approached the front door, Sylvia saw me from the window and came running out.

"Oh, honey, I've been so worried. Are you alright? Is everything okay?"

"Happy days are here again, the sky is blue and clear again."

"Oh, you're so crazy. Tell me what happened."

"We got plenty of dope and plenty of money and your man is good-looking and the rest I'll tell you later."

Just then Sylvia's mother opened the screen door and said hello.

"Hello, Bea, how are you?"

"I'm fine." She didn't ask me how I was. She just glared with a quiet contempt. "Would you like a cup of coffee?"

"Yes, that would be nice. I have to be in Hollywood in forty-five minutes. I think I've got a job selling cars."

"Oh? Where?"

"A friend of mine runs a lot in Hollywood and he said he'd give me a job. We used to work at the same lot a couple of years ago, so I'm pretty sure I'll get the job."

"Have you been playing anywhere?"

"I told you, Mother, he hasn't," Sylvia broke in.

"Well, how have you been getting by?"

"Mother!"

"It's alright, honey," I jumped in. "I got a loan from the musician's union last month and, now with this job, we'll be alright."

She shook her head, disbelieving, as she got up and walked to the kitchen. "I'll heat up the coffee."

When she went to the kitchen, I handed the outfit and stuff to Sylvia. "Don't knock your lights out. Not here. Just get the sickness out of you, okay?"

"Okay, honey." She hastened to the bathroom. A couple of minutes later as she made her way out, she collided into her mom in the hallway. Sylvia was overly apologetic and it was obvious to her mother that a change had come over her, a change she didn't like. She knew. The family dog could have detected the change. To make it worse, Sylvia couldn't stop talking. She rambled on and on, trying desperately to cover her stoned condition, but every word made it worse. I regretted that I had ever given her the dope. I should have let her go sick, at least while she was at her mother's house. Ten more minutes wouldn't have made that much difference, but I had to be a big shot and flash all that dope. What an asshole move. Mommy was going to be a bitch to contend with now.

Just a few minutes ago, Sylvia had had a difficult time walking. Her movements were slow and lethargic, her nose was running, and she looked like she should have been hospitalized for the flu. Her eyes had been like saucers and were dripping. Now they were pinpointed and droopy. Her mother looked at me like a 77th Street detective. Why did Sylvia have to take such a big jolt? I thought to myself. Goddamn her.

I took a drink of the coffee hurriedly, knowing my only out was a quick retreat. I took one last sip, stood up and said, "I really got to scoot, Bea. Don't want to be late for that job."

"Yes, Mom, we really have to go."

Sylvia staggered up and knocked the coffee off the table, all over the rug. "Oh, God, Mom, I'm sorry."

Bea went to the kitchen for a rag without saying anything. When she was out of hearing range, I said, "For Christ's sake, straighten up."

"I didn't mean to knock the coffee over. It was an accident."

"I'm not talking about that. It's your—"

Just then, Bea entered the room.. She got on her knees and started cleaning the rug. There was a vacant stare in her eyes. She couldn't comprehend the change that had taken place in her daughter in the last few minutes. While she was on her knees, she looked up at Sylvia, then moved her head from side to side staring at the floor. There was a long awkward pause, and after what seemed like an interminable amount of time, she turned to her daughter and said, "Don't ever bring him around here again. When you come here, come by yourself. I can't stand to ever look at him again."

"What's wrong with you, Mother?"

"I mean it. Don't bring him with you. Never, never."

"If he can't come here, then I won't come here either."

"That will have to be your decision."

"There's no reason for you to treat him like that. You take a dislike to someone and that's it forever with you. You never liked him because he's a musician."

"That's not true. I don't like him because of the look he has put on your face. Your dead eyes that were so full of life before you met him. I hold him responsible for that look. Do you think because I'm an old woman I can't see what he has done to you? Are you forgetting I raised you? I am your mother."

"But Mom—"

"Please go. Please."

I left by myself, thinking Sylvia would want to talk to her mother, but I was wrong. She followed me out almost immediately.

I opened the door for her. "Whose car?" she asked.

"Ours."

She shook her head almost the same way her mother had. "Damn."

CHAPTER 16

"Okay," said Sylvia "what did you do when you left me?"

"Made a withdrawal out of my private savings account."

"Be serious, what did you do?"

"A Safeway market in Hollywood."

"I guess it went all right or you wouldn't be here."

I filled her in on all the details and how I had met J.B.

"How much money?"

I reached under the seat and handed her the shopping bag. "Count it."

"Let's wait."

"So, where do you want to live?"

""I'd love to live in Santa Monica, close to the beach."

"We rich, girl. We can live any goddamned place we want. Why not Santa Monica?"

"Do you mean it? An apartment by the beach?"

"By the beach, my ass. We'll move on the beach. I don't know how much money we got, but I'm sure it's enough to pay the rent for a gang of months wherever we want to live."

We left immediately to find an apartment. We settled for one with a loft a couple of blocks from the beach. The first thing we did there was count the money. I threw it up in the air all over the living room, then we got down on our hands and knees, picked it up and stacked it very neatly before counting it.

There was over twelve thousand dollars. It looked so good spread out all over the floor I wanted to do it again, but Sylvia was hungry and we had to buy sheets and towels. Everything we owned had been in the car Jessie had driven off with.

"Come on. I'll feed you, then we'll go see my grandmother."

"Wouldn't you rather go by yourself?"

"Maybe that would be best."

I dropped Sylvia at a show in Santa Monica after we ate, and then drove to Hollywood where my grandmother lived, an apartment house in a rundown neighborhood. The owners of her building did little in the way of maintenance, so something was always broken and in need of repair. The neighborhood consisted mainly of old and poor citizens who barely made ends meet. It broke my heart every time I thought of her living there.

I knocked three times, my usual knock, and then called to her by her special name, "Idamommy."

She opened the door and her blue eyes were radiant. They seemed to get bluer every time I saw her. "You took so long answering the door I thought you had a man in here," I said as I gave her a hug.

"He's under the bed."

"He might have to stay there a while."

"He'll just have to get comfortable," she answered. She hadn't lost any of her dry wit. "How are you?"

"I'm fine. Everything is good in my life. Did I tell you Sylvia got rear-ended a couple of months ago?"

"No. Was she hurt?"

"No, but the car was. Today the insurance company settled for eight thousand dollars."

"That's a lot of money."

"I've been working too, so it really put us on top. I'm going to give you more than I usually do because we're doing so good. Sylvia wanted me to. I talked it over with her."

I saw the tension build in her face first before it settled in her neck and shoulders. I couldn't fool her, although I had acted casually when I told her.

"I got a good, steady job.'

"Playing?"

"Yes. They pay over scale and it's four nights a week. Sylvia works there too, as a waitress. At last the dough is beginning to roll in, Idamommy." I tried with a nervous laugh to convince her but it didn't work. She smiled anyway and tried to conceal her embarrassment for my lies. We knew each other so well I couldn't lie to her but I couldn't tell her the truth either. It was an awkward moment.

"Let me get you some coffee."

"All right."

"Would you like a French roll and some cream cheese with it? It's your favorite."

"No, Idah, I just had dinner."

While she was gone I took the money out of my pocket and put it on her desk. Everything on the desk reminded me of her. There was her gold pen that had been there since I was a young boy, her Bible, and a current issue of the *Daily Word*. She was a great one for keeping up her correspondence and still wrote to all her old friends in the circus. On top of the desk were two small silver frames. In one picture she was holding me when I was a baby, and the handwriting on the bottom of the picture said, "My Big Moment." In the other frame was a picture of me when I was fifteen.

After I put the money on the desk I went in the kitchen to see if I could help her with anything.

"We're living in Santa Monica, Idamommy, just a few blocks from the beach."

"Oh, you always liked the beach so much. Do you remember how we used to go down there when you were a little boy? We'd take the trolley."

"Sure, I remember, Idah. I also remember you taking me to the pier on Saturday night and waiting while I'd shoot those guns. You're going to have to come down and spend a weekend with me and Sylvia. Would you like to do that?"

"Maybe I'd come down for an afternoon, but a weekend would be imposing. Let's sit in the front room where it's more comfortable."

When we walked through the door she saw the money on the desk. I felt her stiffen again.

"How much is there?"

"Well, there's fifteen hundred."

She looked at me with those piercing blue eyes and said, "I don't need that much money."

"Well, I have it now, and you know how I am with money. I may not have it tomorrow. Besides, it will make up for the times when I won't have it for you."

"You know all the money in the world isn't worth it if they take you away."

"Idah, there's nothing illegal about my life. Sylvia and I are making good money. You can put that out of your head about anyone taking me away. I am not doing anything wrong."

"I don't like to think of you in those jails. You are too free a spirit to be locked up. Life is such a very short venture. We can only experience it to the fullest if we're free. Money can make us comfortable to an extent, but it only offers us a modicum of freedom. The essence of freedom lies inside us— that's something money cannot change."

"Idah, I—"

"Don't worry; I am not going to lecture." She changed the

subject. "Do you have a telephone yet?"

"I'm having one put in tomorrow. I'll call you as soon as I get a number. It may take a couple of days."

"I understand," she replied.

"Goodbye, Idah."

"Take care of yourself."

CHAPTER 17

Home was a nice place to be, especially with an abundant supply of drugs. Sylvia was either sleeping or coasting. She hadn't moved in hours. I wished I could sleep but there was too much dope in the house to relax. I could never relax when the Gorilla was around:

You would like to rest and take it easy, wouldn't you? A little brother after a hard day in the streets. You've been on a double shift, you big dumb pink trick, and you'll stay there. You can be tired, but it won't do you any good. You could have some time to rest when I was just a little Monkey. That was before you let me grow up. That was where it all began, when I was just a little Monkey hanging on your jive shoulder waiting for you to feed me. It was pretty good in those days. That's when you were playing a lot and I put the rhythm section right in your head. I gave you those heroin chops too and let you play a thousand choruses without getting tired. I always knew how to reach you; you were such an easy trick for music. But now you can't play for shit. If you don't believe me, check yourself out. Try playing a C major scale in tune. Try and make it sound the way it did when I was a little guy. Ah, you see, you won't even try. Of course, you can't play anymore. Dues, my friend, you keep forgetting. I don't know how but you always forget the dues.

And what about the ladies? Think for a moment, if you will, about the ladies. I made you a killer in that department, an all-night affair. The girls thought you were wonderful, didn't they? Be honest now, tell me everything. Check your manhood out now, punk. There is no escaping me, my friend. Or didn't you know I am the dues collector?

Now, I know you're tired, but before you go to sleep, trot on over to the bathroom and feed me one more time. I'll see you first thing in the morning.

Part Two

FLIGHT

CHAPTER 18

We had just come back from breakfast and were looking for a place to park when I saw them.

"How do you know it's them, honey?"

"Because I'm not fucking blind. I saw O'Rourke and a couple of robbery cops, too."

"What makes you so sure they were robbery cops?"

"Take my word for it. All the dope is there. All the money. We're fucked."

"But how did they find us? You haven't been out of the house."

"What name did you put the phone in?"

"Joannie Corn."

"What about the lights and gas?"

"They wanted ID. I had to use my own name."

"Oh, no. I don't believe it. How could you use your own name?"

"They wouldn't turn the gas on without ID."

"Didn't it occur to you to tell them you left it at home, or a dog ate it, or you took a shit on it? Anything but your own name?"

"Honey—"

"Please don't tell me you're sorry. Have you got any money?"

"No."

I had the change from the twenty dollar bill. The rest I had left at home. I got us on the freeway as soon as I could, heading east toward Orange County.

"What are we going to do?"

"I don't know. I'm thinking."

We drove in silence for twenty minutes. By then, I had a plan. "I'm going to see Stan in a couple of days. The job I mentioned was ready to go when I left, but there wasn't time. He told me to call him the day I got back. If that works out it would mean we'd only have to hold on for a few more days. Our habits are too long to try and support because I can't be seen now. It's not routine with robbery. They get out and look. But if I took off a small drugstore we could lay down and kick. By the time the job with Stan will be ready, we'll be close to clean and can leave town."

"God, honey, another robbery?"

"What do you want me to do, turn myself in? God dammit, I'm trying to keep it going."

"Where?" she asked.

"What difference does it make, they all have drugs," I answered. "God, I've got to call my grandmother. I promised I'd call her tonight and I made the mistake of telling her we moved so she'll be expecting to hear from me with a new telephone number in a couple of days. We really have to blow this town after this mess. They're not going to put me in the dead file and wait until I bust myself. They'll be like bloodhounds now that they know who I am. They'll be watching my grandmother's apartment. We've got to get her out of there after I do this job with Stan."

"But won't they be watching her even after she moves?"

"Yeah, sure, but she won't be there long. We're taking her with us."

"Don't you think she's a bit too old to be traveling to Central America?"

"It hasn't entered my little mind to go anywhere without her. We're not going for a week or two and it ain't a vacation. It's forever and when I go she'll be with me."

I took an off-ramp I was not familiar with. "This will do, as long as we remember how to get back on. We're lucky I didn't take the guns out of the car. Goddamn, that was a death blow, losing everything. They must have made me from a mug sheet."

That same feeling was settling in on me that I always had just before I committed a crime. One part of me said fuck the world, whatever I can do and get away with will not affect my conscience. But the other part of me hated what I was doing. These were the feelings I had when I had heroin in my system. When I was drug-free it was a different story. Then, just the thought of committing a crime was frightening to me. But no one knew that. I had kept my fears well-guarded. What I projected to the outside world was a much different picture.

We drove down the main street for about eight or ten blocks until I spotted a drugstore on the corner. I stopped and parked almost in front. "I'll be right back."

"You're not going to do it now, are you?"

"No. I'll be right back."

I walked the twenty yards to the drugstore and stopped in front to buy a newspaper. When I put the money in the vending machine I got a good look at what was going on inside the drugstore. Only a few people were there and it didn't look as if the place did a lot of business. I walked back to the car, got in and drove off.

"That's it? It's right on the main drag, honey," Sylvia anxiously looked back at the drugstore.

"That's where drugstores always are. You want to wait and look for one on a residential street?"

"That's not what I mean."

I had that nervous feeling and energy again. After two blocks I stopped the car, reached under the seat for the gun, put it in my waist and tightened my belt. I pulled my shirt out to conceal the gun.

"Hand me those alligator clips and wire out of the glove compartment."

Sylvia handed them to me and started the car again. She pulled around the corner and parked.

"Wait right here. I won't be longer than fifteen minutes."

"Where are you going to get the car?"

"That parking lot we just passed. I'll probably get it over with before they ever miss the car. Don't worry, honey. I'll be back before you know it. Bye."

I walked around the corner and straight into the parking lot. There was an old Pontiac with the windows down. I walked up to it as if I owned it. I opened the door and got in and sat in the driver's seat just long enough to see if anyone was watching. There was a guy walking in the other direction so I ducked down and started working on the ignition. In a matter of seconds I had it wired. I sat up and looked out. Since it was clear, I tried the starter. The car started up immediately.

"Well, that's the first step," I thought as I drove away. There was no use wasting time now by waiting for the right time. It didn't matter if there were two or twenty-two people in the drugstore. I had to take it.

After driving a block I saw a motorcycle cop giving a guy a ticket on the opposite side of the street. That was a bad break, but at least I knew where the cop was. I pulled up and parked right in front. One quick glance and I was in the store. Luckily there was only one customer, who was being waited on by the clerk up front. I walked to the back and saw the druggist. There was a little half-door separating him from the store. It didn't have a lock, but swung back and forth. I walked through the door and came out with the gun. The druggist was only five feet away.

"Don't put your hands up. Do exactly as I say or I'll shoot you in the stomach. Can you do that?"

The druggist nodded.

"Alright, then, fill one of those boxes with all the dope you have here. I want the morphine and Dolophine first and percodan next. Now be fast because if anything happens while I'm here, I'll shoot you first for fucking it up. You understand me, Mister? Throw some twenty-six needles in, too."

"I will. I won't give you any trouble."

"All right. Move."

The druggist started throwing vials and small cardboard containers of drugs into the box. When it was three-quarters filled, I walked up close to him and said, "Open the register, take the money out and put it in the box. Lift the bottom drawer and give me the money in there too. No change.

"Now I'm going to walk out of here. I want you to lie on the ground and if you say one word I'm going to shoot the clerk on my way out and then come back and shoot you. You got it?"

The druggist nodded. He was scared half to death. I walked out the same way I came in, as unobtrusively as possible, yet alert to my surroundings. The clerk was busy and didn't even look up as I left. I got in the car and remembered to look out the rear view mirror to see if the cop was still there. He was. Good place for him.

I took a left at the first street and drove one block, then took another left until I came to Elm Street, where I had left Sylvia. I pulled in and parked about fifty feet from my own car. I took the alligator clips off with one quick jerk, picked up the box of dope, got out and started walking toward my car. Sylvia saw me and started the engine. I put my hand up like a traffic cop in a gesture that said, "Hold it." After what seemed like an unbearable amount of time I reached the car and got into the back seat with the box of dope. After twenty or thirty yards and a glance up and down the street, I dropped to the floor.

"Get back on the main drag and drive very cautiously to the freeway. We don't have anything to worry about. It went perfectly. Just get us to the freeway and we're home."

After she had gone four blocks or so the police car approached in the opposite direction with its siren and red light on.

"They went right by."

I didn't answer.

"I said they went right by."

"I heard you."

"There's the freeway a block away."

Once the car was on the freeway I climbed to the front seat. I started counting the money. "Six-hundred and forty bucks. It's nothing like what we had, but it's enough to hold us and maybe now we can clean up. When you come to Paramount, get off the freeway. How do you feel?"

"I'm not sick yet. We left the outfit in the apartment too."

"I got some points at the drugstore. Pull over, we'll rent a motel."

"Which one?"

"Anyone, honey, just pull into one." Sylvia drove in and parked but not by the office.

"Here's some money."

Our only belongings were one bag of dope and two guns, but at least we weren't going to be sick.

CHAPTER 19

There was a loud knock at the door. I jumped up, grabbed the gun from under the bed, and motioned Sylvia to ask who was there.

"Yes? Who is it?"

"The maid. We have to change the linens."

"Can you come back in twenty minutes?"

"Checkout time is eleven thirty and I have to change the linens before I go home."

"We're not up and we're going to stay another day, so

come back later."

There was no sound from the other side of the door.

"Go pay the rent, sweetie, and if you see the maid just get some towels. I'll have something cooking when you get back."

Sylvia left and I got the morphine out. I put ten or fifteen half-grain tablets in the spoon and shot them into my arm. Suddenly my face turned pink and puffed up, the skin stretched so tight it felt like it was going to pop. It felt as though a thousand pins and needles were stuck in my face and scalp. My hands and feet itched so fiercely I had to take off my shoes and scratch my feet.

When Sylvia came back the pins and needles had subsided somewhat, but the itching wouldn't stop. I stood up, rubbing my hands together hard as she came in the door. I didn't realize how bad I looked until I saw the horrified look on her face.

"My God, what have you done? Are you all right? Oh, sweetheart, what did you shoot?"

"It's all right now. I'm okay." I could feel my system adjusting to the morphine. It was settling in on me. Actually, I felt quite good. It sure took away the craving for heroin.

"I guess I overdid it a little. The pins and needles are a bitch. I think the key to this shit is to fix more times but not as much. It's nothing like heroin. That initial jolt would knock a mule to his knees if you take too much."

"How much did you take?"

"I don't know. Ten, maybe fifteen half-grains."

"Are you serious? That would kill the average guy."

"I'm wonderful now. It was the first rush. I couldn't hold too good under those pins and needles." I put two half-grain tablets in the spoon.

"I don't want that much."

"It's only two half-grainers."

"I went to the hospital once with a broken arm and they gave me one-sixth of a grain. I was loaded for two days. That's a full grain you put in the spoon."

"Whatever you want to shoot, baby, be my guest. We have a whole box of dope to clean up on. Even if we fixed around the clock, it would still last a couple of months."

I drew about one-tenth up into the eyedropper and fixed Sylvia. I then fixed what was left. I was like a little boy in a candy store.

"How was that? Did you feel it?"

"A little bit. I could go for another one."

"Well, then, Miss Sylvia, we'll cook you up one more little jolt here to get your eyes pinpointed and your big, fine looking ass out of the sand. We also have a taste of that there morphine. Let's see what Dr. Woody can oblige you with on this marvelous sunshine day." I started throwing vials out of the cardboard box and calling out labels.

"Motherfucker," she said, "the morphine has given him back his sense of humor."

I was standing on the bed with the outfit in my hand. "Yes, friends, Dr. Woody just happens to be the very best. I said the very best, yes, I did, the very best fixer in this big ol' state. I will personally guarantee to hit your main geranium in the very first shot and cure all of your ills, both mental and physical, if you will stay with me for three, yes folks, just three of my famous treatments."

"Honey, you're crazy."

"Woman, how dare you call me crazy! Me, Dr. Woody, who has been your provider and your decider since the day we were joined together in wedded bliss. Surely you haven't forgotten so soon what Preacher Abernathy said on the day of our troth? Well, I haven't. He said, 'Watch her or she'll steal your dope.'"

I leapt off the bed and put my arms around her. We were both laughing and holding each other. It was a tender moment, the kind we hadn't experienced in a long time. The prospect of getting away from the heroin had opened me up to a joy I hadn't felt in over a year. The morphine could be just as bad if I got careless. It would be very easy to go from one to the other if I wasn't cool. Then some sleeping pills for a few days would tighten it up.

"Stan's due back today. I'm going to call him. I'll be right back." I made the call and went back to the room.

"Was he there?" Sylvia asked.

"Yeah, he's on his way over."

I put the dope away except for ten half-grain tablets, which I put in my pocket.

"What are you taking those for?"

"I don't know how morphine holds you, but I don't want to get sick out there with this guy. I'll probably be a couple of hours. You better stay here. You never know when the maid is going to come in and start cleaning up."

Ten minutes later there was a knock on the door. I opened it and let Stan in. "Hi, Stan, come on in. This is my lady, Sylvia."

"Hi." Stan greeted her curtly, barely glancing at her.

"Hello."

"Okay, honey, I'll be back soon. How long will we be, Stan?"

"A couple of hours."

"If I'm going to be any longer, I'll call."

We left and got into Stan's car. We drove for ten minutes, talking about trivial things. Stan used to be a plumber before he turned into a thief and he had one of those working-stiff minds. He was totally insecure and tried to hide it by being a tough guy and bragging about his connections in the rackets. His figures were exaggerated; at least I sensed they were. A guy who made forty grand last month wouldn't be taking a two-hour drive for a third of a second-rate robbery.

We weren't in the car five minutes before Stan started giving me a blow-by-blow description of his finances and how he made everyone rich.

"You remember that girl Helen?"

"Yes, that was the first night I met you."

"Well, I put seven grand in her pocket and seven inches in her. She loved both of them."

I found Stan repulsive, especially the way he talked about women.

Stan stopped for some gas and I went to the head and

dropped four tabs. "Two more hours with this asshole and I'll be ready for some heroin. It's the only drug that's an instant asshole remover."

We left the gas station and drove for another ten minutes before we got to Glendale. Stan didn't stop talking and I was half-listening with an occasional "no shit" thrown in to let Stan think I was paying attention. The tabs I took at the gas station were beginning to work, and now Stan didn't seem like such a pain in the ass.

"That's the place over there."

"Laverne's Jewelry Shop?"

"Now when he leaves at night he has someone bring his car in front of the place. In the daytime he parks it in the back. He takes the same route home every night. I'll show you that now." Stan drove two blocks and made a right turn, went almost a mile and turned left into the hills. He drove into the hills for four blocks. "That's it. That tan house with the Spanish roof."

"What time does he leave?"

"Seven o'clock."

"Could I get you to drop me here and pick me up?"

"I don't know. How do you figure on doing it?"

"You could drop me off as soon as it gets dark. I could make my way down to his house and stash myself in the bushes next to the garage. I assume he puts the car in the garage."

"Yeah, he does."

"It doesn't make that much difference anyway, because he has to come to the front door to get in, which is in line with the bushes I'll be hiding in. After you drop me off you can kill some time close by, driving or whatever. The only thing you need to know is when he stops in front of his house. I mean the exact time because when I hear him drive in I'll be coming out the door. You could pick me up on the corner because it's not that far, but you've got to be there on time. Can you do that?"

"That's no problem."

"Does he keep the windows rolled up?"

"Yeah, we checked that. He locks the door too."

"What kind of car?"

"New Cad. What are you thinking?"

"That maybe I could get him at a stop signal. This will work out."

"When do you want to do it?"

"Tonight is fine."

"I can't tonight. What about tomorrow?"

"That's okay. Can you get some handcuffs?"

"I'll have them for you tomorrow."

"You can get me a Halloween mask, too. Not a real big one but one that covers my face. Who's in the house with him?"

"His wife. No maid. She comes in twice a week. She leaves before he comes home, usually about five-thirty. His wife drives her to the bus stop."

"You'd better get me two sets of handcuffs."

"You got it. You want to come out and look it over again before you do it?"

"I've seen all I need to see. Do you know if there's a patrol? It's a pretty uptown neighborhood."

"Not to my knowledge and I've been out here a lot in the last two months."

"I'll bring my old lady with me tomorrow. All you have to do is give me a ride to where she parked. I'll go back with her."

"I'm going to need the ring if I'm going to fence it."

"I'll give it to you, but you're going to have to advance me some dough until you sell it."

"I can do that. You still playing around with that dope?"

"That's where I've been for two weeks, kicking."

"Well, that's damn good. You sure can't get anywhere with one of those habits to support. That must really be hard. They tell me you can't sleep for days. That right?"

"I didn't use that much. It just felt like I had a cold." I didn't want Stan to know the extent of my using so I underplayed everything. I had never yet seen anyone who wouldn't try and play the overs on you if they knew you were hooked up bad.

"What time do you want to go out there tomorrow?"

"I'd like to get out there a couple of hours early. I can drive around and get a feel of the town and find the fastest way to get to the freeway."

"The freeway is on Los Feliz."

"I know where it is. I just want to find the most direct way to get there. You want to have dinner out there?"

"Fine. I'll come over about four and you can follow me out."

"It's a date."

We were approaching the motel. I told Stan not to pull in, just to let me out. "I'll walk across the street."

Stan pulled over and stopped. I opened the door to get out. "You'll have the cuffs and everything?"

"I'll go there right now."

"You know where to get them?"

"I'll get them."

"Okay. I'll see you tomorrow."

CHAPTER 20

I missed Sylvia since I had been gone. Maybe it was because I wasn't on the nod now and shutting the world out. I actually noticed the signs on the street and what kind of day it was. I knocked on the door.

"Who is it?"

I said in a whisper, but loud enough to be heard, "The milkman. Has your husband gone to work yet?"

When Sylvia opened the door she was laughing. "Two hours on the dot. I love a man who keeps his word."

"Then you must be crazy about me. May I come in, my dear, and give you a hell of a ravishing?"

"Only if you're serious."

I walked through the door.

"My word. One day clean and you're putting the burn on me. Does morphine take it away like heroin does?"

"Yeah, but after five days I won't need either one and twenty-four hours after that you better have your laundry done."

Sylvia walked over and put her arms around me. "I promise to be good, sir. And incidentally, I've done the laundry." She pointed to a pair of panties hanging on a chair.

"Well, that does it. Any girl who can get the laundry done five days in advance and make a formal apology when she's wrong, deserves the best. Get ready for a drive-in hamburger." I put my hand in a gesture to ward off anything she might say. "Don't try to suppress your emotions, you've earned it. I know you're all choked up."

"There's only one thing, just one more request while you're being so thoughtful, so understanding, so gracious."

"Yes?"

"May I—"

"May you what?"

"I don't know how to put it in words."

"Take your time. Try to get a hold of yourself."

"Can I have some onion rings, too?"

I lifted her up, walked over to the bed and set her down very gently. We stayed in each other's arms for a long time, not saying anything, just holding one another.

"Are you feeling sick at all?"

"I don't know. How about you?"

"I'm not sick, but I'm not high either. Let's take a jolt and then go out and get something to eat."

"Okay."

I went to the closet and brought out the cardboard box. I put about ten half-grain tablets in the spoon and let them dissolve. The morphine was so pure I didn't have to cook it up. What a difference from that street smack cut with everything including some dealer's dirty socks. The things they use to cut it are worse than the heroin itself. Jesus Christ! I'd overdone it again. I held my head in my hands. The pins and needles were unbearable, but after a while they subsided.

"Are you going to have to go through that every time?"

"I'll have to lighten up. I can't handle too much of that. It feels like my face is going to crack open."

I prepared Sylvia's fix but I only gave her one tab. "Do you feel it?"

"Yes, but it's different."

"It's not heroin, baby. If you were clean you'd feel it just the way you feel smack, and if you were hooked on morphine you wouldn't feel heroin. It beats the hell out of kicking cold. I haven't been sick yet."

"Me either."

"Would you believe we're going to sleep tonight?"

"I already slept while you were gone this afternoon. How did you make out with Stan?"

"It's on for tomorrow night. The caper looks good. I am going to hold up a jeweler at his house and get his ten-karat diamond. Stan says he can fence it in Chicago."

"And if he can't?"

"I don't think he'd be going to all this trouble if he couldn't move it. Are you hungry?"

"I'm starved!"

"Whenever you're ready."

Looking at her I noticed she had been wearing the same clothes for two days. "I want to buy you some clothes before we eat. I saw a shopping center a few blocks from here."

Sylvia put her arms around me. It meant so much to her that I was considerate. "I can wait a few days, honey."

"What about me?"

"What?"

"It makes me happy when I can buy you something."

"Honey, I—"

"Come on, no hearts and flowers over a dress." Sylvia didn't know how to accept my change of attitude. I was feeling alive again. I could tell she had grown so accustomed to living with a dead man that it was difficult for her to make the switch. She was ecstatic.

We left the apartment and found the shopping center. I bought her a dress, a pair of shoes and some panties. I also bought some shorts and socks for myself. We ate a huge Mexican dinner and on the way home I bought a fifth of gin, some ice and Seven-Up. I was still looking to get high and thought maybe the juice would do it.

The first thing I did when I got back to the apartment was fix a dozen half-grains. The pins and needles started again but I was becoming used to them. I fixed Sylvia this time with two tabs. She took off her clothes and lay down on the bed. In a matter of seconds she was sleeping. I fixed another dozen tabs. This time I didn't put it in my arm all at once. I put half in and waited. The blood filled up the eye dropper but I waited a full minute, then delivered the rest to my bloodstream. At last I had the right hookup. I took all my clothes off and decided to start in on the gin. After an hour I was shit-faced drunk. I took the gin bottle with me into the bathroom and ran a hot bath. The room wouldn't stand still for me.

Here we go again... there's got to be more to life than this kind of surreptitious existence. Life had been hiding from me and I didn't know where it was. Maybe no one knew. Maybe it was really Sears & Roebuck.

Pardon me, sir, but could you tell me who that gentleman is over there?

Of course, he's lower Sears & Roebuck.

And the gentleman standing next to him?

He is upper Montgomery Ward.

How about you, Father? You've been a priest twenty years,

and when I was an altar boy, you led me to believe you had the answer. I must have missed it then, but tell me, now, Father, I need it more now anyway. You're cooled out most of the time walking around with a smile on your face. Come on, give me something, God dammit, give it to me.

My son, you must study your catechism, and then you will know that God is the Creator of heaven and earth and all things.

Jesus, Father, that's the same shit you laid on me twenty years ago. I need new material. That stuff never works.

Oh, there you are, Mother, my mother, the one who started this whole thing. You conceived me and gave birth to me. You gave me warmth and comfort when I was a pink bundle of flesh. You made life wonderful, but now I need some different kinds of answers. Answers that will make life right again. How about it, Mom? Come on, I know you know something. You haven't been around all these summers for nothing. What have you got for me?

Son, you need a job.

A job?

Yes, son, a job is the answer.

Mom, go bake an apple pie. I can get a better answer from a street girl.

Hold it there, baby. Where are you taking it to, walking down these streets with your big fine high ass and worldly eyes, which ain't missed a thing? Maybe you know something? You got any of the real shit for me?

Yeah, the real shit is some dough.

But I got dough.

Then you got the real shit.

But I don't.

You're crazy then, boy.

You mean with that fine pooch ass and great looking eyes, your only answer is dough?

That's my answer, boy.

Honey, go turn a fuckin' trick.

"Now where is that fucking gin bottle? Maybe I left it in the other room. No. I brought it in with me. Well, where is that fucking thing? Whoo-ee! Feeling bad. Don't like lush anyway.

What am I fucking with it for? Who turned the fucking water pink? I got to get out of this tub. It's turning me pink for Christ's sake!"

I put one foot on the side of the tub, started to take a step out, slipped and ran into the open medicine cabinet, cutting my eye badly. "Who left that fucking cabinet open? What's that sticky shit on my ass? Where's that gin bottle? Oh shit, it's going to come out." I just made it to the john in time and the Mexican dinner was making a lot of noise.

Sylvia heard me heaving and came to the door. "Oh, my God! Oh, my God. What's happened? What did you do to your eye?" I was on my knees throwing up. Sylvia got a towel and wiped my face. She walked over to wet the towel and saw blood running down my leg. I had a big gash on my ass.

"Will you please tell me where you hid the gin bottle? You came in here and whizzed it while I was in the tub."

Sylvia pulled the plug in the bathtub and shuddered when she saw the jagged edge of the bottle. "I've got to get you to a doctor, honey. You need some stitches in your butt."

CHAPTER 21

"That's his car, the little darlin'. He should be leaving in ten minutes." Stan kept driving and headed for the house.

"I know which way he comes home so on the way back I'll

keep a lookout for him in case he should leave early. In any event, I'll be there, or close enough, to know when he gets out of the car."

I was looking straight ahead as Stan talked. I was nervous, but I knew not to show it. It was a lot easier to rob under the influence of heroin than morphine. Heroin deadened the soul. Morphine gave a different, edgier kind of feeling. We were on the jeweler's street when I suddenly remembered something. "Does the light come on when you open the door?"

"No, I took it out. This is my official case car. No inside lights and the car ain't registered to me."

"Those bushes on this side of the second house, that's where I want you to drop me. I'll make it from there on my own."

Stan had put the handcuffs and mask on the seat between us. I put them in my waistband along with the gun.

"This is it. Let me out. I won't shut the door. You can lean over and hold it until you get up the street some." I got out of the car and Stan drove away.

I stayed close to the ground, took three quick steps combat-fashion and remained hidden by some bushes. I stopped immediately, turned and surveyed everything in the area for a full thirty seconds. I saw Stan drive back down the street. Then I could see him looking around, a dumb move as it made him look lost and out of place. The bushes weren't thick so there was no problem getting through to the jeweler's driveway. I took out the mask and placed it on top of my head so that, with one quick move, I could pull it over my face. It was too dark to see my watch, but there was no need to until I got inside.

The three minutes from there were the important ones. I heard a car approach and tensed, but it drove by. I relaxed but remembered the energy it took to get ready. Before I could wind down completely another car approached. It slowed down. This was it. The headlights engulfed the entire garage. The double door of the garage opened electronically. The Cadillac drove in, and after what seemed like a century I heard the door slam shut. There were short, light steps coming out of the garage. I peered around the side of the garage and saw a man walking toward the front door of the house. Just then the garage door started coming back down. The electric motor that operated the door made a humming sound. I hadn't counted on that kind of break.

I had been poised and ready like a runner on the starting blocks since the door slammed. The jeweler was five feet from the door now. I made my move. One step, two, three, four, and the key went in the door. The door opened. I made the remaining eight steps as I was pulling down the mask. The jeweler had barely one step inside before I reached him, and gave him a shove that knocked him into a hat rack.

His wife heard the commotion and rushed into the living room. I shut the door with my left hand and pulled the gun out. The man lay on the floor looking up at me, scared. His wife had more composure but I could tell she was also frightened.

"I'm not going to hurt you. Get up."

The man did so slowly. I glanced at his watch: seven-forty now. "I want you to take your watch and ring off quick or I'll shoot mommy here right between the eyes." I aimed the gun at his wife. The jeweler had the watch and ring off in seconds, and handed them to me.

"Now, reach in your pocket and bring out the money, slowly."

He handed it to me. I looked at my watch: seven forty-one now. It was going smoothly—just two more minutes.

"Now stand by your husband," I said to the jeweler's wife. "Quick, come on, move! I'm not going to hurt you. I'm handcuffing you so you can't call the police. Alright, walk into the dining room." I had cased the dining room from the hall when I'd first come in. I put the cuffs on the wife first and made her sit so I could handcuff her to the table leg, and did the same thing with the husband. I looked at my watch: seven forty-two.

"Where's your purse?"

"It's upstairs in the bedroom."

I decided not to go up. "All right now, listen to me. When I'm ten minutes away from here I'll call the police and tell them where you are, so just relax and take it easy until they get here. Okay?"

They just glared at me. I walked to the door and looked over my shoulder. I didn't think I could be seen from where they were, so I took off my mask. I opened the door and was about to walk out when I saw the mirror in the hall. They had been watching me since I'd taken my mask off. I threw the mask on the floor. Well, it was almost a perfect caper. As I walked from the driveway Stan drove by and parked around the corner. I walked to the car and got in.

"How did it go?"

"Smooth. Take your time. I handcuffed them to the dining room table."

"Did you get everything?"

"I got everything." I pulled out the ring and the watch. "You want to give me two bills for my end of this watch?"

I handed the watch to Stan. He looked it over. "You got it." Stan reached in his pocket, pulled out a money clip and counted out two hundred.

I asked him, "What would you do if a guy burned you for a ten-karat diamond?"

"I'd probably kill him."

"You sure of that?"

"Yes, I'd kill him."

"Good."

"What?"

"I said 'good.' That's exactly what I'd do and I'm glad that the guy protecting my interests thinks the same way." I looked into Stan's eyes and handed him the ring. "Take care of our interests, partner." If Stan had any funny ideas, he didn't have them now. This bastard would take it all the way.

"You want to count out that five for me before we get to the restaurant?" I asked. Stan counted it out and handed it to me.

"I'm going to Chicago day after tomorrow with the rock and I should be able to move it as soon as I get there. We'll keep Jimmy Jones posted. I'll be in touch with him. I'm going to rent some place to live. Jimmy knows where you can rent a house in our neighborhood. You ought to stay in our neck of the woods. We can make money together."

"I'll call Jimmy when I get home. Maybe I'll move out here. There's the parking lot."

Stan pulled in next to my car with Sylvia waiting at the wheel. I didn't make with a long farewell.

I got into the passenger seat and Sylvia drove off. After a few blocks she asked me if I was going to get in the back seat. "No need to, I handcuffed them."

In a few minutes she was on the freeway. When we got to East Los Angeles I told her to take an off-ramp, that I wanted to make a call. I got out at an all-night gas station and called the Glendale police. I spoke like a black man with a heavy rural accent and told them where they could find the jeweler.

"Okay, let's go."

"What was that all about?"

"I was trying to get in touch with Jimmy. I'll call him when we get home."

"Was it that important to stop?"

"We're cool. The robbery hasn't even been reported yet." I pulled out my bottle of morphine half-grains. "You want a couple?"

"Okay."

I finished the rest. "Jesus, where does the dope go to?"

Sylvia shook her head and smiled. "In my system, right?"

"You said it, I didn't."

We weren't long on the freeway. A few minutes after the off-ramp we arrived at the motel. I went straight to the dope and took a count. "It's getting low, but I think we got just enough to get us through if you don't stay up all night shooting it. I was just kidding, honey."

"You should have had some stitches in your rear end. How does it feel?"

"It's healing up good."

We got into bed. Sylvia went to sleep almost at once but

the Gorilla wouldn't let me alone. I had thought morphine would be the answer and for a few days it was, but in the end it was always the Gorilla.

How about some food in the morning? I'm getting awfully hungry…you've been neglecting me of late. Maybe just a little taste to take the edge off. You've got enough morphine left to get rid of me completely, but it hasn't made you high since you've been taking it, has it? One little ol' jolt isn't going to get you off and running if you don't want it to. In a few more days you'll be rid of me anyway. And you know how hard it is to quit all at once like that. You've been real good. Been trying real hard. Christ, you deserve a jolt, as good as you've been, and then you can put me away for good. Have a good sleep now, you need it. You can get up early in the morning and go into town, score, and be back before Sylvia even misses you. She could probably use a jolt herself, although she'll pretend she's angry. She really won't be. It's not like you're broke. You can afford it. So rest and dream about the feeling you're going to have tomorrow when you feed me some of the real shit.

CHAPTER 22

I didn't need an alarm to wake up. I had been half awake all night thinking about the trip into town. I jumped out of bed, and dressed quickly. It was difficult to contain my excitement, so I swallowed a handful of morphine tablets before I left. I got into the car and then came back to leave a brief note for Sylvia, although I didn't tell her where I was going. I felt it would only upset her.

The drive to town was painfully slow. The thought of a jolt had upset my stomach and I had a hard time not throwing up. Finally, I arrived at Second and Broadway. I drove past once, twice, and a third time but saw no one, so I decided to park. If the connections weren't there now, they would be soon. It was something I didn't want to rush.

I entered from the north side of the market on Hill Street and bought some fruit, a big shopping bag and a baseball hat. That did it: it made me look like an average stiff doing his marketing. While I was buying some of my favorite cheese I spotted Carnation. Carnation always had someone with him. This time he was standing with four guys I didn't want to see, so I waited. Using my eyes, I tried to get his attention, without success. After what seemed to be an interminable amount of time, I decided to approach him and make the buy and then get the hell out of there. I was halfway over there when Carnation saw me. I kept walking, motioning with my head for him to come over.

He followed me and caught up after walking about twenty or thirty feet. That way, walking alongside each other, it appeared that we were not together. Carnation said, "You're burning up, what are you doing here?"

"Looking for my sick aunt. What do you think I'm doing here?"

"They're down here day and night looking for you. They've been to the bucket offering to take guys out of jail to bust you. You better blow out of here, man, they aren't fucking around."

"You got something with you?"

"What do you want?"

"You got five balloons?"

"Yeah, sure."

I reached into my pocket and counted out a hundred dollars which I slipped to him as we were walking through the market.

He reached up to his mouth as if he was scratching his chin, spat out five balloons, and handed them to me.

"Count it; I'll hang out by the fruit stand."

"Man, just blow. I'm not worried about the count. Don't show in any of the joints you been hanging around, they're serious."

"Thanks, Car. Be cool." With that brief exchange, I walked away.

I was even more careful now as I picked my way toward the parking lot. I was about to cross the street when I saw Lee. I didn't want to see anyone, least of all Lee. He rushed up to me like he was my brother. "Hi, baby, what's going on?"

"Hi, Lee. I'm in a real rush right now. You going to be around for a while?"

"Yeah, I'll be here."

"I got to take care of some business a few blocks from here, but I'll meet you back here in an hour."

As we were talking, Lee fell in beside me and now was walking with me. I couldn't let him see what kind of car I was driving so I tried to act natural so he wouldn't suspect anything. "Look, Lee, I got to pick up some dough. I want to make a four or five ounce buy because I'm going to Chicago, so if I meet you in an hour at your cousin's house can you take care of it for me?"

"No problem, man, I'll have it all set up by then."

"I'll see you there at ten-thirty. Be on time because I've got to catch a plane at one." I looked at his face and saw the weakness and low character. It repelled me.

It didn't take me long to get home. Once inside, I took everything in the bathroom and fixed three whole balloons. I waited for the feeling, which started in the mouth, an unmistakable taste that signaled the brain getting ready for what was coming: the rush, a slow, subtle wave of vibrations that worked its way down from the top of my head releasing a peacefulness and warmth that reached every fiber of my body and blotted out all failure and frustration. I put my head back, closed my eyes and whispered, "Thank God."

I put the outfit away and cleaned the brown heroin from the spoon. There was no movement in the front room so I assumed that Sylvia was still sleeping. Why should I tell her? A few more days with the morphine and she would be cleaned up, and then she could make it. The best thing that I could offer her would be the gate. Sooner or later it had to end. Once I got the money from Stan I could leave her with enough dough and just disappear. She would probably hate me for leaving her, but in the end it would be for the best.

"You in the bathroom?"

"Yeah, I'm here."

"You all right?"

"I'm fine. How about you?"

"I woke up with a chill."

"Me too, so I took a jolt of morphine. You want me to fix you one?"

"I guess so." She walked into the bathroom and I got up so she could relieve herself. "It smells like heroin in here."

"I used some matches to cook up the 'phine. I was in a hurry."

She gave me the once over, but how would she know? My eyes were always pinpointed and both drugs are from the poppy. I was filled with guilt, so at once to cover myself I prepared the morphine. When I finished fixing her I got into bed. I knew I was not going to be able to hide the high but I didn't care. It was worth it to lie there in bed with my mind blank.

Sylvia came out of the bathroom. She took one look at me and knew. But, I figured, she also knew it wouldn't do any good to say anything.

"Our little bag of goodies is getting low."

"What?" I was out of it and she had startled me.

"I said, "There's not much dope left. Do you think we'll make it?"

"Sure. We'll be alright." I was really good. I had more moves than a magician. Right now I didn't care two shits for the dope in the bag now that I was smacked down.

"Are we going to look for an apartment today?"

It was an effort for me to speak. My speech was thick. If only she'd leave me alone. "Sure, if you want to." Goddamn, that was a dumb replay. My eyes felt so good closed I could have stayed that way forever. "I'm going to take a quick nap, maybe a half hour, and then we'll get out of here and find a place."

"Do you want to eat?"

"No, I'm a little sick to my stomach."

"I'm going out to eat. You can take a nap while I'm gone."

"Alright. Will you wake me up when you get back?"

"Sure."

I was in nod city before she got out the door.

I was wide awake and feeling good by the time she got back, but one look into her eyes told me that she knew. "You want to look for an apartment, or go dancing? What do you want to do?" I asked lamely in an effort to steer away from the subject of my using again.

She gave me a cold hard look. "Fuck."

So, this was how she punished me for the jolt that I had taken. It caught me off-balance but I was quick to make a joke of it.

"An oversexed woman will ruin a man."

She dropped the subject. "Are you going to stay here?" she asked.

"No, I got some money from Stan. We've got enough to move. I'll give Jimmy a call. It's his turf. He'll know of something." I picked up the phone and dialed Jimmy's number. "Hello, is Jimmy there?"

"Who's calling?"

"It's me."

"Hi, Woody. It's Helen."

"Oh, is this your number?"

"Yes. Where have you been keeping yourself?"

"On the run, as always."

"Well, don't be a stranger. Hold on, I'll get Jimmy for you."

"Okay, thanks."

"My man, how are you?"

"I'm good, but I have to find a place to live and the last time I saw Stan he said that you knew of a house out here that was for rent."

"Yeah, I got just the spot for you if you don't mind living in Hawaiian Gardens."

"What's Hawaiian Gardens?"

"Where are you right now?"

"At a gas station on Paramount, just off the freeway." Jimmy gave me directions to Helen's apartment.

"What happened?" Sylvia asked.

"Jimmy said he has a house in Hawaiian Gardens."

"Hawaiian Gardens?"

"That's what I said. It's out here someplace. We're going to see about it right now. He's at a girl's house down the street and told me to stop by." On the way, I briefed Sylvia on Helen. I told her what little I knew about her and that she was working for Stan.

When we arrived at the apartment I knocked and was welcomed in. After the introductions, Jimmy took over. He seemed exuberant over my being so close by. I noticed the difference in his attitude and attributed it to the way I had handled the jewelry job. Jimmy Jones was the kind of guy who respected someone who could rob and steal. Probably, he would have liked to have been able to do it himself but he couldn't, so he set up jobs and this put him in what rounders called "the life."

He was like a music teacher; he could tell you what to blow but he couldn't do it himself. He was in heaven when he was surrounded by criminals who weren't committing crimes on a whim but ones who depended on crime for a living. For some strange reason he had the need to be accepted by people on the wrong side of the law. He wanted something for nothing, like the housewife snitching a can of pepper, or a gambler or a thief. But despite this, Jimmy had a quick mind and was likable. He probably could have been successful in anything he tried.

"Where are you trying to stick me, Jimmy? Where is Hawaiian Gardens?"

"It's perfect for you. It's a neighborhood that the cops never go into."

"Who lives there?"

"It's a mixture of crazy Okies and Texans. On Saturday nights they all get drunk and fist fight, even the women. It's got to be a real emergency for the cops to come in there."

"But I don't like to fist fight on Saturday nights."

"Oh, they'll give ya a good leaving alone once they see where you're coming from, but you can also have more trouble there than the Second World War if you want it. Some streets aren't even paved. Half of the people who live there work and the other half just hang out. The ones that work are hod carriers, longshoremen, cement workers, or do some kind of work in construction."

"But where is it?"

"It's only a mile from here. It's an area about three miles square at the end of Paramount."

"That close?"

"That's it."

"What's the house look like?"

"It's a one bedroom stucco, maybe twenty years old. It's my sister's house. It's only a hundred a month and I'll get it for you without a deposit."

"Furniture?"

"There's a bed, stove, refrigerator and the rest we can pick up at a used furniture store I know of. I'll get you everything you need for practically nothing. Let's go over there and I'll show it to you. Let's all go. You want to go, Helen?"

"Sure, I'll go."

Sylvia and Helen had hit it off good together and had been talking ever since they were introduced. We all piled into my car and drove to Hawaiian Gardens. Ever since I had been talking to Jimmy about the house in Hawaiian Gardens, I had my doubts, but when I got there it looked like any other working neighborhood. The house didn't look bad. The lawn was run down but a little water was all it needed. Jimmy had the key so we went in and looked around. Sylvia loved it and immediately saw the possibilities of making it into a home. If it was as cool as Jimmy said, it would be a good place to stay instead of leaving town. If the cops never came around and Sylvia and I never left the house, we could live off that diamond ring for a long time.

"I like it, Jimmy."

"You want to take it?"

"Yeah, I think so. What do you think, honey?"

"It's great."

"Okay, ya got it?"

"Just up me a hundred and I'll call my sister when I get home and tell her it's rented."

I reached into my pocket and handed Jimmy a hundred.

"You gonna stay here tonight?"

"Yes, I want to get out of that motel."

"That wraps it up, I guess. Why don't you drive me back to Helen's? I got to be in Long Beach in an hour."

"I'm ready. Come on, ladies, let's do it."

Sylvia and Helen had been going over the house and intuitively knew what changes to make. They had changed things a half-dozen times and were in the process of rearranging the bedroom when I told them it was time to leave. Back at Helen's, Jimmy said goodbye and left for Long Beach. Helen asked us if we would like to stay for dinner and we accepted. We decided to get our things from the motel while Helen was preparing dinner.

When we got back to the motel I quickly took stock of the drugstore dope.

"Is it going to last us?" Sylvia asked.

"We got just enough to get over, if we don't get hoggy."

She gave me a funny look and I was sorry I said it.

"You got everything, hon?"

"Lately it doesn't take long to pack."

"Good times are coming."

"I know. I was making a joke."

We left the motel and got into the car. On the way to Helen's I was starting to get sick, but decided to hold out as long as I could.

Helen's house felt comfortable, a reflection of her personality. The dinner was fabulously prepared but by now the chills were on me, and I had to force the food down. Helen sensed a change in my personality and asked me if something was wrong. I said no, but then decided to tell her the truth. "Helen—"

"Yes?"

"I've got to tell you something. I don't know how you're going to take it but I want you to know what's going on with me and Sylvia." I waited a second for her reaction and then said, "We're hooked."

"You mean on dope?"

"Yes, but we're tapering off and trying to quit completely."

"Do you get sick when you stop?"

"I'm sick right now."

She looked at me not knowing what to say. "Is there anything I can do?"

"Would it spook you if Sylvia and I did it here?"

"No, not at all if it will make you feel better."

"Thanks, Helen. I'll be right back. I'm going to the car to get it."

I returned moments later with the bag of dope and the outfit. I prepared two tablets and fixed Sylvia. I got up to clean the outfit but suddenly felt a pounding in my head. With every heartbeat it felt like my head was going to explode. Now came the sickness to the stomach and I barely had time to get to the bathroom. Everything came up, fast and hard, as if I had a pump in my stomach pushing it out. After a while there was nothing left to vomit, but my stomach kept pushing. Sylvia came crashing through the bathroom door and I moved to the sink. She didn't stay over the toilet long, not as long as I had.

"Oh my God, it's coming from the other end." I took my pants down and brushed Sylvia away from the toilet. Now she moved to the sink.

"What is it?" she asked.

"I don't know."

She was very short of breath and could hardly talk. The discharge from my bowels was as rapid as it had been from my mouth, and sweat was pouring off me even faster. The pounding in my head was getting louder and my ears were ringing. I got off the toilet and Sylvia got on. It had all happened so fast and I was so fucking sick I couldn't concern myself with what to do. I put my arms over the sink. Holding on, I dry heaved. I felt like something was going to rupture. The throwing up began to subside but the rest of the symptoms remained the same. Maybe this was it; I thought I was going to die. What a way to fade… couldn't even fight it.

Helen stood by the door and asked if there was anything she could do. It was humiliating but I was so sick I couldn't even apologize.

"Under the seat on the driver's side wrapped in a cigarette package are a couple of balloons."

"Is the car in front?"

I just nodded. Helen left returning two minutes later. She placed the balloons on the sink in front of me.

"Get me the outfit."

"The what?"

"The eyedropper and needle. It's in the kitchen." She brought it to me. "Oh, please, a spoon and a match."

I had a difficult time standing, so I sat on the floor and opened up a balloon. Helen came back in with the spoon and matches and placed them by me. I emptied the balloon into the spoon. As I was doing this, Sylvia placed her hand on my head in a sign of affection. Jesus Christ, I thought, as sick as we both were, she was still concerned about me.

There was no use trying to hit the main line. I was too sick for that. Instead I drew the heroin up and shot half of it into my shoulder. The other half I gave to Sylvia. The heroin had practically no affect on me. Nothing, it seemed, would stop the terrible pounding in my head. My clothes were wet and now both Sylvia and I had the chills. I looked at Sylvia and she was shaking. "Honey, let's get into the shower."

We took off our clothes, got into the shower together, and turned the hot water as high as we could stand it. Helen came in and asked if there was anything she could do. I told her to turn the heat on. We stayed in the shower until the hot water ran out and then reluctantly got out and helped each other dry off. Helen took our clothes out of the bathroom and hung them up to dry. She also brought in fresh towels.

We were starting to feel a little better but we were exhausted. In the front room we lay on the floor and Helen covered us with a blanket. I was so spent I couldn't even say thanks, but I felt a great indebtedness to her for helping us. She would be on my forever list now, and that was right up there with Grandma. The chills had subsided somewhat and the sweating had slowed down. The heroin had worked.

CHAPTER 23

The next morning the sun was beating down on my face. I had a terrible taste in my mouth and my throat was sore from throwing up, but I was alive. Last night I thought it was all over. Now I knew how it felt to get a hot shot.

I looked at Sylvia still sleeping, and remembered that, at the height of her sickness last night, she had shown concern for me. The sickness was still on me but not like it was last week. The morphine had helped. In a way I wished I didn't have any heroin but now that I had it in my possession, I knew it was impossible to give it a pass. However, I would try and fix it up by taking a jolt in the morning and then using the morphine throughout the day. If I gave Sylvia some in the morning with me I would only have enough for two, maybe three more days. I heard the back door open and Helen appeared carrying a laundry basket with my clothes. "Hi. How do you feel?"

"All right. I want to apologize for last night."

"Don't say anything, it's all right. What kind of dope was that?" Helen asked.

"I don't think it was dope. I think it was embalming fluid."

Sylvia opened her eyes. "Well, Sylvia's with us."

Sylvia looked up apologetically. "Oh, Helen, I'm so sorry about last night. I don't know where to start."

"Well, don't try. The big thing is that you're both all right."

"I've never had anything like that happen before," I said." I guess it serves me right using something I didn't know anything about."

"Where did you get it?"

"A friend of mine gave it to me along with some morphine."

"Can you find out what it was?"

"It doesn't make any difference now. I'm still alive and what's left I'll throw away."

"You're not angry with the guy who gave it to you?"

"I'm sure he didn't do it intentionally."

"Are you guys hungry?"

"I could go for some coffee but I'm still a little sick from last night."

"How about you, Sylvia?"

"Thanks, Helen, but I'm sick too."

"Helen, do you have those balloons I gave you last night?"

"It's all in the bathroom."

"Well, the first thing I'm going to do is throw that dope away."

"That's probably a good idea."

I wasn't real sick but I was so anxious to get to the bathroom that the small talk was making me nervous. Helen sensed my irritation and said, "I'll make you some coffee. How do you want it?"

"We both like it black."

"Here are your clothes. I'll get the coffee while you're getting dressed."

"Helen?"

"Yes?"

"I'd just like to tell you you're a super lady and if you ever need any kind of favor, I hope you'll ask me."

"Thanks." Helen walked into the kitchen.

I got dressed and motioned for Sylvia to follow me to the bathroom. We fixed, but not the usual amount. I couldn't help feeling guilty about starting all over again. When we came out of the bathroom Helen told us that Stan had just called and was coming over.

"Did you tell him I was here?"

"That's why he's coming over, to see you, not me."

"Oh, I thought you were going with him."

"No, it's not like that. I went out with him once. Why, I don't know, and now I can't shake him."

"Just tell him you don't want to go out with him."

"He gets pushy. When he left town he said he'd see me when he got back."

"What did you say?"

"I told him I was going through some things where I didn't want to date anyone and then he said, 'We'll straighten that out when I get back.' He scares me."

"Just tell him you don't want to be with him."

"It sounds so simple when you say it like that, but it's not that simple."

"How long before he'll be here?"

"He said he was coming right over."

"Is he aware you're turned off by him?"

"I'm sure he is but that doesn't stop him. Why do you ask?"

"Because I don't think he would come on to you with Sylvia and me here for fear of looking bad."

Helen heard a car drive up and went to the window. "He's here."

"Helen, you're so nervous."

"He makes me nervous."

I opened the door as Stan was walking up the stairs.

"Hi, Woody." He reached the door and I made way for him to come in. Stan acknowledged everyone and sat down on the couch. "You got some coffee, Helen?" he asked.

"Sure, I'll get it." As she went to the kitchen, Sylvia followed so Stan and I could talk. Even though we knew each other's business, she knew we would both feel more comfortable by ourselves.

"How did it go?"

"Howie got popped for receiving stolen property the day I got there so he can't make any moves. I didn't see him. I called him on the phone and talked to his wife. I figured there wasn't any reason to hang around. He might have a tail. I don't know. I told his wife to him call me when he gets some air."

"When will that be?"

"What she told me in a roundabout way was that he'll not be doing anything until he goes to his preliminary hearing. He wants to find out what they have on him before he makes a move. He's been a fence since God was a pup, so there's no telling what they got on him."

"What do we do now? I mean, to the rock?"

"I'll make some calls. We won't have it for long."

"When we talked this caper over you said you could move it in three days. I wouldn't have gone in there on the come."

"I know."

"Why don't you buy my end out right now?"

"I can't do it today. Not right now."

"Well, are you going to wait until Howie cools off to move it or do you have some other connections?"

"I've got a couple of other guys I can call, but I wanted to move it out of town because of the heat and besides, we'd also get a better price in Chicago."

"Look, Stan, I didn't go into that robbery and put a gun in that guy's face to be told I got to wait until some jerk fifteen hundred miles away cools off. You got to come up with better answers."

"Do you want to try and move it?"

"That wasn't part of the deal. I would never have considered taking it off if I thought for a minute there was going to be a hassle unloading it. I don't know where to fence it or I'd have been robbing jewelry stores long before this. If you've got someone to call, then let's call now." I knew Stan would take an edge if he could so I laid it out clean from the start. There was a small chance that he might try to bully it out for more time. I was very definite when I said, "Shall we call?"

"Yeah, I can do that. I'm just as anxious to dump that rock as you are." No one was home on the first call and the second call was also a bust-out because the guy didn't have the money. "I don't think it's smart to sell it in this town but if you want me to, I'll keep trying."

"What's happening in Chicago?"

"I can sell it there for sure, but it will be another week before Howie will take it. If we keep asking around it could get out and some jerk could drop a dime on us to the insurance company for a cute piece of change. I can give you a grand right now and let me work on it in Chicago. Believe me, Howie will buy it."

"That sounds respectable. I can live with that."

"All right. By the end of the week I'll put a grand in your hands and I'll stay on the phone to Chicago until I put it together. Hey, Helen, did you go to Brazil for that coffee?" Helen entered with the coffee.

All the time I had been talking to Stan I had been careful that his voice hadn't carried to the kitchen so the girls wouldn't hear the way I had been leaning on him.

"I hear you and Woody moved into Hawaiian Gardens?"

"We haven't really lived there yet, but we're living there, if that makes any sense."

"It'll take you a while to get settled but you'll like it there. It's a good neighborhood. Everyone stays to themselves."

"So we're told."

"You got a phone yet?"

"I'm going down for it today."

"Call me when you get your number. In the meantime, if I get any news I'll be right over with it. How about some dinner tonight, Helen?"

"Thanks, but I'm going to bed early. I'm really tired."

"You and me are going to hook it up sooner or later, baby. You better accept that and quit fighting it."

Helen shrugged her shoulders as if to say "big deal." She was not frightened with me and Sylvia there, but nevertheless, Stan still made her feel uneasy.

"Well, don't plan anything for tomorrow night and I'll be by early."

"Stan, I—"

"Look, bitch, I'm trying to treat you nice but don't give me a hard time. I'll be here at seven tomorrow night. Just be ready."

Helen lowered her eyes and said in a frightened whisper, "Stan, I don't want to go out with you."

"Well, you just don't have that much to say about it, honey." He drew the word "honey" out sarcastically. "I was alright to date when I put some money in your pocket, wasn't I? Wasn't I? Do you think you got some fucking trick here? 'Cause you ain't, baby. If anyone's the trick, it's you, because if I want you I'll have you and you don't have a fucking thing to say about it. Is that clear enough for you to understand?"

Helen hadn't said a word in answer to his last question so he repeated it once more, saying it more slowly. "I asked if you understand."

"Stan, I don't know why you want to be with me if I don't want to be with you. You can have other girls. It's not like I'm your only choice. I'd like to be your friend. Can't we keep it on that basis?"

"I asked you if you understand how it's going to be, that's

all. Nothing else. Answer that."

He was really pressing her now and Helen was frightened. She looked toward me for some support. It was a delicate situation. I didn't want to make a move that would affect my business with Stan, but I was not about to let him abuse Helen. Stan got up quickly but before he reached Helen, I rose. Stan hadn't expected me to help her. He stopped and looked at me.

"Come on, Stan, take it easy."

"This bitch thinks I'm some kind of trick."

"No she doesn't, Stan."

"If I tell this bitch to jump, she better jump. She ain't got no say-so."

"Yeah, she does, Stan. She can speak her mind." I said this in a low voice and looked straight into his eyes.

"You takin' this cunt's slack, that what you doing?"

"Call it anything you like. She's my friend."

It was now or never. The challenge was on and Stan knew it. There was an awkward silence that was up to him to break. "Now, wouldn't that be a bitch for you and me to get in a jackpot over a broad?" Stan said.

"Yes, it would be, Stan."

Stan looked at Helen and said, "Forget it, baby. Besides your coffee is too good to get barred from the house. Well, then, I'm off to take care of some things. I'll see all of you people later." Stan made his goodbyes and left.

As soon as the door closed, Helen ran over to me and put her arms around me. "Thanks."

Sylvia looked at us and smiled. She knew Helen was a friend.

CHAPTER 24

Sylvia opened her eyes and asked what time it was.
"Ten thirty."

"We're going good, honey. Have you fixed yet?"

"No, I've been thinking about it. You ready?"

Sylvia nodded.

"We've come a long way from fixing morphine every twenty minutes to once every twelve hours. We got some left. You want that or smack?"

"I think the morphine holds me longer."

I slipped out of bed and got the dope from the dresser. I prepared everything and hit Sylvia first. I felt good now that we were only shooting quarter grain tablets. I hit myself and settled back. I had not lived a drug-free existence since I was twenty.

It seemed like five lifetimes back when I took my first jolt. Back then, I was playing with Joe Abrams, who was a bitch of a piano player, and during a break we fixed in the back of a car. I remembered throwing up all over his gray suede shoes, and also that I played forty choruses without my chops getting tired. In the beginning, it made me everything I ever thought of becoming. It made me look better, play better, and feel self-assured about any situation. It didn't take much to fix me. I thought that state of heaven would never leave. How did it get so turned around? Now it was all in reverse. All the good feelings had left. I hadn't been straight in twelve years and the prospect of living without drugs terrified me.

I heard someone at the front door, and immediately took the gun from under the bed and placed it in my waistband. I walked to the door and peered out the curtains, and was relieved to see it was Stan. I opened the door and invited him in.

"How you been?"

"Good. What's going on?"

"I got some work for you. Can we talk?"

"Sure, c'mon in. Sylvia's the only one here."

"Why don't we talk in the car?"

"Sylvia knows all my business."

"I don't mean that, Woody. I want to show you something."

"All right. You want to go right now?"

"If you're not too busy."

"Let's do it." We got into the car without saying a word to each other. This was the first time I had seen Stan since I had pulled him up at Helen's. If Stan had any feelings about what had happened there, he had let them pass, or so it seemed.

"I heard from Chicago this morning. He told me to come back with the rock on Monday and he'll take it off our hands. I've already made reservations for a six a.m. flight out so I should be able to wrap it up and be back by Monday evening at the latest."

"Well, that's good news. You know, I was thinking I may just stay here in Hawaiian Gardens, even after I get the money. It's quiet and there's no heat. I'd probably be just as safe here as in a farm town in Nebraska."

"Sure you would. All you have to do is stay out of LA. I'll print up some ID for you and Sylvia. We can do that now. It's on the way to the place I want to show you."

"You mean you can do it right now?"

"Sure, no problem."

"That really is far out. I'll feel a lot more secure with some good ID in my pocket."

"You can't go anywhere without good ID. If you get stopped, it's all over."

Stan pulled off the freeway and after going down a few side streets, he stopped in an alley and parked. "Come on. We'll walk it from here." Stan produced a key which opened a door to a small warehouse and we entered.

The room was bigger than a garage. There was an old-fashioned bed in one corner with a cheap quilt thrown over it. In the middle of the room stood an impressive looking duplicating machine. "There's your driver's license," Stan said as he pointed to the machine. "They don't do any better than that in Sacramento. That will print anything that goes on paper."

"I believe it. It must have cost a fortune."

"It didn't cost a cent. But that's a two-hour story. What name are you going to use?"

"Think I'll use a Jewish name."

"Why Jewish?"

"How many Jews do you see when you go to jail? And if you get rousted, the rollers treat you a little different. You could easily be the son of a doctor or a stockbroker who owns half of New York City."

"Well, what name?"

"Give me, uh, Art Weinstock. Make it Arthur Weinstock."

"Age?"

"Thirty-four."

"Birth date?"

"One-three-twenty-five."

"Height?"

"Six feet."

"Weight?"

"Two-ten."

"Where do you want to live?"

"I'll make it Beverly Hills. Oh, 450 North Roxbury Drive."

"Here, fill this card out for Sylvia. I'll go print this one." Stan turned on the machine and ran off a half-dozen licenses. By the time he was finished, I had filled out the card on Sylvia. Stan handed me the licenses and went back to the duplicating machine to do hers. In a few seconds he handed them to me. "How do you like them?"

"Man, they look real. Stan, can you do something with birth certificates?"

"Of course. I've got the seal and the blanks. You want one for you and Sylvia?"

"Yeah, and one for my grandmother."

"What about mom and dad?" he said in a sarcastic tone.

"Grandma's mom and dad in one package. I am not going

to be too comfortable living in LA. and if I leave the country, I'll be taking her with me."

Stan shrugged and got the typewriter and seal out and asked me again what names I wanted to use for grandma. I decided to use her real first name, Idah, and told Stan to spell it with an H. "Idah Haas will be good, Stan." In a few minutes Stan had them all together.

I put everything in my pockets and stood up ready to leave. "This job in town?"

"Yeah, it's on Eighth Street near Vermont. You know the neighborhood?"

"Like the back of my hand."

We reached the car and drove the first few blocks in silence. I finally broke the ice. "What's in this place we're going to look at?"

"Money."

"How much?"

"Anywhere from eight to twenty big ones."

"Who has seen the money there?"

"Let me start from the beginning. It's a waiter's union and they pay their dues on the first of the month. I found out they have a membership to twenty-five thousand. I don't figure all of them working, but the ones who work got to pay their dues or they don't get a card. I've been in the place twice. Once was with a friend of mine and once on the pretense of joining the union. Both times they were collecting money like confetti. On the third day an armored car picks up the loot."

"How do you know that?"

"I make it my business to know."

"You saw them pick it up?"

"Yeah, I saw them."

"How many people in the office?"

"Four. Three chicks and a guy."

"Where do they keep the money?"

"In a double-door safe. There are two cash drawers in the front office and that's where the safe is. There are two small offices on the north side of the building where they probably do the bookkeeping. You have a view of everything once you get inside."

"You think they got any guns there?"

"If they do, I don't know who would use them. The guy looks like Clark Kent and he's built like a pear and the chicks aren't going to shoot you. No, I don't make them for having any guns around. But let's look at the worst of it and say they did. They couldn't even get them once you make your move because they're all right there together. If I was doing it, I'd go right over the counter and get control, put everyone on the floor and have one girl open the safe."

"When did you figure on doing this?"

"The money is there today. It's up to you."

"I didn't bring my piece with me."

"I got a .38 Police Special in the trunk and an army bag to carry the loot in."

"You think of everything."

"Like I said, that's my business."

"I suppose you know the route to get out of there?" I was looking straight ahead and thinking, weighing it out. The money would give me enough air to lie down for a year, maybe two, with the ring. I had already been on one job with Stan and he had been there when he said he would be. I was still thinking it through as he parked the car.

"There it is. It's that white building next to the alley by the gas station."

"Has it got a back door?"

"No. You got to come out the same way you go in. I can park over there on the side once you get in and be waiting for you. You come out and fifteen steps later you're in the car."

"Let me look at it for a few minutes, Stan."

We both sat in silence for five, ten, fifteen, minutes. I had already made up my mind that I was going to go through with it. It was now only a matter of getting the tempo together. Four people had come and gone since we had started watching the building. "Get the bag and piece, Stan. When the guy who just walked in comes out, I'll take it."

I didn't take my eyes off the building. Stan got out of the car and in a few seconds came back with the gun and the bag. I put the gun on the seat between us and placed the bag on my lap. I put the gun in my waist and pulled my shirt over it. I took the ID Stan had printed and put it in the glove compartment. "I won't need that right now."

I experienced a slight nervousness, but I was not frightened. I knew it had to be done. Somehow the game had changed. It was not a thrill anymore. It was too serious now. Now that the revenge I once felt toward the O'Rourkes of the world had disappeared, I had to summon a different kind of strength from a source that was alien to me. I could feel the change in my body; the tenseness, the concentration, the alertness were all overwhelming.

The last man came out the door, and I got out of the car. "I won't be longer than five minutes, Stan."

"I'll be waiting. Good luck."

I nodded and was off. Crossing the street, I felt perfectly calm. I wondered how this could be. My life would be on the line in the next few minutes. I could be shot and killed, and yet I felt as relaxed as if I was going to the grocery store.

I opened the door, walked in and exploded. With one hand on the counter, I vaulted it and as I landed on the other side, I pulled the gun out. "Everyone on the floor, except you, honey. You get on that safe and open it before I count to thirty or you're all going to heaven. Twenty-nine, twenty-eight, twenty-seven—"

It had all happened so fast that none of them had a chance to think. The lady opening the safe was so startled she just stood there. When I hit "twenty-five" she went to the dial and started turning it. Knowing I had everyone under my control, I put the gun inside my pants and started emptying the two cash drawers. I hadn't stopped counting, and was now down to twelve. "Eleven—"

"It's open."

"You can join the others on the floor. Come on, baby, snap to it."

She got on the floor with terror in her eyes and I wanted to tell her not to be afraid, that I was not going to hurt her. I walked quickly to the safe, and started throwing money in the bag I had brought with me. It seemed like I would never get it all and there was some in the envelopes, too. I put all the envelopes in my bag. I knew they couldn't all have money in them, but I put them in anyway.

Finally, it was over. I had all the money and was about to vault the counter again when I saw a window in one of the offices that lead to the alley. It was open and didn't have a screen. If I went out the window I could walk down the alley ten feet and get in the car. I took the gun out of my waist and put it with the money.

"All right, everyone, stay where you are. I'm going into this office and count the money before I leave." I walked into the office and closed the door. I didn't slow down but put one foot on the window sill and jumped out, holding the bag of money. It was only about three feet to the ground. I unconsciously looked to the right and couldn't believe my eyes: there were six squad cars in front of the place and the street was blocked with black and whites; two other cop cars pulled up. The only cops I had seen were the ones who had gotten out of the car, and they both had sawed-off shotguns which they laid over the hood and pointed in the direction of the building.

There was a small picket fence separating the gas station from the alley and people were gathered in the gas station looking and watching the building. I was standing right by the fence. I backed over the fence, one foot at a time, and cautiously backed toward the crowd, the few precious feet I needed. I kept staring at the building like the rest of the crowd.

I saw a cop get behind a black and white with a bullhorn. "All right, clear out of that station if you don't want to get hurt. Officer Scalise, get those people out of there right now."

I was in the main stream of citizens. It was a thousand miles to the other side. I couldn't rush. I had to look casual and do what the rest of the crowd was doing. They were looking at the building as they walked away. Only a few more feet to go until I reached the curb. But before I got there I heard the voice through the bullhorn "All right come out with your hands up high in the air." I continued walking. I passed a few stores and then an apartment house with a "For Rent" sign in the window. There was no chance to make it if I didn't get off the streets. It was not going to take them long to discover that I was not in the building. My only chance for time depended on whether the people in that building thought I was still in the office, and were too frightened to move. I quickly ducked into the doorway of the apartment house and knocked on the manager's door. An old lady in her seventies opened it and said in a suspicious voice, "What can I do for you, honey?"

"I'd like to see the apartment for rent."

"It's a two bedroom, one thirty-five per month, first and last and a thirty-five dollar cleaning deposit. You still want to see it?"

"Yes, I'm looking for a two bedroom for me and my wife."

"Well, it's on the second floor. Wait until I get the key." She reappeared after what seemed like hours. She shuffled ahead wearing worn-out-at-the-heels slippers. I wanted to pick her up and carry her upstairs, but I played it to the end. I was thinking now that I should have run. We finally got to the second floor and she opened the door to a dingy looking apartment facing the street. I looked out the window and saw an army of cops out there.

"What's the neighborhood like?"

"Oh, it's so-so."

"The reason I ask is that my wife is a writer and she'd be here most of the day by herself. I'm a sheet metal worker and I work the day shift. I just came in from Portland to work for Douglas. I worked for them up there for four years. My wife's parents live close by and I've been walking around the neighborhood most of the day looking for a place I like. I would like to live upstairs. I feel it's safer, don't you?"

"Well, I ain't lost nothing yet, sonny boy."

"Let me look at the bathroom, and if it's all right I'll take it." I walked into the bathroom, opened up the canvas bag and quickly pulled some money from the bag, folded it and put it in my pockets. I came out of the bathroom in seconds. "I like it. I'll take it."

"The lights and gas is extra. You know that?"

"Yes, of course."

"And ya can't play no loud music."

"We always go to bed early. You don't have to worry about us. I didn't catch your name, dear."

"Gracie."

"Well, Gracie darling, do you think I could use your phone to call my wife and tell her I found a place for us?"

"Sure thing. I'll write up a rent receipt for you, too." We walked down the stairs and I put my hand under her arm to help her along. By now she was completely at ease with me. The phone was on the desk with a short cord so I was going to have to talk with her right there.

I counted out the money and handed it to her. She sat down at the desk and started writing out a receipt for me. "There's the phone. Help yourself."

I dialed the number. After a couple of rings Sylvia answered. "Hi, sweetheart. I found a place for us over here on Eighth and Vermont. What? Right. Near your parent's house. Real nice landlady named Gracie." I winked at Gracie.

"You can't talk? Something's wrong?" Sylvia asked anxiously.

"That's it. Stan may send John over to pick you up and I don't want you riding with him. I don't know him that well so go over to Helen's right now and I'll pick you up in a few hours. I'm so tired from looking at apartments all day, I'm going to have to rest a couple of hours before I pick you up, but leave now."

"Can you tell me anything?"

"No, honey."

"Are you all right?"

"Yes, at the present time."

"What happened to Stan?"

"Gee, I don't know. I sure wish I did."

"Are you trying to tell me Stan could send the man over here when you use John's name?

"Yes, I am."

"But they don't have you?"

"That's right."

"You did something with Stan and you don't know where he is?"

"Right. That's about it."

"Are you going to be able to get to Helen's? Should I pick you up?"

"No, I'll be home in a couple of hours. I'll call a cab when I'm ready to leave. I'll need my vitamins."

"I got you."

"I'll see you in a few hours, sweetheart."

"Can't I do anything?"

"Hurry. Bye now."

As I hung up Gracie handed me the keys and a receipt. "You'll have to fill out this paper."

"Sure, Gracie. Just give me a pen and I'll fill it out in the apartment. I'm going to rest for an hour before I pick up my wife. Thanks for everything." With that I turned around and walked upstairs.

Once in the apartment I pulled the shades down, then got to my knees at one corner of the window and looked out. The cars were moving on Eighth Street again and I counted two black and whites. I stayed at the window for two hours, watching. In that time I saw three police cars but one hadn't passed in the last thirty-five minutes.

I put the dead bolt on and started counting the money. Another twenty minutes passed and I was eleven thousand richer. Well, Stan had been right about one thing: there had been some money there.

I looked out the window again. I looked for things the average person wouldn't notice. Detectives riding in straight cars; the flow of traffic. There were three local riders standing on the corner. That was a real good sign. If there had been lots of cops out there looking for me they would have been sure to stop the riders and ask questions and the low riders had been there for over an hour. It was becoming dark and the street was no longer hot, I could sense it. I took one last look before leaving for Gracie's apartment downstairs. I knocked twice, and she opened up the door.

"Hi, Gracie. Will you call a cab for me? I'll get us a couple of beers while you're doing that."

"Sure thing, honey boy. Make mine a Bud."

"I'll be right back."

She closed the door and I went upstairs again. I waited five minutes and came back to Gracie's and knocked once more.

"What happened to my Bud?"

"Well, I'm going to give you three bucks to get your own because I am on a diet and if I see you drink one I'll have to have one myself, so—here." I handed her three dollars. "You can get yourself a six pack after I go. You wouldn't want a fat tenant, would you?"

"You don't have to—"

"Here, come on. Take it." I thrust the money in her hand. She accepted it without much show.

"Is the cab here?"

"Yeah. I figured you'd want to wait here."

I was nervous. They could have put a line on all the cabs.

"This city sure lights up at night, Gracie." I said this as I casually walked to the window and looked out.

"Well, it ain't exactly Portland, you know. You really took a long rest."

"I had been walking all day and I was tired. You know, I fell asleep up there on the floor."

I saw it, the beautiful yellow cab that was going to take me to freedom. But God dammit, the cab was parked on the other side of the street and the bastard was honking his horn. Oh that fucker! I couldn't cross the street with the bag in my hand; too much open real estate. I waited it out. The cab waited it out. I walked out of the apartment without saying anything to Gracie, whistled and motioned the driver over. He reluctantly made a

U-turn and while he was turning I walked back and said goodbye to the landlady.

"I'll see you tomorrow, Gracie."

"Okay, sonny boy, and thanks for the beer money."

"You're welcome."

I stood at the top of the steps for a brief second, looking both ways and then I was in the cab.

"Where to?"

"The Santa Ana Freeway."

CHAPTER 25

I closed my eyes and leaned back on the seat. Freedom City. Somehow I had gotten away but so had all my hopes. After today there was no chance of ever straightening out my beefs with a high-powered attorney. I had to make an out-of-the-country move to survive. There was going to be so much heat on me by tomorrow morning I wouldn't even be able to go into a supermarket for a pack of cigarettes.

The pressure of getting away had taken all my energy and I hadn't had time for anything but escape. But now that it was all over I realized I was sick. My eyes and nose were running like crazy and I couldn't stop yawning. My insanity took over and I thought of stopping the cab to score. The only reason I didn't was that I knew there were some drugs at home with Sylvia. I couldn't stop yawning and had that tingling between my legs again. I had to laugh about that. The drugs made everything happen in reverse. I could be in bed with Sophia Loren and not be able to get it up, but my prick got hard in the back of a taxi after spending the afternoon being chased by half of the Los Angeles Police Department. Or I could be in one of the better restaurants with a pocketful of money and not able to eat, and then I'd come home and eat a jar of peanut butter, ravenously.

"How far from the freeway is it, sir?"

"You can take the Paramount off-ramp and stop at the drive-in on the left."

"Got it." Not long afterward the cabbie pulled up in front of the drive-in and let me off. I gave him a five buck tip. It was a long way out and the cabbie had probably missed a lot of rides.

I called Helen's house and told her where to pick me up. It was only a few blocks away so they got there in a few minutes. They were both happy to see me and even more so after I started telling the story of what happened.

"Do you think Stan drove off when he saw all those cops, or that they got him there?" Sylvia asked.

"Come on. What would they arrest him for, sitting in the car? Of course he drove off and left me."

Once we got home I got the drugs from Sylvia. On my way to the bathroom I said, "This is to be continued, girls. I'll be right back."

After fixing, I called Jimmy Jones and filled him in. I asked if he had heard from Stan but he hadn't. "I called jail for him," I lied, "and he's not there. Maybe he had to run for it himself."

"That doesn't make any sense at all. Why would he have to run if he was sitting in the car? It looks awful phony to me. It looks like the sonofabitch saw all those cops and left you there." Now I knew where Jimmy was at. "That's really what I been thinking all along."

"What are you going to do?"

"I haven't decided yet."

"Well, let me tell you something first. I've been looking at a job worth over two hundred thousand for the past three months and today I was able to put it together. Now it's yours if you want it, but you're going to have some steam after tonight, and I mean steam. They might even make a movie star out of you on the eleven o'clock news, so you've got to find a hole and crawl into it for a while.

"You got any suggestions?"

"If I was in your shoes I'd go to Mexico tonight, right now. This job I was telling you about will be ready within a week. You can stay down there until it comes off, then ease it back into town, take it off and have enough dough to get completely out of the country. I have a friend who owns a motel in Tijuana where you could stay and be safe. I'd have to go down there with you."

"When could you go?"

"I could be ready in ten minutes."

"All right, Jimmy, I'm at Helen's. Come on over."

"I'll be right there."

"Okay. Hey, wait a minute, Jimmy."

"Yeah?"

"Thanks."

"Okay, man."

I didn't have any idea what Jimmy was like until now. Jimmy could have gotten half a dozen guys for the job he mentioned. That was not his reason for helping me. He was a friend, as simple as that. I put the receiver in the cradle and looked toward Sylvia. "We're going to Mexico."

"When?"

"Right now."

"What about our things at the house?"

"We'll have to leave them there. Jimmy is coming over right now and following us down there. He has a friend who runs a motel and we'll stay there for a week."

"You mean we're going to leave everything we own here?"

"That's it, honey. I don't want to take any chance of getting popped. I don't understand anything about what happened today and I'm not going to press our luck."

I went into the bathroom again, fixed, and counted out a thousand dollars in small bills. I hadn't realized the seriousness of what had happened today until I had gotten away. But once I was temporarily safe I was able to reflect on what had really happened and realized it was all over. Money couldn't fix it anymore. Maybe a couple of crimes back it could have, but not now.

Could I really get out of the country? Of course I couldn't, it was a wishful dream. A small part of me embraced the danger of it all because now I had nothing to lose. All the blue chips were in the pot. I was certain of one thing, and that was that I was going to get Stan. It hadn't entered my mind not to. It was the one thing I was willing to remain cool for.

Sylvia knocked on the bathroom door. "Are you all right?"

I opened the door. "Yes, I was coming right out." I folded the money and came out of the bathroom. I handed the money to Helen. "Here's some pin money, Helen."

"What's that for?"

"For being a sweetheart."

"Come on, now."

"You've been a friend to us. I want you to have it. We're going to Mexico and probably won't see you again."

"But—"

"Please take it. I wouldn't offer it if I really didn't want you to have it." I shoved it into her hand.

Helen looked at me and there was a feeling I loved so well in her eyes, a feeling of caring. Jimmy broke the spell by ringing the doorbell, and Helen let him in.

"You ready?"

"Ready as I'll ever be."

Sylvia put her arms around Helen while I walked to the door and waited for Jimmy. Helen and Sylvia walked toward the door as Jimmy opened it. I said to Helen, "Take it easy."

"You, too."

CHAPTER 26

The trip down took a couple of hours. It was a pleasant drive once we reached the shoreline. The moon was so full we could see the waves breaking, and for a moment I forgot the mess I had gotten myself into. We crossed the border with no problems and met in a bar which was in the motel.

Jimmy Jones had to eat all the time and he invited us to go with him to a quaint Mexican restaurant he had been to before. He continually tried to impress everyone with his limited Spanish.

"What's this guy like who owns the motel?" I asked.

"He's people."

"Where do you know him from?"

"From Los Angeles. We cut up a few scores together. He took his dough and put it in heroin and dealt around town for about a year and made lots of money. When he started getting some heat he slipped out in the middle of the night and came down here. He bought the motel, married the chief of police's daughter and squared up. Well, not completely. That was five years ago. He does all right."

"Can he take care of business?"

"He can take care of anything down here, but he doesn't turn his hand. Why should he? With his father-in-law he has everything locked down. What he does now is mostly legit. He sends workers to LA. and gets part of their salary on both ends. He's a smart guy. You'll like him."

"Well, that settles the heroin question." I was not going to have to go out on the streets looking and that was a big relief. "When are we seeing him?"

"We'll check you into the motel first and he'll come over when I call his private line."

"Did you talk to him?"

"Yeah, I called him before I picked you up. Let's get the check and get out of here." We left and in five minutes got back to the motel where I registered. We went to the bar for a few drinks and waited while Jimmy called.

"What's his name?"

"Del Hunter."

"Seems as though I know a Delbert Hunter—"

"You might. He was dealing in LA. for a couple of years."

"What part?"

"Venice."

"I don't know too many people in Venice. What does he look like?"

"He's real good-looking, about six foot, one seventy-five pounds—put together pretty good and talks real soft. A real smoothy."

After about ten minutes Del came in and I sensed that everyone in the bar came to attention. He had his act together. He had on a black suit and looked all business. He walked right over to Jimmy and gave him a warm welcome. Jimmy introduced everyone. As soon as he sat down a young waitress brought him some kind of tall, cool one. He evidently drank a certain kind of drink, because he didn't even have to say anything. It was just there.

He said to me, "How long you going to be staying here?"

"A week, maybe ten days."

"You been here before?"

"A few times."

"Just how hot are you?"

Jimmy broke in. "He's steamed up."

"Well, it might be good to stay in your room. I can have meals brought in to you and your lady. There's a few places you can go and I'll take you around, but stay away from downtown."

"I won't go anywhere unless I see you first."

"That would be best. You like to shoot guns?"

"Yeah, I like them."

"I shoot almost every day. If you want to go tomorrow, I'll pick you up."

"Fine." I sensed I could talk to this guy without holding anything back, so instead of waiting for Jimmy to leave I decided to put it on the line. "Look, Del, I got a lightweight problem I got to resolve before I settle down in that room, and I think you can help me."

"What do you need?"

"Some heroin."

"Some heroin? You hooked up?"

"Not bad."

"What did you want to get?"

"A piece if I can."

Del thought about that for a minute and then looked at Jimmy, who had heard everything. Del was looking for some confirmation and Jimmy gave it to him. "I wouldn't bring a lop down here, Del."

"I think the going price is a deuce. Is tomorrow all right?"

"I didn't bring hardly anything with me."

"You need it tonight?"

"If it doesn't inconvenience you, I'd like to get it out of the way."

"What room are you in?"

"Number eight."

"Let me make a call and see if I can reach this guy." He left and we saw him making a call on the pay phone.

Jimmy said, "You didn't fuck around putting that together."

"I can't be running around those streets trying to score."

"It's all right; it just took me by surprise."

Del came back and sat down. "A guy by the name of Ralph will stop by to see you at ten tonight."

"That was fast. Thanks, Del."

The waitress brought Del over another drink.

"How long you staying, Jimmy?" Del asked.

"I'll probably be going back tonight."

"You got to see the dog races before you leave."

"I forgot what time they start."

"They're already on but they got nine races, so we'll see the last half, maybe five or six."

"You're talking to a man who loves dog races."

"Come on, then." Then to me, he said, "I'll pick you up in the morning."

I nodded and stood, then we all walked out.

"Where are you parked, Jimmy?"

"Right there."

"Come on, we'll take my car. It's over here." Jimmy and Del walked off. "See you and Sylvia tomorrow, Woody."

"I'll be down next weekend, Woody. I'll have it all put together."

"I'll be ready."

"Jimmy?"

"Yes?"

"See if you can find out anything about Stan for me."

"I'll check it out."

"Check it out good, will you?"

"I will."

Sylvia and I left for our room. As we were walking, Jimmy and Del drove by in a new Cadillac.

"He really does have it together, doesn't he?" I said.

"It seems that way, honey."

I stopped by the car on the way to the room and picked up the canvas bag and the dope. The room wasn't bad, not bad at all for Mexico. Once inside, I dumped the contents of the moneybag on the bed and started pulling it together in neat tidy piles. I gave the dope to Sylvia to hold. I counted out three hundred and put it in my pocket. The rest I put in the dresser. "You know that one of us is always going to have to be here, or else take the money with us."

"I know."

I took the gun out and put it on the dresser. I felt like fixing, but decided to wait and see if Ralph would show. We watched TV for a while, and were almost asleep when we heard a knock at the door. I got up and put the gun in my waistband and then opened the door. A small Mexican guy stood there. He had one gold-capped tooth in front and straight black hair. He was wearing a white shirt and a pair of pants out of the forties, with pleats no less. The shoes were scuffed and a size too big.

"I'm Ralph."

"Good. Come in. You got it with you?"

"Yes." I knew Del wasn't going to send anyone to burn me so I counted out two hundred and handed it to him. Ralph came out with the stuff and set it on the table.

"Is there some place I can reach you, Ralph, if I want to do this again?"

"You could have the same person call me."

I hadn't gotten very far with that shit. "I don't have any more money with me now, but when I come back next week I'd like to buy ten of these if I could get a deal."

"Have the guy call me. We can talk when you're ready."

"Okay, Ralph, I'll see the guy when I'm ready. Do I need to give you a couple of days' notice?"

"Just have him call."

"Well, okay, Ralph. I'll see you." I walked toward the door and opened it. "Good night." Once he was gone I went directly to the package.

"Get the outfit, honey, it's in my coat." I already had put some in a spoon.

"Where did that come from?"

"The restaurant."

She went into the bathroom and came back with the outfit and a glass of water. I didn't look up, just put out my hand for it. She set the glass of water down and handed me the needle. She had already fitted on the end of the dropper.

Without looking at her I said, "Give me your arm, girl." I fixed her first, but she was the only one who got that consideration. I was always first with anyone else. The needle found its mark and she had to sit down.

"How about it?"

"Man, you're not going to believe it."

"Good?"

"Oh, shit." She started scratching her eyes and face and then her cunt. I knew it was good when I saw her scratching herself like that. She couldn't stop; she just dug in. I watched her briefly, and then prepared my jolt and fixed it. God, she was right. This was it, this feeling. It was a non-feeling. To feel nothing was the highest form of being high.

"Honey, what are you doing? You just fixed."

"Yeah, I know, I must have missed."

She lay back on the bed in a state of bliss and I fixed again. This time it was enough to turn everything off, almost all my lights. I walked over to the bed very slowly and lay down beside her. No pain, no shame. No nothing. I could hardly keep my eyes open. What a wonderful feeling, no feeling.

CHAPTER 27

A man and a woman were speaking Spanish. I didn't know what they were saying, but their voices had woken me up. I got out of bed and went to the window to look out but didn't see anyone. Last night I had been almost ready to give up. I'd been acting like a weak punk. I thought it was all over. Now, I was thinking and making plans and calling the shots. What's to stop me from getting out of the country? Nothing but by own thinking. I couldn't stay here; too close. But I could go to South America or maybe Canada. When I get the money in my hands, I'll make the necessary moves.

Being half-sick most of the time for over two weeks was what had caused all the trouble. I couldn't think right with that sickness on me all the time. I'll make some money with Jimmy, and money can do anything. I got myself caught already with that fuckin' give-up attitude. That American way of thinking—that every crime will be paid for—is so much bullshit! Money's the key.

I got up quietly, shaved, and then took a jolt. I cleaned up the room and put the dope and money together in the closet. There was a knock at the door and I asked who it was.

"The maid, Señor."

I opened the door and was about to tell her I would make the bed myself if she would leave me the linen.

"Señor Del is waiting for you downstairs."

"Thank you. I'll be right down."

Sylvia woke up. She stirred lethargically, but couldn't get it together. "Come on, honey. I'm leaving now with Del. Wake up."

"I'm awake." She sat up in bed faking awareness, but I was hip to her.

"Come on, baby, go to the bathroom before I leave. I put the dope and money in the closet."

She finally got out of bed, reluctantly, and went to the bathroom. She had splashed some water on her face and looked a little better when she came back out.

"You got it together? I'm leaving with Del."

"I'm okay now."

I put my arm around her and kissed her on the head. "I'll be back in a couple of hours or so. Don't worry."

"Bye."

When I got downstairs I remembered the gun so I ran

upstairs again. After Sylvia let me in, I got it out of the closet, put it under my shirt and left once again. Del was waiting for me. "Good morning. Where's your gun?" I patted my stomach.

"Did Ralph come by?"

"Yes, after you left. Thanks, that was a sweetheart of a move."

"If you don't know what you're doing you don't have a chance. Most of those creeps that hang out down there will sell it to you and then blow the whistle on you, and for that they get their dope back, or most of it. They keep enough to convict you and give the rest back to the guy who sold it to you, plus he gets to keep the money. It's conceivable a pusher could keep on dealing the same ounce for months and make money every day."

"Jesus, that's cold."

"That's Mexico, my friend." We were driving toward the outskirts of town throughout the conversation. The terrain was bleak, there was nothing growing. It all looked dead and desolate.

Del turned on a dirt road between two mountains and drove for perhaps five hundred yards. The road behind us had completely disappeared from view. When he stopped the car there was an eerie silence. Against one mountain there were several target boards and spent shells on the ground.

"You come up here a lot, Del?"

"Every day."

"You must like it."

"I do. I've always liked guns. I was raised in Arizona. I remember shooting coyotes when I was eight and my dad always had handguns around so I learned all about guns before I started school."

Del got out of the car and took a large box out of the trunk. Inside were four guns: a .357 magnum, two .22 target pistols, a .45 automatic, and several boxes of shells. He placed the box on the seat and took out the .357. "Come on, we'll start at the end. I got some cans and bottles left over from the other day."

I took out my gun and got out of the car. "Is that a magnum you got?"

"That's what it is."

"I heard they're hard to shoot."

"They are. You have to get used to them and they take lots of practice. It's a powerful gun. If you hit someone in the little finger it would be enough to put his lights out." As we were walking Del aimed his .357 at a can about twenty yards in the distance and blew it away. He made quick work of three cans in the general vicinity.

"Jesus Christ, do you ever miss?"

"Like I said, I practice a lot. Try that can over there."

I stopped and took aim. I squeezed the trigger and instead of a bang there was a click. I aimed the gun in the air and squeezed the trigger again and again, producing a series of clicks.

"Let me see that gun."

I handed it to Del who took the shells out and examined it. "Where'd you get this gun?"

"A friend of mine." I didn't want Del to know Stan had given me the gun because I was uncertain of how tight he and Del were.

"He must have been some friend. The firing pin has been filed down."

"How can you tell?"

"Look, right here. That's the firing pin and it's been filed down."

"My friend had it around the house. I just wanted it for show anyway."

"Come on, Woody, I'll let you use one of my guns. Which one do you like?"

"The .45. No, wait a minute, let me use the .22."

"Whatever you want."

"Yeah, make it the .22, Del." I was thinking about what kind of gun to use on Stan. I didn't want to shoot him with a .45, it would be too easy. What I really wanted was to shoot him a dozen times with a .22 and never in a vital spot. That was what he had coming.

Del got the .22 from his case along with a box of shells and gave them to me. We walked back down the road. On the way down I loaded the gun and started shooting at objects lying on the ground. Somehow guns didn't appeal to me. I thought jokingly that I was in the wrong profession, like a racecar driver who couldn't stand cars.

Del put up some targets and we both shot for a little bit. I lost interest almost at once. I would rather have been back at the motel with the dope, but I feigned interest. I could see Del enjoyed everything about guns and it gave me an insight into his character. It had been my experience that people who associated themselves with weapons, as Del did, were usually cowards or at the very best afraid of something or somebody.

After a while Del finally packed it in. We drove back making light talk until we got about a mile from the motel. Then I asked Del to get me a gun.

"What kind do you want?"

"A .33, just like the one you have."

"That's not the best gun in the world to use for business."

"You're probably right. Can you get me a .357 like yours and the same kind of .22?"

"Yeah, no problem. I can pick both of them up this afternoon."

"You want some money?"

"You can pay me when you get them. What do you want the .22 for?"

"I'm going to give it to a friend of mine."

We pulled into the motel and I got out. "What time this afternoon, Del?"

"I'll meet you at the bar. And thanks for the target practice."

"I had fun, too."

CHAPTER 28

I envied the way Sylvia could relax. I knew it was not the drugs because she was the same way when she was sick—stretched out like a cat; it was an ability I never had. I watched her and examined the lines on her face. The lips were full and soft, free from hate. She looked the same now as she had when I first met her. It relieved me to think that the heroin hadn't left its stamp yet. I made a mental note to change the money into large bills so I could carry it with me. She slept too soundly to leave it in the room when I went out.

I took the outfit and the heroin out of the closet, cooked up a large jolt and hit myself. It was good. Since it was on the table, I prepared one for her. Drawing it up in the dropper, I walked over to the bed and stood there just looking at her, and I knew. I knew that I loved her, and I also knew that we didn't have a chance. She was my woman, that was for sure. But I hadn't asked to be loved this way. I wondered why she couldn't have given that stuff to a nine-to-five accountant or any kind of working stiff. All of my brilliant thinking and planning had reduced our existence to the confinement of a dingy motel room in Mexico with half of the Los Angeles Police force looking for me. I reached under her arm very gently and put the needle into her vein, very delicately squeezed her arm and injected the drug. As she opened her eyes, she felt it. It raised her up into a sitting position. "What a way to wake up, honey. How long have you been home?"

"Only a few minutes."

"How was it with Del?"

"It was okay. I tried to fire the gun Stan gave me. The firing pin had been filed down."

"I don't understand."

"He filed the firing pin down so it wouldn't shoot. He sent me in there to get killed."

"You think he did that over Helen?"

"Either that or he was thinking he'd have one hundred percent of the ring if anything happened to me, or probably a little of both. He's an evil sonofabitch and he gets away with murder in the first in that little hick community. When he barks, all those dummies stand at attention, which might be the reason he wanted me off the scene. I was ranking his bully hand. Who knows, but I'll find out when I see Jimmy. He's going to give me a lot of answers before anything happens to him. I'm going to call Jimmy when we go downstairs."

"Are we going to eat there?"

"Well, we could. I think we should stay out of downtown. In the evening we'll have dinner at that place Jimmy took us to. How do you feel?"

"Now that I'm awake, wonderful! I was so tired today I had to take a resty."

"Baby, you always need a resty. That ought to be your middle name. Come on, Miss Resty, let's eat." While she was getting ready to leave, I put the dope away. Until I changed the bills I would have to carry the bag with me. No use taking chances, even if Del did own the motel. It only took Sylvia a few minutes to get ready, and we went downstairs to eat.

"Honey, order me some eggs. I'm going to call Jimmy."

"That's all?"

"Some coffee, too. They serve beans with everything. Probably with doughnuts too, if you ordered one. I'm not too hungry. Be right back."

The phone booth was out in the open where anyone could pick up on the conversation. I got some change from the bartender and placed the call. "Hey, Jimmy."

"Man, I'm glad you called. I just called Del to reach you, but he wasn't home. It's all together on this end, and it can be for the day after tomorrow, if you're ready. I can come down this evening and lay it all out for you."

I waited a minute before saying quietly, "Well, come on down then."

"Can't you talk?"

"Not too well. The phone's in the motel restaurant."

"I got ya. Alright, I'll be down about ten tonight. You'll love it."

"What about Stan?"

"I haven't seen him."

"Have you tried, I mean really tried?"

"Yes, I've been over to his house a half-dozen times."

"Jimmy?"

"Yes."

"Try harder. Like your life depended on it."

There was a pause on the other end of the phone. "I am really trying, Woody, honest."

"I know you are. I'll see you around ten."

"Okay, Woody. I'll have that together when I see you. See you at ten."

"Goodbye." I placed the receiver in the cradle gently and pensively walked back to the booth.

"What's wrong?" asked Sylvia.

"Nothing."

"Why so quiet?"

"Jimmy hasn't found Stan, or if he has he won't crack."

"He's not going to give you Stan. He's afraid of Stan."

"You're right. He won't while I'm here, but when I see him in town, he'll take me right to him."

"It will depend on who he is most afraid of, you or Stan."

"He's coming down tonight at ten, said he'll have it together in a couple of days."

"I thought you said it was going to take a while longer."

"So did I, but he said he had it wrapped up."

"Why don't we stay here for a while? We have money."

"Because Jimmy is ready to go on it now. If I wait around he's liable to get someone else. There's no way that I can put anything together like he's got because I got so much heat I can't show myself anywhere. I'm not exactly excited about committing another robbery, especially after what happened on the last one, but this is big money and that's what we're going to need to make it. If I get over on this one, we'll have enough dough to do anything we want. You want some more coffee, Sylvia?" I looked over at her, but I could see she wasn't listening. She was miles away. "Honey where's your head? You've been on a trip the whole meal."

Sylvia sighed as she gazed out at the mountains. "I've been thinking how nice it is here in Mexico."

CHAPTER 29

I devoured Sylvia with my eyes as she got dressed. She caught me. "You aren't getting any ideas, are you?"

"Just checking you out." I didn't want to start something I had no way of finishing, so I didn't press it any further.

I heard Jimmy coming up the stairs. I hastened to put the dope away and met him at the door. "You're early."

"My main man, how are you? Del been treating you good?"

"Like a champ. Couldn't ask for more."

"Yeah, I finally got hold of him after I talked to you. He said you guys were out taking some target practice and your gun wouldn't fire."

"Yeah, it wouldn't, but I bought two new ones through Del."

"Well, it's on for this morning."

"Christ, you're fast."

"I didn't want to crack over the phone about everything. I don't trust long distance calls."

"What happened to change it so quickly?"

"I got one of my boys working in the joint, which is what I've been trying to do for months. I figured we could pull it off without inside help if we had to. I was going to set it up when I left here, but the day I got back in town there was an opening which I got through the vine so I sent one of my boys in and he got the job."

"Well, run it by me."

"When I put 'em together, Woody, they're sugar-sweet. My grandmother could take this one off herself, it's that sweet. Your mother would love me, Woody."

"That depends on if I ever find out what you're talking about."

"Okay, here it is. It's six restaurants owned by one guy. He picks up the weekend receipts on Sunday and puts everything in one safe. He makes five different trips for the dough and his son takes two, sometimes three, but they both pick up the loot on Sunday and bring it to the safe in Westwood. The joint in Westwood does a good bar business and doesn't close until two in the morning, and they clean up before they go home. They got a manager there who's an ex-fighter from the East Coast and he counts out the receipts before they go home and then he puts everything in the safe."

"Then he's got the combination?"

"Right."

"How do I get in?"

"That's the sweet part. There's a screen door in the back alley. The guy who started working there today will leave it open for you, but on your way out you carry this with you." Jimmy took out a medium-sized pocket knife and tossed it to me. "Cut the screen with this so it doesn't look suspicious for our boy."

Jimmy opened his briefcase and produced some eight-by-ten glossy photographs. "Look these over and then I'll explain it all to you. They're all good pictures, taken from every angle."

"Where did you learn to take pictures like that?"

"In the army. All right, let me go over this with you. The door that you enter opens to the outside, not the inside. Right now it's being oiled so it won't make any noise when you open it. When you get inside, stand by the refrigerator. The fridge shields you from anyone seeing you, but you can see the guy when he's counting the money at the bar because he's got his back to you. How you get from the back door to where he's counting is the sticky part, and you can do it any way you like. He's got a gun, and if he gets a chance, he'll use it. I've checked him out. He's for real. If he has a chance, he'll have a go at it, but he's no fool. I mean if you've got business pointed right at his head, he's going to give it up."

"How far is it from the back door to where he sits?"

"About fifty feet."

"That means I've got to get closer."

"I would. It's a straight path through the kitchen. What I'd do is watch him from behind the fridge for a minute or so until I got the feel of the place, and when I see he's really into counting that dough, I'd advance until I get right up on him. Then I'd say, 'Freeze or I'll take the top of your head off.' You've got all the advantage in the world because he'll have his back to you. He won't know if there's one guy in back of him or twenty-one."

"You sure, I mean really sure he's the only one there?"

"Positive. I've checked it out every Saturday night for two months."

"Where does he carry his gun?"

"In a shoulder holster on his left side."

"He's right handed?"

"Right."

"I'm going to need some handcuffs." Jimmy took a set of handcuffs out of the briefcase. I looked at him and smiled.

"And some tape." Jimmy produced the tape.

"What kind of end do you want?" I asked.

"One-third."

"We're in business. Where am I going after the job?"

"We'll meet at my sister's house."

"Where does she live?"

"Westwood. She lives two blocks from the job. I'll drive you there myself. We'll all stay at her place until the next day. After that, you can call the airport and go where you want to."

"I was going to buy a van in San Diego and live in the interior of Mexico."

"That's no good, Woody. You can't live in Mexico without some juice. I can get you a passport if you wait another day. Your only chance is leaving the country. You're steamed up."

"That sounds good, Jimmy. Can I stay at your sister's until you get the passports?"

"Sure. I'm not going to dump you after the job."

"What about Stan?"

"I found him. I'll take you to him after the job."

"I want to see him before the job."

"There isn't enough time."

"I won't need a lot of time. That gun he gave me had the firing pin filed down. If I hadn't gotten away on the last job they would have blown me to pieces."

"How do you know that?"

"Del looked at the gun and told me."

"I guess there's no doubt, Woody, but why put your future in jeopardy for revenge? The tab is too high."

"It's something I have to do, Jimmy."

"Okay, all right, but let's get the job done first and then I'll take you to him."

I thought about it, then agreed. "Okay. I'll wait until after the job."

"That's using your head. Now we're talking. Here's my sister's address. You won't have any trouble finding it. It's a block west of Westwood Boulevard. The porch light'll be on. Take your time driving back. We got six hours before it comes off. I'll be waiting for you. I'm leaving now."

"I'll be out of here in five minutes, Jimmy. I want to thank Del."

"He's in Los Angeles on business."

"When you see him, thank him for me."

"I will. Remember, don't set any speed records. We got six hours."

"I'll see you then, Jimmy." Jimmy left and I got everything ready.

"I walked over to Sylvia where she had been sitting on the edge of the bed. "Are you ready, sweetheart?"

"Yes, I guess so."

I put my arms around her. I could sense she was frightened. "This is the last one, honey. I won't have to do it again. It's going to be all right."

Part Three

THE GROWLER

CHAPTER 30

There was always a lot of activity in Tijuana on a Sunday night and this night was no exception. If I could have picked a night to come back on, this would have been it. The tourists were all returning from the bullfights, in a rush to get home. If the border patrol stopped a car to shake it down, traffic would be held up for hours, and tourists didn't like to wait.

I had a good feeling about going back to LA. I believed in leaving nothing to chance. The way Jimmy put a caper together was almost a work of art. Anyone else would have told me that the guy counting the money was a patsy, trying to make the job look easy. But Jimmy was smart enough to know that you've got to give that ex-fighter a lot of respect or you'd wind up in the clouds and no one would get any money.

"Christ, the line is four blocks long!"

"We've got until two a.m. to get there."

"You're right, and the more people the better."

"You really look loaded, honey."

"I am, but I'll straighten up when we go through the gate."

After ten minutes of driving at a snail's pace, we finally reached the check point. A skinny guy about forty years old, who looked like a farmer, was waiting for me to come to a stop. "Hi, how are you doing?"

"Fine." I smiled at him. But before I could do anything, a .38 special was inches from my face. I was so thoroughly taken by surprise I couldn't believe it had happened.

"Hands on the dashboard and don't make any funny moves or I'll blow your head right through the windshield."

A cop came from the other side of the car and jerked open the door with his gun drawn. "All right, sister, out of the car, slow, real slow." He pointed the gun at Sylvia. A look of stark panic swept over her face. "Let's go." She got out of the car and stood by the door.

By now three more officers had arrived with their guns drawn. One of the three appeared to be the leader. "Shake him and then get him inside. We don't have a matron to shake her down so just make her take off that coat."

"You heard him. Take the coat off." She did and handed it to him.

With our hands over our heads, we were marched to the substation. Once inside, they sat us down on a long wooden bench. Within minutes three detectives came out and stood in front of us. "You're a pretty active fellow," one of the detectives said.

I knew that, unless I could make it out of this police station in the next few minutes, I would never get another chance. Just then the lady cops entered. "Take her in the back and shake her down." Sylvia followed the matron through a door, but as she left she turned around and looked at me. She was dazed, it had all happened so fast.

Since I first walked into the police station, I hadn't missed a thing. I saw a window at the end of the hallway and knew there was a mountain directly in back of the station which I could get to by going through the window. It was dark out there and anything could happen in the dark.

The big detective spoke to the other officers. "We'll take it from here."

It was a large building, sixty feet long. There were three desks in the building at which clerks were busy typing. I assumed the cells were in the back behind the door that Sylvia had been taken through, and that a window would be the only way out for me. It was forty feet away, a lot of real estate. I had to make a move before they shook me down and took all my money. I had about three hundred dollars in cash. Not much, but enough to do something with if I could get away.

Then I noticed that a water cooler was just a few feet from the first clerk's desk. It would cut fifteen feet off the run if I could get there. I turned to the detective nearest me. "Officer, do you think I could have a drink of water? I'm dry as hell."

"When you get in your cell you can have all the water you want. Stand over at the desk and take everything out of your pockets."

"Okay, officer. Say, could I talk to you for just a minute?"

"What do you want?"

"Well, you see, I know I have a lot of charges against me and I sort of wanted to get it off my conscience. There were three burglaries you don't know about that I'd like to get off my chest and a string of robberies you don't know of and there were—could I have just a sip of water? I really am thirsty. Officer, just one sip and I'll tell you guys all of it. Now that you got me, one robbery is as bad as twenty, right?"

"Yeah, you're going away for a spell, that's for sure." Oh, I was going to love hitting this guy, even if I didn't get away with it, it would be worth it. "All right, let's go." The three detectives and I started toward the drinking cooler.

"I'm glad it's over. Every day was a nightmare the last couple of months." I was playing it so well I could see the disgust in their faces at my being so weak. Even cops hated people who couldn't keep their mouths shut.

We reached the cooler, one cop standing in back of me, the other two facing me. I got a cup, filled it with water and drank it slowly, trying to get in a position where I could see the other cop out of the corner of my eye. If I was too obvious, I'd blow the whole thing before it got started. I went to get another cup of water and the fat cop said, "Come on, that's enough."

I hit him low, below the waist, right in the fat part. I moved my right foot a short step as though I was starting to walk backwards, which put my left foot in a perfect pivot position to throw a left hook to the other cop's jaw. I spun around and brought a left from the floor and destroyed the third cop. All three were stretched, but I didn't bother to look, I could feel it in my hands. The last left hook turned me in a half circle and I had to take a step back to get on the track for the window. The clerk at the second desk jumped up and tried to tackle me but I put my shoulder down and knocked him back over the desk.   But when I reached the window I saw I couldn't dive through it because it was more than half down and it wouldn't allow my chest any clearance. I stopped and jerked it up in one movement, put my head through and shoved off on the outside with my hands to pull myself through. But someone had my foot and I couldn't get loose. I put everything I had into it but couldn't break the hold. The last clerk was holding on to me. I saw a cop run around the side of the building with his gun out aimed right at my head. "One move, just one move, you motherfucker, and I'll kill you right here."

The second cop inside had recovered and come to the window where I was half in and half out. He grabbed me by the other leg and pulled me inside. Once in, he ordered me on the floor and handcuffed me behind my back. I could hear the cop with the big stomach coming and I knew what was in store: six, seven, or eight kicks in the ribs, until they got tired. When they were done kicking me they dragged me to the front and through the door, and put me in a cell.

It was quiet in the jail, only one other guy in the tank. I didn't feel anything. I didn't feel bad and I didn't feel good. I knew it was over and that didn't affect me either. I would be awake for a lot of days by the time I kicked this one. I wondered where they had taken Sylvia. There was probably a woman's side on the other wing. I didn't want to think of her now. Tomorrow it would all come down on me, the guilt, the sickness, the sore ribs. I knew the dues would start in the morning, so I lay on the bunk to get what sleep I could.

CHAPTER 31

The smoke was getting thicker as I entered the driveway. I got out of the car quickly and ran toward the front steps. Fire leaped out of the top windows; the entire top of the wood-frame house was engulfed in flames. For five, ten, maybe fifteen seconds, I stood there dazed, not knowing what to do. The front door opened, creating a draft, which intensified the fire and smoke. There, in the midst of the holocaust, stood my grandmother. Her clothes were not burned, the fire had not touched her, but her face was pasty-white and she had the look of death. The roaring fire was everywhere around her but she looked straight into my eyes, searching for an answer. I knew what her eyes were saying and it made me cringe. My body shook and I felt myself losing control as the words thundered in my head, "Why have you deserted me? You are from my blood." I took a half step backward in shame. My grandmother lowered her eyes. She could not look at me. She was the strongest woman I had ever known. And she was ashamed of me. I put out my hand and took a small, unsure step toward her. Suddenly she went up in smoke and disintegrated right before my eyes. I was stunned. Swaying back and forth in a trance-like state, I fell to my knees. The tears ran down my cheeks and my mouth contorted in an agonized expression. I looked at the ground where she had been standing moments before, but only ashes remained.

My words began to flow softly, chant-like, as I pleaded, "Oh, God, please, give me another chance. Please, God, let me in that house to save her, please. God, let me die for her instead. I am not afraid to die for her. Please, God. God, the bells are so loud— Please stop the bells." My head was exploding.

I looked up to see a tall, thin sheriff running his keys across the bars. I sat up quickly and tried to clear my head. But I was still disoriented. With my hands cuffed behind my back I stood up and waited for the sheriff to open the cell. Somehow reality wasn't nearly as bad as the nightmare I had just had, but I felt very weak and didn't have the energy to give either one much thought.

The turnkey opened the cell door and I walked out and waited for directions. He directed me toward a door fifteen feet away. Upon entering, I discovered that I was in the same room that I had previously tried to escape from.

Every inch of my body ached. They must have put the boots to me more than I remembered. The sick feeling that I had in my stomach when I first woke up had now reached its peak. "I have to throw up. Where is it? Quick, where is it?"

"The first room on the right," the jailer answered. The detective took me by the arm and quickly escorted me to the toilet. I just had time to reach the bowl. For five minutes I threw up and continued to throw up even after there was nothing left in my stomach. I sensed that the detective knew what was happening. He stood there waiting for me to finish. He didn't rush me. I felt weak and my bones ached. I knew that the full strength of my sickness wouldn't reach its peak for a few days, but it had started and I dreaded the thought of it. I washed my face and the water felt terrible. I was beginning to get the chills.

The detective's every move was thought out in advance—no one was going to catch him sleeping. He was big, well over six feet, with big hands and feet. He definitely bought his clothes at the "Big Man" stores, had probably played guard or tackle in college. There was a cold-bloodedness about him which was typical of all robbery detectives, it went with the job.

He hadn't taken his eyes off me since we entered the

bathroom but I wasn't offended by him. They hadn't sent a rookie to bring me back. This guy looked like he could transport a saber-tooth tiger and get it to the jail on time. He hadn't said anything since we entered the toilet, only watched, but finally he asked, "How long is your run?"

"About two years."

"A straight two-year run? With no jail time?"

"I've been booked a few times but I've always made bail."

"How much are you using at one time?"

"About a spoon every jolt."

"Man, you're going to have a bitch."

"Going to have?"

He looked me straight in the eyes. "Look here. I'm going to tell you where you stand. I'm going to give you some pannapon for the ride back. Not because I'm a good guy. I just don't like to get thrown up on, okay? You ever take pannapon?"

"Yes."

"Will it keep you together?"

"Yeah, about twenty of them would."

"I can't give you twenty."

"Take your chances."

"Goddamn, twenty seems like an awful lot."

"I've got a two-year run, man."

"Sylvia hooked up the same way?"

"Same way. Is she going back with us?"

The detective nodded.

"What kind of charge?"

"A robbery warrant." I knew they couldn't make that stick. Once they got back to LA and to court they would have to release her.

The detective produced a small bottle from his pocket, counted out the pills, handed them to me, and told me to take them. He watched me closely as I put all twenty in my mouth and swallowed them. This was something entirely new for me—a cop giving me dope in a police station!

"Now I'm taking you back to LA County Jail. I know you're facing some bad robberies and I can imagine what's going through your mind, but don't get the idea that I'm easy because if you try to get cute on me I'll put you straight in the ground. I came down here to pick you and Sylvia up with two things in mind, to get you back to LA and have a nice, comfortable ride. Now, you think we can do that?"

"Yeah, thanks for the pannapon." Then I added, with a smile, "I never got any drugs from a cop before." I saw a smile play around the detective's mouth, and I understood him. For a brief moment I had the thought that somewhere down the line if I'd gone left instead of right, up instead of down, I might have been a detective instead of a dope fiend and a robber. And if I had, I probably would have been just like the one I was standing with right now.

The pannapon was beginning to work. My stomach had quieted down, my energy level was back and my bones had stopped aching.

"Are you ready?"

"Yes."

"How do you feel?"

"Well, I don't think you have to worry about me throwing up on you."

"That's exactly what I was worried about."

"What about Sylvia? She really throws up."

"Don't worry, she'll be alright." He didn't have to explain. I knew he had it covered, so I left it alone. I walked out of the bathroom a different man from when I had walked in.

As soon as I opened the door I saw her. She was sitting with a female detective. She saw me and tried to put on her best smile. She always made the effort to please me, whatever it took, but now all she could give me was a sad smile. She did her best with it but it had the opposite effect of what she had wanted. It stirred up feelings of remorse like I had never known. That smile showed the goodness and the honesty of her feelings for me, giving all and asking for nothing in return. I was so completely devastated by this I could not smile back. The end was too close, and this was really the end of it. There was no comeback, no more chances. It could never have been any other way. I had known that from the beginning. I had known how it would end: throwing up sick in some police station with the feelings of fear and remorse and guilt pounding in my head, driving me close to madness, but wasn't that the bargain? My life and all lives connected with me in exchange for no feelings and no fear.

As we came out of the bathroom, the big detective walked close to me. He was all business again. He had his detective "tough guy" mask on, the one he'd been wearing when I first saw him. I walked over to Sylvia and instead of kissing her, put my hand on her head and gave her an affectionate pat. The pannapons had started working and I had a lightweight glow through my body. As I sat down next to her I said, "How do you feel?"

She dropped her eyes and slowly moved her head from left to right.

"Don't worry; it's going to be all right."

"All right?" she looked skeptically at me.

"Trust me," I said in a whisper.

After following me over to the bench where the other two detectives and Sylvia were sitting, the big detective acknowledged everyone and walked over to the desk to talk to the two officers. He produced an envelope from his coat pocket, obviously the warrants. Within a matter of seconds he was back. "We're ready to go," he said. He handcuffed me, and we left the police station together and got into a four-door sedan. The big detective got into the back seat with Sylvia and me. Everybody was acting overly cautious and the atmosphere was tense. We drove the first mile or so in silence and I hoped the ride would stay that way. I had nothing to talk about. The drugs were making me feel warm and peaceful and I wanted to enjoy it while I could. Finally the woman detective broke the ice, saying something about her husband being transferred to a day shift in Compton, and how she would never see him. I could do without her crying. There I was going to the joint for a thousand summers, and I had to listen to her story about only being able to see her husband on weekends.

I turned to Sylvia and asked her how she was feeling. She was too sick to answer. I looked at the big detective sitting next to me and then back at Sylvia and said, "It's starting to come on bad with her."

The big cop just nodded as if to say, "I'll take care of it." I was reassured. I understood that he couldn't let the other two detectives know what was going on. After a few more miles and the incessant chattering of the woman cop in the front seat, the big cop's left hand eased into his pocket and brought out the bottle of pannapons. Placing it in his lap, he gently unscrewed the top, slowly poured a handful of pills out then screwed the top back on the bottle. He handed me the pills. Goddamn if this big ol' cop wasn't the smoothy of all time. I couldn't have made the move any better myself.

I passed the pills to Sylvia and, just as smoothly, she got them to her mouth and swallowed them. She had known I had a surprise in mind but she never expected anything like this. She was more relieved to discover it wasn't another escape. In ten minutes we were both drowsy. Just before we went to sleep I looked up at the big cop sitting next to me and said quietly, so the two up front wouldn't hear: "Thanks."

CHAPTER 32

I was coasting, not sleeping, as we drove into the alley of LA County Jail. I knew every exit, every entrance, every tank. I dreaded the thought of going through the eight-hour ordeal of the booking office: the fingerprinting, mug shots, shower, and disinfectant spraying. Nothing is as depressing as the booking office of LA County Jail. The pushy cops are always on their mark for a fight, any kind of action to show they're tough. They always look so uncomfortable in their tight, altered body shirts, short haircuts and shined Navy-surplus shoes.

We left the car and walked down a tunnel-like driveway past the morgue to the elevator. I knew this was the last time I was going to see Sylvia, yet I didn't know what to say. It was always different before. There was a chance of making bail or taking care of the right business to get out, but there was no hope now. I finally said, "Get in touch with Royce, honey, when they give you that phone call, and tell him to file a writ for your release."

"I'll be up the day I get out."

"Don't come up for a couple of weeks. I'll be kicking and I won't have the energy to make it to the visiting room."

"Should I see anybody about bail?"

"You know somebody with two hundred big ones? That's what it's going to take. Just go to your mother's house and get yourself together. Wait until you feel better. We'll talk about it."

The elevator doors opened and we waited for the two plainclothesmen to get off before we entered. I could tell Sylvia was confused by what I had just told her. She had seen me cold before, but not like this. I was going to be in jail for five or six months, and then in the joint for years, and I acted like I was just going to the corner for a newspaper. But I had to be that way in order not to upset her.

No one said anything on the way up. The elevator stopped. I looked at Sylvia for a brief second. It was hard to form words. I had no idea what to say. I wanted to comfort her, make it easier for her. Just before the doors closed, I blurted out, "You'll be all right." Then she was gone, it was gone, whatever we had together was gone, disappeared when the elevator doors closed. I took a big breath and dismissed her from my thoughts as I always did with anything that was painful to me. She would be all right. Absence did not make the heart grow fonder.

We waited for a guard to open the iron grill gate. I hoped the dope would last until the booking was over. I put on my jail mask, looked straight ahead, and walked on through.

As I was leaving the booking office, on my way to the tank, I felt the weakness coming over my body and I knew what was in store for me. I entered the tank and saw the cells were all occupied. There were men sleeping half-way up the walkway. I spread out my pancake-thin mattress on the floor, looking at the winos and listening to them snore. I felt envious. Looking at the prisoners sleeping, I marveled at how childlike they appeared. It was hard to imagine them committing crimes. When they awakened their masks would go on again: tough guy, comic, intellectual. There are as many masks as there are prisoners. But in sleep they revert to children. I wished I could sleep but sleep was way down the list.

Every addict has to face kicking sooner or later. I knew I couldn't get any heroin now, so I accepted it. I could no longer control the shaking of my body. My eyes were watering and my nose was running, sweat poured out of me, making my clothes damp and my skin clammy. It got worse every second.

I was still up at six a.m. when the shift changed. The jail was like an echo chamber. The officers talked loud, walked loud and slammed gates, getting men out for early court appearances. Just as soon as the other prisoners were getting up, I felt the nausea hit me. The toilet everyone used all night was the only one available. The food in my stomach roared out. It splashed the toilet water back in my face but I was too sick to care. I threw up for twenty minutes and my body continued shaking. When I finished I cleaned the toilet and floor immaculately, washed my hands and face and walked out of the cell, looking straight ahead like nothing had happened.

It took all of my strength to nonchalantly roll up my mattress and put it in cell six. I had difficulty standing but I managed to walk to the end of the tank and waited there while the trustee swept and mopped. They had just put the mops and brooms away when the runs hit me. I was cold, freezing cold. My breathing was reduced to a series of gasps. Every breath was an effort. The sneezing started and I couldn't control my body from twitching. My entire system jerked out of control every five or six seconds. I took another trip to the toilet to throw up but nothing came out except a loud retching noise. By now everyone in the tank was aware of my sickness and I could sense their disgust. Most prisoners, unless they're addicts themselves, show little or no understanding toward a junkie. I was thankful no one said anything.

The trustee was talking to the officer at the front of the tank. The officer looked around the trustee to get a better view and I knew I was being told on. I made a mental note to dump the trustee as soon as I got my strength back. The officer walked down the catwalk and called to me over the bars and said, "You want to go to the hospital?"

"I'm all right," I answered.

"Are you kidding?" the officer asked.

"Yes." At that moment I had to throw up again. When I came back the trustee was waiting for me. "The officer wants to see you up front." I walked to the front of the tank in a daze. I didn't remember kicking being this bad before. Reality eluded me. I didn't know what I was saying but I felt my mouth forming words as I answered the officer's questions.

The smell of hospital disinfectant was strong. There was cold metal on my cheek and a pan to throw up in but nothing was coming up. "I can't find this guy's veins," a male nurse said. "You got any veins, fella?" Seven, eight, nine, ten jabs. My worn out veins wouldn't accept a 20-gauge needle. "Well, God dammit, the doctor ordered glucose. I don't know how to give it to him. The doctor's left." Another nurse said, "You got any veins in your leg, fella?"

I looked up from a hospital bed, wearing a white cotton gown that stuck to my skin. "The needle is too big," I tried to explain, but they weren't listening.

"Put it in his thigh. It will get in there," a voice said.

"Well, I can't get it in his arm, that's for sure. Raise his leg up," he told the other male nurse. Feeling a sharp jab, I opened my eyes to see a rubber tube coming out of my leg connected to a bottle of glucose. The nurses left. I heard a heavy iron gate shut. It was quiet. For some reason my body wasn't twitching, which was a welcome relief, and the glucose began to have a calming effect on me. The pain was still there but I could bear it now. It was very quiet. I could almost hear the glucose dripping into my leg.

Recalling the events that had led up to my arrest was painful. I thought of the people I had hurt. I had surely killed my grandmother this time. Sylvia would never be the same, I had ruined her. Every person who had been a part of my life had been destroyed. My thoughts wandered back to my childhood and my grandmother. When did it all happen? There was plenty of love in my home. What made things different for me? No chance for a comeback this time. Oh God, my legs hurt.

Catholic school, that was what did it. I was all right until the nuns. I'd be on my knees for two hours at a time. Maybe I had always had a black heart. That was it. How could I be good when I was born with a black heart? I cared for no one. I didn't even love my grandmother despite what I just said. How could I? She lived in poverty while I put thousands of dollars in my arm. I deserved what was happening to me; I should accept it. It should have been worse. The pain didn't compare with what I had done to the people who loved me.

They kept me in the hospital for two days. Two days without sleeping, two days of thinking, thinking, thinking.

On the way back to the tank I had to walk slowly. I was so weak every step was a triumph. Entering the tank I saw the trustee, but I was still too weak to bother him. I was better off in the tank. The constant noise made it harder to think. I got a blanket out of my bed roll and wrapped it around myself. The chills were back. I sat huddled with the blanket around me at the end of the tank and spoke to no one. The only time I ever got up was to go to the toilet.

I walked a little each night while everyone else was asleep. My body was experiencing such waves of pain from lack of sleep that I was semi-delirious. I was consumed with a deepening, indescribable melancholy.

On the fourth day, still barely able to walk, I was taken to court and arraigned on three counts of robbery. I remembered hearing something to the effect of $25,000 on each count but even if it had been twenty-five cents I still couldn't have made bail.

When I got back from court, the deputy gave me a letter from Sylvia. She had been charged with possession of one of the guns in the car when we were arrested in Mexico. It was a harassment charge to hold her and also put pressure on me. Once the case went to court the charge would be dismissed, but the preliminary hearing was weeks off. The district attorney's office filed my prior, a conviction for forgery over five years ago. It had been my first forgery conviction and I had gotten probation, with the joint suspended, but it only took a couple of months for my probation department to discover I was using drugs, which violated my probation and sent me to Quentin. They must have known I couldn't make parole because I got a discharge after serving two-and-a-half years. They were right, because I used heroin the first day I got out. With the skillful maneuvers of attorneys and plea bargaining, I had managed to stay out of the joint for five years. I had nothing to bargain with now. Even if Clarence Darrow were alive, and offered to defend me, he couldn't do me any good.

The days were endless; the nights were even worse. At least in the daytime there was some activity, prisoners coming in or going to court. I spent the nights watching the cockroaches scurrying across the floor, the walls, everywhere. Somehow I was able to get through fourteen sleepless nights and my preliminary hearing. The hearing produced a number of witnesses who positively identified me on all three robberies. The trial was set six weeks off. I thought about calling my attorney but without money it was useless. The public defender assigned to my case looked like he had graduated from law school the week before and was in a hurry to get everything over with. He wouldn't make an attempt at any plea bargaining but I knew if I got enough postponements, I'd have some bargaining power. They would, I thought, make some kind of a deal to save the expense of a long, drawn-out trial.

On the fifteenth day, I was able to eat some food, but still hadn't been able to sleep. My day was interrupted by a petty, hustling junkie who, as soon as he walked through the gate, let everyone know he was kicking a habit. He didn't know I was sick and in a whining voice told me he needed a bunk. I looked at him with hate and said, "Get the fuck away from me, punk." I just wanted to be left alone. I wanted to sleep. If only I could sleep.

I began to think of Sylvia and how much I missed her. Our life together had always been hectic except for the very beginning. I remembered the night I met her. I was playing in a small club in East Los Angeles. The rhythm section was on fire and I had so much fun playing with those guys I would have worked the gig for nothing. I was using drugs, but at that time, the drugs were working for me. They hadn't started going in reverse yet. Life for me was one big, beautiful, ongoing party.

I had just finished playing a solo and had stepped back to listen to the rhythm section when I saw her walk in. It was August and the night was hot and muggy. She wore a flimsy print dress that clung to her body. Her stance was very erect and she seemed to be trying to decide where to sit. She spotted a table near the bandstand and walked toward it very slowly trying not to disturb anybody. She lit a cigarette and then looked up and saw me staring at her. I claimed afterwards that she smiled when she first saw me, but she denied it. It was something we always laughed about later on.

When the rhythm section was finished, I took the tune out and then made a brief announcement that the band was going to take a short break and would be back in twenty minutes. I wasn't sure of how I was going to do it, but I knew I had to meet her. Walking over to her table, I was nervous and didn't know what I was going to say. When I finally got to her table, the way she looked at me put me at ease, and when she told me she liked the way I played, I relaxed. "I like the way you look," I said. We both laughed and I had the feeling I had known her forever.

When the gig was over, I took her to my apartment. It was all so natural. No questions, she just went with me. We talked and made love until the sun came up and then fell asleep in each other's arms.

CHAPTER 33

I hadn't anticipated seeing anyone, so when I heard my name called I was surprised. I walked up front and was told to report to the officer at the attorney room gate. Once there, I was ordered to take a seat and wait. After about five minutes the officer opened the gate and motioned for me to come out. "Those men over there want to talk to you."

Before I could take a step in their direction, they approached. "Hello, Woody."

"Hi."

"We got somebody downstairs you might want to see."

"Oh, yeah?"

"We're taking you to the ninth floor. We want to talk to you."

"I don't have anything to talk about. It would be a waste of time."

"We have an order signed by a judge so you'll have to come with us. We're going to have to cuff you." I put out my hands, but the detective walked in back of me and put the handcuffs on from the rear. We reached the ninth floor, walked down a long corridor, and entered a door marked Bureau of Detectives. Sylvia was sitting by herself but there were two more detectives in the room. One of the detectives who brought me said, "You got ten minutes with her." This was Trap City. What were they being so nice for? I didn't say anything and one of the detectives, named Dunn, continued, "I saw a friend of yours yesterday." I remained silent. "Did you know Stan is here in the jail? We brought him in this morning."

"I didn't know."

"I'd like to play a tape for you. I think you might be interested in it."

"Who's playing piano?"

"Ah, you're getting your sense of humor back. This won't take long and it will probably clear up a lot of things for you." Dunn reached over to the tape recorder and pressed a button. It took a few seconds to start. A gruff voice on the tape said, "There's nothing we can do."

Then I heard Stan's voice say, "What about the information I came up with? I went way on a limb for you guys and now you're telling me you can't do anything."

"I'm sorry, Stan, we've done all we can do. It's not like you got a simple forgery."

"God dammit, I could have been killed by that sonofabitch. It wasn't my fault you didn't get him on Eighth Street. And then I told you he was in Mexico and what kind of car he was driving so you could get him at the border. What if I go to the joint? If he doesn't get me, he has friends just like him who will."

Dunn turned off the tape and said, "Nice guy. You're fortunate to be here, don't you think? God knows how you got away from that job on Eighth Street, because when you went in the front door, Stan got on the phone and called us. He was an informer for us, but then he started working both sides. He snitched on a couple of my officers and now there's a department investigation going on. Of course it'll be cleared up, but I want to put him away, and with your help, I can. Right now, you've got three robberies against you. I'm willing to drop two of them and you can plead to one second degree robbery. I'll also see to it that Sylvia's charges are dropped, but you'll have to take a stand against Stan and tell us everything you know about him so we can build a case."

I looked over to Sylvia, and she quickly looked away. She refused to influence my thinking although her freedom depended upon my decision. God, I loved her. At that moment, I had never loved her more in my life. Most women would have begged and pleaded, done anything to influence me. But she just turned her head. I totally ignored the officers in the room. I was only concerned with the answer I would give to her. The room was very still. It was the quietness a salesman experiences before he hands the customer his pen. Sylvia's head was still turned. She wouldn't look at me. I said her name softly, almost in a whisper. She turned her head slowly, her eyes cast to the floor. "I don't know if you can understand what I am about to tell you, but I want you to try. You see, if I do what they want me to I won't be what you think I am. I'll be just another Stan, the same kind of man. Can you understand that?" Sylvia nodded her head very slowly. I would remember later how very innocent she looked at that time.

Dunn spoke, "Woody, this isn't a question of honor among thieves. This guy tried to get you killed. What chance do you think you would have had if you had that gun in your hand or they were ten seconds earlier in getting there? Use your head. You're no dummy. And what about her? You want her to go to prison, too? I am not asking you to testify against your brother, but a rotten sonofabitch who deserves to be in jail.'"

"Lieutenant, we don't have a deal."

"I can also lean on the other side, Woody. We want to help

you, but if you choose to make it difficult—

"Lieutenant, have you got a dime?"

"A what?"

"A dime?"

"Yes, why?"

"I thought you might want to call around and try to find somebody who gives a fuck."

"You're going to play the comedian with your life on the line? That's not too smart. Think it over, and I'll see you in a couple of days."

"Save yourself the trip."

He motioned with his head to the two detectives who stood up and opened the door.

CHAPTER 34

It took twenty-seven long days before I slept, and at the beginning it was only for a few hours, but each night from then on I slept a little more. After a few months I slept every night and my body felt like a body again. The days were long and dull, especially the weekends. With the continuances it would probably be another two or three months before I got to the joint.

I made a fast transition to jail life. It was what I was most comfortable with. I held a high place in that society, so I didn't mind going back.

Jail is a lot different from prison. In jail things are still moving fast because there's more direct contact with the outside world. There's a steady influx of new prisoners coming in every day, and with them comes a constant flow of information to the inside. Most of the men in jail have a chance of getting out in a relatively short period of time. However, once in prison, it's a different type of living, with a different set of principles. One is gradually consumed by the society within. No one escapes it.

I heard the officer call my name up to the trustee and he walked toward the front. "They want you in the bullpen to clean up some traffic tickets."

"Traffic tickets?"

"Yeah. They come by every couple of months and write them off the books."

"You're jiving me. I won't be on the streets to drive anyway."

"The cop on the deck says it saves them a lot of paperwork."

"Man, I've been coming to jail a long time and I've never heard of that."

"It's a square business, Woody. I'm not putting you on." The officer appeared at the gate. He was almost twenty-five years old, very G.I. haircut, shoes and smart remarks. Also very cute.

"Woody?"

"Yes?"

"You know where the bullpen is?"

I could tell I couldn't say "sir," and I might get some static if I said "Yeah" so I said "Yep." The officer had wanted a "Yes, sir."

"Button up your collar and no talking to any of the other prisoners or loitering. Got it?"

"Yep."

The officer opened the gate and let me out. When I got to the bullpen, the afternoon court line was coming in. I signed the papers for half a dozen moving violations and was told I could go back to the tank. The officer who was handling the traffic was so preoccupied with the list that I decided to see if I could get any information on Stan. I knew Stan was back in jail from a newspaper clipping I had seen. I asked the clothing room trustee if there was a Stan Singer on the court list. The trustee asked me what Stan looked like. I produced the newspaper clipping and handed it to him. Very nonchalantly, the trustee said, "That's him over there." My stomach turned over and my heart wouldn't stop pounding. I turned slowly and saw Stan.

He was talking to some wino, probably trying to keep a low profile. I walked toward him, not fast, but easy and deliberate. When I got in back of him, I put my hand on his left shoulder. He turned around and was greeted by a left hook from the floor. I felt the impact in my shoulder and it felt good. I took a step back, knowing from the feeling that Stan could only fall forward. Stan's knees and then his head hit the floor. I stood looking down at him for a moment, then grabbed him by the shirt and pulled him up to a right hand that split his nose in three places. I let him drop again with a thud.

The prisoners were very quiet. The officer who was handling the traffic cases had left and there wasn't a cop anywhere. I could ruin Stan right there. By the code, I should have, but I didn't carry it through. I walked over to the bench and sat down. I lit a cigarette and watched Stan bleed. Revenge wasn't as sweet as I thought it would be. In spite of what Stan had done to me, I somehow didn't feel hatred. My action was merely part of the code. My entire existence was based on the rules of the code. If I hadn't had to live by it I would have had two years to do in prison instead of ten. Sylvia would have been on the streets and Stan wouldn't have been lying on the floor covered in blood.

When Stan came out of it, the look on his face was one of pure panic. He screamed, "Help me! Please help me, officer. Please. Please. He's going to kill me. Please help. Help, help, help, help, help me, please!" When I saw him holding on to the bars and screaming I knew I should have done a better job, something he would have really remembered me for.

Big John, a black cop, ran to see what was going on. By now Stan was on the gate screaming like a woman for help. Big John opened the gate and led him out toward the elevator to go to the hospital.

In twenty minutes Big John came back and called out my name. He was an okay cop. He didn't have the pettiness that practically all the cops working at the County Jail had. If a prisoner didn't bother him, John wouldn't bother him either. He didn't pick his shots and he would get it on with anybody if he was fucked with. He wouldn't do anything illegal like run a letter out or bring anything in, but he turned his head a lot if he liked a guy. I liked him as much as I could like a cop, and I knew Big John liked me too. "Hey, hey. That cat's all busted up. Looks like a steam roller got in his ass."

"What did he say?"

"He said you tried to kill him."

"Shit! I never touched him, John."

"You didn't hit him?"

"Never touched him, John," I insisted.

"Well, run it on by me then. The sergeant wants the story."

"Okay. Here's what happened. You know the motherfucker is a rat."

"Yeah, he's got a 'keep-away-from-you' stamped all over his property slip."

"Well, he didn't only rat on me, he didn't spare anybody. He put it on a couple of cops in South Gate. He isn't particular who he puts it on."

"So what happened? You punched him out?"

"No, John. I didn't hit the asshole. The guy's a nervous wreck in here from giving up half the city and he stays on his mark. I spotted him when I came through the gate but he didn't see me, so I walked up kind of casual and said, 'Stan!' Well, would you believe what that cocksucker does? He bolts and runs straight into that fucking grill gate and busts himself up like that."

Big John just grinned and shook his head. "You are a

toughie, Woody. You mean you want me to take that jive to the sergeant?"

"John, that's the only story I got."

"Well, I guess a jive story's better than no story. I'll be back."

"John?"

"Yeah?"

"Don't forget the part about him snitching on the cops in South Gate."

"I'll do what I can, but you better smoke as much as you can before I get back."

The conversation between John and me had been in hushed tones and intimate. Big John knew I had busted Stan up, but if he could help me, he would. However, he didn't want the prisoners to know he and I were on such familiar terms because, except for a select few, John kept everyone at arm's length.

The prisoners were milling about, getting closer and closer to me in an attempt to approach me for information. They waited for eye contact, a signal that it was all right to ask me what had happened, but I didn't give one to them. I stood by the gate looking straight ahead as if I were the only one in jail. The prisoners saw Big John come back and inched their way closer to listen. But John waved them off and told them to get back. He opened the gate and told me, "Come on." We walked the length of the corridor and stood there for a moment before John said anything. I had accepted the dues of going to the hole when John said, "You gotta be the luckiest sonofabitch in the world."

"Why?"

"He got on the sergeant's ass. When I went back he was screaming at him about a lack of protection, saying we set him up to get killed, that we'd all be in Norwalk substation. He got the sergeant so hot I thought he was going to get downed again. His face looked like a watermelon. You did a job on him."

"Who's the sergeant?"

"Comstock."

"Oh, Christ, I am lucky."

"I'm telling you."

"What did he say about me?"

"His last words were, "Take this fucking punk to General Hospital and get him sewed up," and when he left I asked him what I should do with you. He said, "Put him back in his tank." I didn't even have time for that jive story of yours."

"It's over?"

"Yeah, you're home free. And when they bring your friend back he'll most likely be put in the rat tank." I had to laugh to myself. It was the first time I had ever come out on top getting snitched off in jail.

"You can go back to the tank, killer."

"Thanks, John."

"I didn't do nothing."

"Well, thanks for nothing then. See you."

CHAPTER 35

"Drop your cocks and grab your socks, reveille, reveille. Shake it out of those racks, motherfuckers, chow is on the line."

I wondered how they invariably picked the loudest-mouthed sonofabitch in the tank to be trustee. I was so sick of that "drop your cock" number I could throw up. They had been doing it ever since I could remember and would probably be doing it long after I was gone.

I had been sleeping straight through the night for a couple of weeks. I usually didn't eat breakfast, only a cup of coffee, which the trustee passed through the bars. He was an Okie out of Bell Gardens. He had a look of arrested intelligence and was the loudest of the three trustees who lived in the first cell. It was an effort for me to speak to him, but I threw him out a "what's happening" a couple times a day. He set down the coffee bucket and said, "My partner told me you threw the best left hook he ever saw yesterday. What happened?"

"I don't know."

"Was he fucked up? You think you broke his jaw?"

"I don't know what happened to him."

"I heard the cops on the midnight shift talking about it early this morning."

"Well, then you know all about it. You got a dime? Never mind."

"What?"

"Never mind, I just don't like my business all over the jail."

"I ain't going to tell no one."

"I know you're not, because if I said anything to you it would be like putting an ad in the Los Angeles Times."

"Man, you're cold, Wood." He walked off mumbling to himself.

Those were the real dues of jail, putting up with assholes. It was not the absence of women, the sexual aspects of the confinement or the guards and their insipid rules. They were bad enough, but it was the society of prisoners one couldn't escape from. Sleep was the only escape, but unless you had proven yourself to be one tough motherfucker, men would bother you all the time. So, even sleep wasn't sacred. After clean-up was usually the quietest part of the day and I decided to take advantage of it by taking a nap. Just then, someone shouted: "Hey, Woody! Woody, wake up!"

"What in the fuck do you want, asshole? Is this your first

time in jail, punk? You don't wake anybody up in—"

"I'm sorry, man, the cop told me to wake you up. They want you down at the Chief Jailer's office."

"All right. I'll be down there in a minute. I've got to splash some water on my face." As I walked up front, I thought, "This has got to be bad news."

The cop opened the gate and said, "The Chief wants to see you. You know where the office is?"

"Yep."

"Okay. Go on."

I had never heard of anyone seeing the Chief Jailer, maybe a captain or a lieutenant, but never the Chief. I stopped at the gate of the attorney room, where his office was located. It was closed off by two-way mirrors, which spanned a good twelve feet. When the officer on the gate saw me coming, he opened it and pointed to the office.

"Just knock on the door. They're expecting you."

It took me twenty more steps to reach the office and I knocked. A tall, dignified lieutenant opened the door and told me to come in. Inside the office sat two lieutenants and the Chief, a large man with the physical appearance of one who kept himself in good shape. He was well dressed in civilian clothes and didn't look like a cop. He told me to have a seat.

"We have a problem here. It seems we're being sued. Yes," he said, with a grimace, "being sued."

"By whom?"

"The Los Angeles County Sheriff's office. And you, Mr. Woodward, are being sued by a Mr. Stan Singer for conspiring to have him killed."

"Are you serious?"

"I am dead serious. I was served the papers this morning."

"Is Stan still in the hospital?"

"No. He came back last night and the sergeant put him in the informer's tank. When he entered the jail his attorney spoke to the booking officer and requested he be kept away from you for fear of his life, and we complied by following the usual procedure that we use for informers. We stamped in red letters 'KEEP AWAY FROM' and then we typed in your name, but somehow that didn't keep you away from him. You popped him a couple of good ones and now we're all in somewhat of a mess. I talked to his lawyer just before I called you in." There was silence. "What he wanted to know, I mean, what he asked, was what we had done with you."

"And what did you tell him?"

"I told him we had put you in isolation."

"I hope you were kidding."

"I would like to tell you I was."

"You mean after the red carpet, I'm going to the growler? What did you call me down here for? You could have had one of your officers just stop by my tank and take me to the hole."

"We don't want to put you in the hole. We have a real creep here who is claiming we set him up to get killed. You know what he's doing. Maybe he's trying to beat the case, using this petition for leverage. I doubt if he will ever take it to the courts, but if he did, it would look strange if we hadn't taken any action against you. The facts are if we let it go without doing anything, then it does begin to look like a conspiracy. Try to understand our position."

"You're running the jail. I just don't understand why you have to explain it to me at all."

"Because we didn't want to put you in the hole today for something that happened yesterday, and off the record, the sonofabitch probably had it coming. I'm sorry, Woody. We'll make it five days and we'll count today." I smiled at the Chief. He asked, "What is it?"

"I was just thinking that I've gone to the hole before, but never under such elegant circumstances. Well, it's not just anyone who can get sentenced by the Chief, right?" I stood up, "Well, let's do it."

The Lieutenant escorted me out of the office and to the gate. He told the guard on duty to call the prowler and had me wait by the gate. The prowler was an officer who roamed all over the jail and might be called on to do any number of things pertaining to jail security, but mostly, he was an errand boy.

The prowler showed up almost immediately. The officer on the gate opened it and the Lieutenant motioned me out. All three of us proceeded to the elevator, with me walking in front.

The hole was on the fourteenth floor across from the nut tank, two cells side by side in an enclosed area resembling a room. It was quiet and desolate and the vibrations of human misery could be felt as soon as you entered the door leading to the cells. Places like these were the breaking point for many men. Ten days in the hole had a way of taking a lot of fire out of a tough guy's ass. The cell was eight feet by five feet. It was just large enough for the guy to be able to take two steps back and forth. The toilet was a hole in the floor, and sleeping accommodations consisted of a pair of longjohns and one blanket.

The lieutenant opened the cell door and without a word, I walked into a world of darkness. The clang of the door being slammed rang in my ears for a moment. I heard the outer door open and the footsteps gradually disappear.

I was alone, more alone than I had ever been before, surrounded by darkness. It was not like going into a movie and waiting for your eyes to dilate; in here there was absolutely no light. I felt the walls with my hands, front and back, until I became familiar with the two spaces. My feet were already cold so I sat on the blanket yoga style and tried to warm them with my hands. It took all the character Grandma had given me to hold on. The hole wasn't new to me. It had never been pleasant, but I had been able to psyche myself out when I had a ninety-day sentence. The attitude was, "ain't nothing for a stepper." I could have done every day of the ninety in the hole and still come out smiling and popping my fingers, however, the pressure of my current cases had demoralized me completely.

I knew better than anyone what was ahead: a dog-eat-dog world of hairy convicts and sadistic guards and a daily living routine that was maddening, where life was worth a pack of cigarettes, where men turned into punks and informers, where nothing was real except a murder, and the worst of it was having to live in hate, for without it one could not survive. The guards hated the convicts, and the convicts hated the guards. The longer the sentence, the stronger the hate. The punks, the informers, the tough guys, they all had it. It became part of the convicts' personality and robbed the soul of all human feelings.

A cockroach ran over my foot. I put my hands in front of my face, but couldn't see them. "It wasn't like this before. Motherfucker, cockroaches in the hole are a part of the deal. If you can't fade it, then you shouldn't have sat down at the table. Fade it or check out, but do one or the other. Well, what about summing it up? What could you present to the world that would make it worth going on?

"Here you are, a thirty-two-year-old bebop saxophonist who, in the last five years, hasn't had the chops to play a dozen choruses of any tune and sound good. Be real, motherfucker, you never really played. Woody...it's hot licks...fill-ins, and breaks. It's what the fools play. Your musical ability might be there, but your musicianship sucks! Your ambitions in music never materialized because it was always a half-assed commitment. The only thing you ever committed to was heroin. You've taken everything you could from people; their money, their feelings. Your life's like a pimp's, but at least a pimp comes up with a pat on the ass now and then. You come up zero."

These were the thoughts echoing in my head; they were all true. There was nothing like the hole to help discover the truth. The silence was frightening. Fade it or check out. Fade what? Fade ten years of miserable living. Ten miserable prison years, and for what? For what purpose? It wouldn't be over then; it would only start all over again.

I brought my arm up to my mouth and with my teeth I felt for the big rope-like vein that ran down my arm. One quick bite. The decision didn't rest on the pain. I was past that. One quick bite and it would be finished. Gone would be the jails, the prison time, and the Gorilla. I ran my tongue down the vein. It would be so easy to bite it right out of my arm. A sudden calmness overtook me. I hadn't any desire to go on living; yet, I didn't want to kill myself, either. There was no fear of death for me probably because there had been so little joy to my life. I stopped feeling the vein with my teeth. I would have to endure it all. Strange how I could openly court death with such frivolousness but could not indulge myself in it. This fact that I could not take my own life blocked my last and only escape.

In the quiet and dark I started humming the bass line to my favorite tune, "Round Midnight." I started out softly at first. The cell acted like an echo chamber and it sounded good to me. Hearing the bass line in my head excited me and encouraged me to explore different changes and to make up little melodies of my own. Thank God for music.

CHAPTER 36

I waited right up to the day of the trial for them to make a deal, which was usually what the state did to save time and money. But with me, they didn't care about savings. The prosecutor looked exactly like what he was—a professional prosecutor. He was a small man, very meticulous in his dress and manner, and one could feel a sense of order about him. He reeked with intelligence and gave the impression that every phase of his life was planned, even his bowel movements. In the courtroom, he had little notes stuck into every pocket, never confusing any of them. He reminded me of a chess player who, after relieving his opponent of all his major pieces, plodded down the board and took twenty unimaginative moves for a checkmate that could have been accomplished in three. He was not concerned with flash or brilliance, only with winning.

I had a hopeless case and no defense whatsoever. Therefore, the prosecutor would get a chance to shine. I knew it was useless to ask my attorney to make a deal; nevertheless, I said I would cop to three robberies if they would sentence me concurrently. While my attorney was talking, I saw the prosecutor shake his head slowly with a sardonic grin. After a few moments of conversations, my attorney came back to me and said, "He said that you already had a deal and didn't want it." I didn't need an explanation.

The trial lasted two days and was merely a matter of procedure. The jury was only out two hours before finding me guilty on all counts. It was a relief for it to be over.

Three weeks later, I appeared in court again. As I stood in front of the judge waiting to be sentenced, I saw my grandmother. She was sitting in the front row. I could feel her saying her prayers and hoping for some kind of miracle, some kind of lenient sentence. She always thought the world saw me as she did. I didn't want her in court but she had come for every appearance. She had been visiting me once a week, taking the bus downtown and waiting in line for hours. It was always crowded and noisy, but she came anyway. I enjoyed seeing her face, but I knew that once I went to prison, the journey would be too long for her.

The judge sentenced me consecutively on each robbery and each robbery was aggravated by the prior robbery, which meant I would have three ten-to-life sentences. I didn't expect anything less, but hearing it read off in the bleak atmosphere of the courtroom was something I wasn't prepared for. Nonetheless, I dealt with it as I did everything else, by the code. I stood there looking right through the judge without showing the slightest trace of emotion. When it was over, the bailiff led me out of the courtroom. A casual observer would have thought I was in traffic court and had received a ten dollar fine. I didn't look at my grandmother. I looked straight ahead as I walked out. No one in the courtroom, not even my grandmother, knew what I really felt.

I was led back into the anteroom with the other prisoners to wait to be taken back to jail, and was handcuffed to a short black man who had just been sentenced for second-degree murder. I could tell he had not been in jail too many times because he kept asking me stupid questions. He was a carpenter named Tom, who had killed his old lady in a drunken, jealous rage. He was a likable guy with huge hands and his eyes had a kindness to them. He wasn't streetwise and he had an unusual innocence about him that most black men of the streets didn't have. Poor bastard, I thought. He'll get swallowed up when he goes to the joint, and it will take him at least a year to learn how to take care of himself.

We reached the jail without saying too much and were given back our jail blues. When we had a few minutes before we went to our separate tanks, Tom was the first to speak.

"You think I'll go to Folsom?"

"You might. But you could go to Quentin."

"What about you, Woody? Where do you think they'll send you?"

"Straight to The Pit."

"The Pit?"

"Folsom."

"Which one is the worst?

"I don't know. I've never been in Folsom, but I heard it's a bitch. They don't call it 'The Pit' for nothing."

"Are you sure you'll go to Folsom?"

"The only thing that will beat me there are the lights on the bus."

"Alright, no bullshitting down there. Back to your tanks." Tom and I looked up to see a young crew-cut deputy looking at us. He had his hands on his hips in a defiant stance. I knew I was going to have to handle a lot of cops like this one before I ever saw the streets again. It had to start here or I would never be prepared for the joint. Once they spotted resentment, it was over. The word would go from one cop to the other and they would make life unbearable. "Yeah, okay, we're on our way." We started walking toward the tanks.

"What tank you in, Tom?"

"Twelve EL. You?"

"Eleven C2."

"Maybe I'll see you up there."

"Yeah, maybe. Take it easy, Tom."

"You too."

CHAPTER 37

In the past, I had been resentful toward the deputies, but now they were comical to me. The way they were so serious about trivial things made me laugh to myself.

"He had his socks on the line at count time, Sergeant."

"His socks on the line?"

"Yes sir, his socks on the line."

"Woodward, did you have your socks on the line at count time?"

"You know, Woodward, you were given a set of rules when you came in. Have you read them?"

"Yes, sir, I have."

"Then why did you have your socks on the line—"

I interrupted, "—at count time."

"Yes, at count time?"

"I guess I wasn't thinking, Sergeant." I said with utmost sincerity.

"What do you think would happen if everyone had their socks on the line at count time? I'm giving you a warning, Woodward. Watch yourself from here on out."

"Yes, sir."

My time didn't begin until I got to the Guidance Center, but I wasn't thinking about when my time started. Completing my sentence hadn't even entered my mind. My only thought was escape. I knew there had to be a way to get out, regardless of what joint they sent me to. Being well-connected up there was going to help, but only five percent of the prison population could keep their mouths shut, so I had to be careful. Just to get the opportunity, I knew I was going to have to have a complete change of personality and it would probably take two years just to get in position for an escape. I had to play their game, be a model prisoner, take correspondence courses, pretend I was trying to prepare myself for release, go to church, become friendly with the priest, join the Gavel Club, the Toastmaster Club, join every club I could join. I knew what I had to do, but could I fake that kind of action for two years?

Christ, after following that kind of program, I would deserve to get out. However, I knew there were no other choices open. I had seen guys who had done ten years and they had become so perverted and out of touch with life that they didn't fit in anywhere, even in prison. I'd rather take my chances getting shot off the wall than end up like some guys I had seen.

The key to the whole escape move was in my association with the inmates. There was no way I could be involved with any kind of drugs, or more importantly, the guys who used them. The word got out; it always did. There wasn't one man in the entire prison system that the staff didn't have an accurate profile on two months after he got there, especially dope fiends and gangsters. The game had to be so tight that when the captain called on one of his informers, the answer would sound something like, "He said he gave it up."

"You believe that?"

"Haven't seen him loaded."

"What about gambling?"

"Doesn't play cards either."

"Is he loaning money or bookmaking?"

"I think this jolt bought him, he's a different guy. You know he's going to school and he's studying animal husbandry." That was the kind of profile I had to project and that was going to take every ounce of nuts in my sack. Could I be that straight for as long as it took? It was like having one sentence on top of another. The plotting and scheming had kept me going these past five months in jail. I had a secret that no one knew. I had set my time at three years and that was something I could live with. Thinking about escape every night before I went to sleep, I was able to shut out any thoughts of jail.

For professional convicts who did over five years, there could never be a return to any form of normal society. I knew I would not let that happen to me, whatever it cost. I would wait. It was only a matter of time.

CHAPTER 38

"Eleven C-2, Eleven C-2. Woody, roll ' em up."

"Oh, sweeet Jesus! I'm leaving this nuthouse. The vultures came around to see what I was leaving behind: toilet articles, stamps, cigarettes, etc. I took my grandmother's letter with me, but left everything else to a little wino named Howie. The deputy was waiting by the door.

"Woody?"

"Yep."

"Let me see your wrist band." The deputy knew me but followed procedure and looked at my wrist band. I had never had any words with him and didn't want any. He had a know-it-all attitude and on top of everything else, he thought he was tough.

I was about to pick up my bedroll when he said, "They finally got your ass on that ol' bus, did they?"

"Yep, it's me and the bus ride."

"It probably won't be your last trip. They must have lots of dope up there the way you guys keep going back. How many cases are you taking up with you?"

"Turnkey, do you ask everyone who's going to the joint what they're going up for?"

"Not all of them."

"Then, what the fuck are you asking me for?"

"Hey, you watch your mouth, man," he said.

He was really agitated, and I loved it. The guards would never tolerate any form of aggressive attitude, but this guy couldn't very well hold up the bus to put me back in the hole. He knew it, and I knew it.

"Yeah, tough guy, this won't be your last trip," he sneered. I picked up my bedroll and without looking at him, walked toward the bathroom.

The deputy just glared and said, "You're going to the right place, asshole."

I would never lull them to sleep if I didn't keep my mouth shut. I had to start here, now, in the jail, on the bus, everywhere I came in contact with them. If I made a slip like that in the joint it could mean the loss of my escape chance. I walked to the bathroom with a new resolution. I would make it work. But I had to learn to keep my mouth shut.

The bathroom was always crowded. It was the point of

arrival and departure for court or release and was a beehive of activity. There were always three to five deputies and maybe thirty trustees working the bathroom, cleaning, sweeping and mopping. It was where the blankets and bedrolls were issued and where you were assigned. Leaving, it was the same thing, because you had to go to the bathroom to pick up your street clothes. There were two exits from the bathroom. It all depended on whether or not you were being released. If the case was dropped or beat, or bail was made, you walked up a winding steel staircase to the twelfth floor and were released from the booking office to the outside elevator. When you were being taken to prison, you walked up to the tenth floor and took a special elevator down to the garage. A host of deputies was waiting to usher everyone into an old, dismal bus, commonly referred to as the Grey Goose.

As I entered the bathroom, I saw Tom. His face lit up, and he motioned me to come over. "I saved you a seat."

"How'd you know I was coming?"

"The trustees have been calling a roll since I got here, and I heard your name."

The deputy, with a clipboard in his hand asked for quiet, and said, "Everyone in blues get your street clothes from the trustee so we can get you out of here."

I got my clothes and put them on for the last time. There was a strange smell to them, a combination of drugs and disinfectant. These were the same pants I had been wearing when I was on my knees in front of the toilet in the Mexican jail, the same pants I had been dragged around in by my hair, and now finally, the pants I would wear to prison. I had gained twenty pounds in jail and both the pants and shirt were too tight. As I was dressing, I wondered if everyone else had the same bad feelings about their clothes.

Standing there, I took it all in; the cracks in the walls, the corny "No Loitering" sign painted in red and white, the lines painted on the floors for direction. I looked at the iron staircase, never again for that. There was misery all about this room. Nevertheless, it held a strange fascination for me. In a way, I didn't like to leave it. It consoled me because it let me pay my debts, the debts owed for taking and not giving, the debts I could never repay. The smell of cockroach disinfectant added the final touch.

And there I was, waiting to go to prison, sitting on a little bench, wearing my mask and waiting. Fear was the predominant emotion among first-timers The young boys in their twenties were trying to conceal it by laughing, being loud and overly hip. To cover this fear, their masks displayed arrogance and toughness. Should anyone try to test them, they would try to kill to prove they were not afraid. The hardened criminal had less use of a mask and was usually so full of bitterness that his was a face that had been chiseled by years of resentment. Hardened criminals didn't talk a lot, except with their eyes. They didn't have to play a game or wear a mask; it was all in the eyes.

The roll call was taken again and everyone was paired off in twos and led through a gate where we waited for the elevator. Once again, we were counted, and then walked onto the bus two at a time. I was anxious to get to the Guidance Center. It would probably be easier to escape from the Guidance Center than it would be from the joint, especially Folsom. After being in the County Jail for six months, seeing the sunrise was almost enjoyable. It had been a long time since I could appreciate the world without heroin in my veins, and it felt good. Just looking at the sky was a treat.

We arrived in a little over an hour and spent the rest of the afternoon being processed through. I finally got to a cell a little before dinnertime. Tom was sent to another unit at the opposite end of the institution, but we would probably see each other on the yard. Tom hung on to me for support.

He was the squarest black man I had ever seen; a working stiff who never hung out, didn't know any games and didn't want to learn any. I would have liked to look out for him if we went to the same institution, but I knew that was impossible. The whites hung out with the whites and the blacks with the blacks. Our friendship wouldn't cause trouble but it would be strained. I knew all the heavies who ran the black end of the joint and I would put Tom in with them. Without my help, he wouldn't stand a chance. Tom was the first black man I had opened up to in a long time. I didn't hate blacks, but I didn't exactly like them either.

At twenty, I had been one of the only white boys hanging out around Central Avenue. I knew the black man almost as well as I knew my own race. The blacks gave me the music game, not the technical part, the feelings. They taught me chord changes and to rely on my ears for everything in music. I copied their walk, their talk. I was a brother and had lots of sisters for girlfriends, which I thought was hip. I saw the white man's prejudice and didn't like it. I was anti-white, not to all whites, but definitely to the rednecks. That was in the early fifties.

A couple of years later I got my first conviction for forgery, and the judge sent me to San Quentin, where my attitude toward the black man gradually changed. I still had black friends, but somehow, they weren't the same as the ones I knew outside. Then one day, I got into an argument on the basketball court with a black guy called J.C. It all started out slow and almost died until J.C. put mama into the conversation. J.C. was a ring fighter who worked out in the gym everyday. He challenged me to settle our squabble in the ring. The rules established were three-minute rounds and the first one to quit or get knocked out was a punk. By the time we reached the ring in the gym, everyone in the joint knew what was happening; even a few guards were there to check it out.

In the first few seconds of the fight, I got hit with a left hook and went down. It hurt bad and I knew I was in trouble. Then I made a terrible mistake; I got up too fast and got downed again. This time, I was flat on my back. I heard three, four, five. I lay there for a few more seconds trying to get the fuzz out of my head. I looked up and saw my black friends. They were screaming and yelling, in a frenzy, but it wasn't for me. They were shouting to J.C., "Fuck him up, J.C., kill the motherfucker, J.C., teach that pink punk something. You the man, baby, teach that white motherfucker, you the man!"

When I reached my feet, I was so close to being out that all I could see of J.C. was a blur, so I did something I had never had to do before; I tied him in a clinch and held on. I was holding on like some punk, but at that point, it was my only chance to survive. I got hit a few more times that round but when the bell ended the round, my legs were straight and the fuzz was gone from my head. My strength was back. I didn't sit down when I went to my corner. I just stood there and glared at my black friends.

The bell signaled the second round. We met in the center of the ring. J.C. threw a jab and I went under it to tie him up. In the clinch, J.C. said, "I'm the man, white boy, the man."

"You the punk, pooch-mouth, the big black punk." I wanted him angry. I had it all planned. J.C.'s big weapon was his left hook and I showed him enough jaw to throw it. As he did, I rolled in underneath it and threw my own left hook, followed by a right cross, a left uppercut to the heart and a straight right hand that ended it. J.C. started to fall forward but I wouldn't let him. I held him onto the ropes and worked on his body. I knew he was out but I kept pounding him. Finally, I took one step backward and when he started to fall forward, I hit him with a right that drove him into the canvas. I stood over him for a minute like a Roman gladiator, but I was looking at the faces of the black men who had been shouting for my blood. The ones I was closest to wouldn't look at me and started to walk away.

That was a long time ago. By now, my attitude toward blacks had been reformulated by prison principles. My feeling of hatred since the fight with J.C. had gradually diminished, at least enough to take a black man in as a friend.

The buzzer for the count was loud and startled me. Over the loudspeaker, I heard, "Count time, count time, everyone up to bars for count."

CHAPTER 39

It took six to eight weeks to be processed in the Guidance Center. There were shots, physicals, and interviews with a psychologist. The prisoners who had committed the more serious crimes like robbery, rape and murder had to see a psychiatrist for evaluation. At the conclusion of this, all prisoners went before a Classification Committee. The Committee consisted of a custodial officer, a psychiatrist, the Supervisor of Education and a few miscellaneous caseworkers. The Classification Committee determined what prison he would be sent to and also what type of program was to be followed. In essence, it was a miniature rendition of the Parole Board, only with less power.

Drug addicts were not considered for any trades. They usually worked in the kitchen, laundry or on the yard crew. This was unfortunate for the few drug addicts who wanted to straighten up because they got out the same way they came in; unqualified for anything but factory work, and ol' dopey never stayed in a factory for very long.

I had been in the Guidance Center for five weeks. There was a list posted everyday that stated where and when prisoners would be leaving. The list came out right after lunch at noon, and everyone who hadn't been classified yet went to the bulletin board after his meal. I knew I could only go two places; Folsom or San Quentin. I checked the list after lunch and was not on it so I decided to go to the yard. As I was walking down the corridor, I saw him: Stan, with three officers. He saw me almost at once and said loud enough for me to hear. "That's him, there."

One of the officers walked over to me immediately. "Stand right there. Don't move." The officer stood directly in front of me as the other two officers continued to escort Stan down the corridor.

I said, "I'll see you later, Stanley," and then added, "you rat bastard." I had to say that. There went my resolution.

I walked outside. There were some diehards playing handball in the rain. I ran a few laps, not talking to anyone. I heard my name over the loudspeaker, "Woody, 63570, to report to the control room." I knew what that was. I took another lap before going in. I stood by the control room and waited. A guard looked out of a little window. "Woody?"

"Yes."

"Through the door."

I entered a room through an electrically controlled door. Another guard appeared. "The Captain wants to see you." The guard motioned toward a door, and I entered.

The Captain was a large man in his forties. His hair was almost white. The eyes were cold, stamped by years of institution work. "Sit down, Woody, I am Captain Townsand."

"How do you do, Captain."

"We got a friend of yours here," he said, shuffling through some papers on his desk. I didn't answer. "The guy whose jaw you broke in the county jail."

"Yes."

"He's asked for protection and we've complied with his request by housing him in the holdover cell. However, he's going to have to be interviewed and staffed, which mean's he's going to have to be escorted out of that cell from time to time. I don't want to have any trouble here."

"There's not going to be any trouble."

"You called him a rat bastard a little while ago, right?"

"Yes, that's right."

"You came here on the fifth?"

"Right."

"You're going into your sixth week, so you'll probably be

leaving the end of this week or the first of next. I am going to move you to another unit and put your cell on deadlock until you leave. At the most, it will only be a week, but I'll try and rush it through and get you out of here by the end of the week. You can do what you want to him somewhere else, but not in my institution." I didn't say anything. The Captain rang a buzzer under his desk and an officer appeared. "Take Woody to Cypress Hall, a cell on the bottom floor, and put him on deadlock. He'll have his mailing and visiting privileges, and escort wherever he goes, and he'll be fed in the cell."

"Yes, sir."

I stood, and the Captain motioned with his head toward the door. The guard and I left, stopping by the control room to get a cell number. In a matter of twenty minutes, I had moved everything to Cypress Hall and was locked in my cell. I should have kept my mouth shut; it had been my own fault. I was suddenly exhausted. I lay on the bed, too tired to read, but more determined than ever to escape.

CHAPTER 40

"Woody, wake up. You're taking a bus ride."
"Yes."
"What's your number?"
"63570."

"You'll be eating breakfast in twenty minutes. You're being transferred this morning. Come on now, get up."

"Transferred? Where?"

"Folsom."

There were about forty guys waiting there already. One of them was Tom. Christ, I hadn't thought Tom would go to Folsom, being a first-timer. But murder was murder.

"Hey, Woody. Thought I missed you when you didn't come out on the list today. I looked on the yard and went by your wing when I found out I was going, but no one knew anything. What are you doing down here?"

"It's a long story. I'll explain it on the bus. Come on, let's get some coffee."

The aroma of bacon and eggs was strong as we walked into the mess hall. There were two fry cooks behind the counter. One of them turned around, "How many eggs, fellas?"

"Can we have as many as we want?"

"You got it."

"What's this, the last meal?"

"I guess they figure anyone going to The Pit deserves a good meal."

"Well, give me and Sammy Davis here a half-dozen each. You can fade a half-dozen, Tom?"

"Yes, Lord."

"How do you want them?"

"Scrambled is fine. Tom?"

"Yeah, that's good."

I walked over to the table and poured a couple cups of coffee while we were waiting. In a few minutes, the eggs and bacon were ready and we sat down and started eating.

"I didn't think you'd go to Folsom, Tom."

"One's as good as the other, I guess. Since I haven't been in any joint before, I wouldn't know the difference. You're going to need some company on the bus anyway."

The mess hall looked different early in the morning, almost mystical. I had never been in a dark mess hall before. It had always been daytime, when the place was noisy and crowded.

Now everyone was talking in hushed tones like in church. Everyone, it seemed, was accepting the fate of The Pit. Once the guard saw that we had finished eating, he said, also in a hushed voice, "Let me have your attention, men, I'm going to call the roll. When I call your name, step outside and form a column of twos."

Outside the mess hall, Tom and I stood by each other so that we would sit together. When everyone's name had been called, the other guard opened the door of the wing and we proceeded down the corridor to the Sally Port gate, the same gate we had come in by. The Grey Goose was just pulling up as we arrived.

Everything connected with the Grey Goose was bad news. It brought you to prison, it transported you to the other prisons, but it never took you home. It reeked with such bad vibes, it should have been called the Misery Bus. The ride alone would be enough to destroy the average guy. Fourteen hours on the road, straight through. If we were lucky, we could stop overnight in Soledad and get a hot meal. Otherwise, the meal would consist of two horse cock sandwiches and an orange.

The morning dew was fresh, and I could smell cows in the distance. There was something about the smell of cow shit that had always attracted me. I should have been a dairy farmer. I should have been anything but what I had become; a dope fiend, armed robber, bebop saxophone player.

The leg chains were being put on while another roll was being called. In a matter of minutes, everyone was on the bus and ready to go. The last guard on the bus said, "Let me have your attention. We're going to be on the road for some time. You can get up and stretch when you feel like it, but don't stand up for any length of time. The john's in the back. Use it anytime you have the need. No communication with anyone outside the bus and keep your hands inside at all times. Lunches will be passed out at eleven. Any questions?"

No one said anything. The guard sat down and motioned to the driver to go. I looked at Tom and said, "Get comfortable, baby, because we got a motherfucker of a day to fade."

Part Four

THE JOINT

CHAPTER 41

We were on the road for twelve hours. The last two miles were spent driving through mountains of granite. The sound of tires was all that could be heard. All the talking stopped when the bus passed a sign that read, "City of Folsom." The driver slowed down to five miles an hour as he climbed up a slight hill. The joint looked like a fortress against the dark sky, a granite medieval castle. A light could be seen in the distance as the bus got closer, revealing a gun tower. Below the tower to the left a large gate opened as we drove up.

A wall, approximately forty feet high, surrounded the bus. After thirty feet, we came to another gate which looked like it had been built by the Spaniards in the fourteenth century. The squeaking hinges on the gate added to the atmosphere. After passing through the last gate, we were surrounded by yet another wall, and, at last, were in Folsom prison itself. Both walls ran completely around the prison so that if anyone had designs on leaving, he would have to escape twice to get out. Guards were stationed on guard rails on the second wall, but there was no guard on the first wall.

After passing through the last gate, the bus traveled up an incline and stopped in front of a row of buildings underneath a sign which read "Receiving and Release." Three guards stood inside the small gate in an area approximately twenty by twenty that was enclosed by a chain link fence twelve feet high.

No words were spoken as we all filed out of the bus. It seemed uncommonly quiet for a prison at this time of night.

We were counted, and then led through a large steel door, which opened into a cell block. Each cell door had a hole in it about the diameter of a coffee cup, to allow vision both in and out. I didn't hear any sound or movement in the cells. I wondered if anyone was living in them until I saw an eyeball in the first small opening. Walking down the rows of cells and seeing just the tired and vacant eye of a man behind each door was like a scene from a horror movie. Fifty yards further down, we turned left and passed the mess hall. A corridor ten feet wide separated the mess hall from another cellblock five stories high. Along the corridor was a chain link fence with circular balls of barbed wire strung on top.

Still no noise or movement of any kind could be seen or heard. But there were windows on one side that ran almost to the ceiling in which I could see the reflection of men in the cells.

The guards who had accompanied us had not said a word since we got out of the bus; they only made gestures. The guard who led the procession had a clipboard with the prisoners' names and cell numbers. Against the wall of the cellblock were bedrolls, mattresses, blankets and towels. The silence was finally broken by the guard with the clipboard, "I'm going to call off your cell number. The first number is the tier number, like five-ten would be fifth tier, tenth cell. Now, when I call your cell number, pick up a bedroll and walk up to whatever floor you're on and wait at the front of the cellblock for an officer to let you in. Don't walk down the tiers, wait for the officer. Any questions?"

Both Tom and I were assigned to the fifth tier. The guard started opening the cells on the first floor and working his way up, so we had some time to talk in whispers before the guard got to the fifth tier. Tom said to me, "What do you think?"

"About what?"

"The place here."

"Well, it's not the LA Country Club. Just keep your mouth shut when we come out tomorrow. I'll introduce you around."

"I'm not going to say nothing."

"Everybody in here has a spot where they fit and feel

comfortable. The sooner you find it, the easier the time will be for you."

"What do you mean, spot?"

"A place where you can get away from the guards and most of the convicts. It might be a job studying, weight lifting, something, but you'll find it. Some guys play dominoes all day, that's their spot."

"I don't want to play dominoes, I want to work."

"I'm not saying that, Tom. Just hang loose. We're not going anywhere but the cell for a week anyway."

"We're going to be locked up all day?"

"For a week, at least."

"Man, I'll go nuts in that cell all day."

"Hang in there; it's only for a week or two."

"It's a cold motherfuckin' joint, huh, Woody?"

"Yeah, it's cold; it's the daddy of cold joints."

We heard the guard coming up the stairs and stopped talking. Just before the guard got there Tom said, "I'll see you tomorrow." I nodded and we both went down the tier to our cells and disappeared.

CHAPTER 42

"Water, hot water." I heard the water boy on the tier below. Folsom didn't have any hot water piped into the cells, so every morning before breakfast a convict delivered it in a five gallon bucket which had a long spout that fit easily through the bars. Those wanting hot water to shave and wash placed a can by the door the night before. If they forgot, the convict passing out the water would say in a quiet voice, "Water, hot water." He was careful not to offend anyone by making too much noise. Most of the old-timers didn't bother with it, having accustomed themselves to shaving and washing without it. This was connected with their antisocial behavior, like not going to picture shows or asking for any favors. To the old timers, favors, picture shows, and hot water were a sign of weakness.

Except for the sounds of flushing toilets, it was still eerily quiet. Almost everyone in Folsom had to learned to respect what little privacy one had. No loud talking was permitted in the buildings. These rules were enforced by the convicts, not the guards. When the rules were broken the result was usually a stabbing. Sometimes people were talked to beforehand, sometimes not.

The convict who delivered the water stopped in front of my cell. "Woody?"

"Yes?"

He handed me a small jar of coffee, three packs of cigarettes and six envelopes. "From Joe Shipps. Says he'll see ya in the mess hall."

"All right. Thanks." I loved Joe Shipps; everyone did. He was the sweetheart of the joint. I had known Joe in Quentin. He spent every minute of the day trying to put together a deal that would produce some drugs. He could have been a brain surgeon with half the effort it took to hook up one deal. He had plots and counter plots, long and short range results. His schemes were so utterly outrageous that they sometimes worked, and the incredible thing was that he could keep a dozen of these going in his head at once.

I made my bed and shortly afterwards, the main bar was pulled, releasing the door. I waited at the end of the tier for Tom. Tom walked up, shaking his head. I asked, "What's wrong?"

"Man, this place is creepy. I mean creepy. It reminds me of a morgue, and those two walls last night. I thought it was because it was dark when we arrived, but I had the same feeling when I woke up today. It's so quiet here. Some of these guys look too old to commit a crime."

"They've probably been here a long time, Tom. Come on; let's get to the front of the line. I want to see a friend of mine."

Joe was waiting on the first floor as we came down the stairs. He was with Fat Phil and Hog Jaw. Fat Phil was the clown of the joint, always on the bad end of the joke. In his late twenties, well educated in the convict code, he was big enough to be tough, but couldn't hold his hands up. Phil had been on heroin since high school and hadn't stopped since his first jolt. He came from money but had worn his parents out with bails, lawyers, and recovery houses. They finally decided he wasn't going to recover and wrote him off as a bad investment. In spite of his heavy drug use, there was a soft youthfulness in his eyes. He was extremely intelligent but concealed it by acting the buffoon. Wearing the clown mask suited him, enabled him to get along without any serious trouble, and concealed his sensitivity.

Hog Jaw was the Louella Parsons of Folsom. He somehow managed to collect every intimate detail worth knowing of everyone's history. He had an unusual, quick sense of humor, biting and direct, and shame on anyone who challenged him verbally. The best had tried and walked away shaking their heads. He went for the throat.

There was nothing delightful or charming about prison humor. The dominant themes were suffering and misery. One's weaknesses and intimate feelings were constantly on the line, and there could be no bailing out with anger. Hog Jaw was the master of this art. He was in his early thirties, a professional convict since reform school, meaning he had lived by the code ever since he was a kid. The Jaw was a robber, though not a very good one considering he had been getting caught all his life. His lack of success was due in part to his impulsiveness and lack of imagination. Prison didn't frighten him because there he had status and respect. Consequently,when he returned to prison, he could accept being there, practically embraced it.

Prison had taught him how not to live. To him, life was a game of cops and robbers, and when he lost, he didn't lose that much. Outside of prison, he didn't fit; he was out of sync with the outside world as were most men who did substantial amounts of time. But he accepted prison gracefully, with a smile and a repertoire of jokes. Nothing was taken seriously. Not even the Parole Board. He wore the "life is no big deal" mask. Hog Jaw, like Joe, was well-liked because he was able to make the dull existence of life in Folsom somehow bearable.

Joe saw me first and his face lit up. When Hog Jaw saw the expression on Joe's face change, he turned around and they all greeted me. Jaw, who was always first at everything, said to Joe, "Well, goddamn, I told you the big ol' broad would show."

"I'm sorry, daddy, I got here as soon as I could," I answered. "Hey, Joe, Phil, how are you guys?" All three nodded with a smile. They were glad to see me and it showed on their faces. I was happy to see them, too. Folsom was cut off from the world outside and they were eager for news of what was going on in the streets.

"I got the things you sent, Joe. Thanks."

"If you need anything else, holler."

"I'm okay."

I introduced Tom around and explained quickly about our meeting in the jail and riding up together. I sensed an undercurrent of uneasiness when I introduced him and I knew Tom felt it too. We got in the chow line, talking and making light conversation. I noticed the mess hall was segregated with all the blacks on one side, the whites on another. I hadn't known that Folsom was segregated. I wondered if Tom had noticed, but as we were walking through the line, he whispered to me, "I'll see you on the tier." As he walked toward the tables where the blacks were seated, I made a quick downward motion with my hand to affirm it and said, "Cool." But it was awkward.

When we sat down, Jaw said, "What are you doing with him?"

"He's all right, Jaw. Lighten up." I gave finality to the words, "lighten up." I knew how all my friends felt about blacks. It was the way of life in prison.

Hog Jaw changed the subject. He said, "What did you bring up?"

"Wall to wall time."

"Consecutive?"

"Yeah. Four counts aggravated by priors, the whole bit. It breaks down to four ten-to-life sentences. How long have you been here, Jaw?"

"Six summers."

"In Folsom?"

"Right here."

"Haven't you tried to get out? I mean transfer somewhere else."

"Not really. The only place I could go would be San Quentin and there's too much fucking noise up there. Folly is bad, but you get a lot of leaving-alone here. In Quentin, you're always fucked with. Either some dumb kid or the goon squad shaking you down."

"How much you got left, Jaw?"

"I'll probably round out ten."

"That's a taste."

"Yeah, but I got six of it in and when you see me go you'll only have six left if you're lucky. I mean real lucky. The spread you had in the LA Times called for ten."

"Don't depress me at meals, Jaw. You ruin my appetite."

"Ha, ha. You want to use that dope and pick up those pistols, you got to pay the dues. Whatever happened to that sucker you smacked in the County?"

"I don't know. I left him in the Guidance Center."

"Standing up?"

"They had him on protection. I doubt if they'll send him here. I got locked up the day he came in and they shipped me the next day."

"You don't need to worry about him anymore. They won't put you two together."

"What's going on with you, Joe?" I asked.

"I'm going to the board next month. Taking these three years on a violation."

"You got action?"

"I could."

Hog Jaw broke in, "You got about as much chance of action as Woody has of getting a date next month."

"Jaw, can't you keep your jibes down to a roar for the first couple of years until I get used to you again? Just coming off the street, it's hard to make the adjustment to your vocal chords. What's with you, Phil? What are you doing in Folsom?"

"Suspicion of using in Quentin."

"Marks?"

"No, I was fixing in the leg. They picked me up with Dave Malone on the yard and he had an outfit on him so they locked us both up and sent me here two days later. That was two years ago."

"You been to the board?"

"Last month. All they talked about was the bust in Quentin."

"What happened to Dave?"

"He only had four months left to flatten it out so they kept him locked up until his time ran out."

The mess hall was practically empty. Joe stood and said, "You'd better get back, Woody. We'll send you some books."

"How long will I stay in quarantine?"

"Anywhere from two days to two weeks. You're going to go behind the screen."

"What's that?"

Hog Jaw broke in again. "Where they keep all the gangsters."

"I thought that's all they had here."

"It's where all the heavy beefs go so they can keep an eye on you for a year or two," said Joe.

"It ain't a big deal. Little tighter security and there's a screen on the outside of each tier. You'll probably like it better than the main line. As everyone was walking out, I asked, "What's happening with the music here?"

Hog Jaw answered, "If you play guitar, great. Otherwise, forget it. No horns on the yard."

CHAPTER 43

Quarantine lasted for ten days. I read books and jerked off most of the time, but the time still passed slowly. What a place to get my sex drive back. But wasn't that the way it always was? Hustling in reverse, everything backwards.

I sensed the quiet gloom that prevailed in Folsom. Even in quarantine I felt it settling in on me. Almost every movement was slowed down. Although I had only seen a small part of the prison, I knew it was impregnable.

At the Classification Committee, they talked about the robberies and my trouble with Stan in County jail. They didn't recommend a work assignment and classified me maximum custody, meaning I would live behind the screen. I moved my belongings out after breakfast. I didn't have much to move; still the fellows were there to help.

As I walked across the yard, I saw men I hadn't seen in years. I said hello to a big guy named Gene. Gene had his head and eyes to the ground, but acknowledged me timidly. "Oh, you know Good Head Gene?" said Jaw laughing.

"What do you mean, Good Head?" I asked. "I've seen Gene in action, fighting two guys at once. He's a bitch with his hands."

"Yeah, he's a bitch all right, pure bitch."

"Hog Jaw, come on."

"I'm telling you, he got caught on a rod up to the moustache a couple of years ago and he's been on that kick ever since."

"You got me on the rib."

"Joe, tell him."

"He's right, Woods."

I wondered what would turn a guy like Gene, whether it was Folsom or just the years without sex. Gene couldn't have been pressured into it—it must have been his decision. It was obvious that he felt guilty about it, the way he lowered his head and wouldn't look anyone in the eyes.

"Did I bust your bubble, Woody?"

'Yeah, as a matter of fact, you did. I just can't picture Gene a fruiter."

"Not a fruiter, a dick sucker."

"All right, Jaw, give me a fucking break."

"Oh, he's a lightweight. I'll open your eyes up around here. Half the fucking joint will take it in the ass, while the other half will snitch on you. Ninety percent of these motherfuckers would do anything to get out after they've been here a while. You have a harder time finding out about them because they've learned how to be real cunning, but there ain't ten guys in the fucking joint worth two dead flies. When you get your shit put away I'll take you on a grand tour and introduce you to the world of Folly."

I walked to the screened-off area in Number One Building where the extreme cases were housed. Most of the men living behind the screen didn't work, but those who did had jobs where they could be accounted for at a moment's notice. I was lucky to get a cell on the ground floor. I put my things away and returned to Hog Jaw on the yard.

"Come on, I'll show you the handball court." Jaw said.

"I'll see that later. Let's go sit on the bleachers. I want to talk." We selected a spot on the bleachers where we couldn't be heard. I started it off, "You know what I'm looking for?"

"You can forget it. You're talking about blowing the joint, aren't you?"

"That's what I'm talking about."

"You got no action here, too fucking tight, especially with your custody. If you could get in the shops, you might have a shot, not a good one, but it's going to take you three years to get there. Two guys got over the wall about a year ago, but they were lucky as hell. There's a fifty caliber machine gun on that wall. The Sacramento River runs by the far end of the machine shop, cold as a motherfucker all year round. The two guys made it over the wall into the river, but they got busted the same night by a farmer. They were both frozen half to death. Lucky they got nailed, they could have died out there."

"The shops, is that all there is?"

"If you want to blow, you better try getting transferred out of here. You got anything wrong with you physically?"

"Yeah, a bad knee."

"They don't do too many operations here. They refer them to Quentin. How bad is your knee?"

"Cartilage. Sometimes it swells up."

"What makes it swell up?"

"I don't know, it just does."

"Well, you're going to have to make some trips to the hospital. We might have to hit the motherfucker with a bat. Are you game?"

"From what I've seen of the joint, I'm game to cut it off."

"The chief medical doctor is a religious fanatic. If he thinks you're a Christian he'll go for a story, but you'd have to play a heavy role. Carry one of those religious pamphlets in your shirt pocket when he interviews you. Let it stick out so he's sure to see it. And for Christ's sake, don't swear in front of him or you're through. He can be the coldest motherfucker in the world if he doesn't like you. He was giving a friend of mine aspirin for the last stages of cancer and that's what he went out on, aspirin. I had to stop seeing him. He was in pain every minute for the last six months."

"What's my first move?"

"Make sick call, and complain about your knee. They won't do anything for it, but it will get on your medical record. You'll have to attend his church every Sunday for an hour-and-a-half and let him see you there. You can fall down right in church and have them take you to the hospital. In the meantime, don't pick up any beefs. If I were you, I wouldn't get high. It brings heat on you and that's the last thing you need if you're going to pull this off."

The sound of a rifle echoed, then another shot, and a third. I saw two black guys fighting near the end of the bleachers. A fourth shot hit one of them in the leg, but it didn't stop him. One of the guys pulled the other to the ground and bit his ear off. The whistles from the gun tower were blowing like crazy as guards poured out of the control room with clubs in their hands. A shot hit the earless man, but still that didn't stop him. Finally, the guards reached the scene and with a few deft blows, got the situation under control.

"Come on, let's blow to the handball court," Hog Jaw said, totally unconcerned.

I couldn't believe what I had just seen, yet the Jaw acted as if nothing had happened. "Jaw, what the fuck did they shoot those guys for?"

"There ain't no fighting here, baby. You keep your hands in your pockets, especially in the yard."

"But to shoot a fucking guy over a fight?"

"What are you so upset about, for fuck's sake? It's just a couple of rugs."

Anywhere else, fights would have attracted attention with people clamoring over one another to watch, but not in Folsom. When I heard the first bullet fired, I saw men scattering in the opposite direction trying to get as far away as they could. They weren't interested in seeing a fight at the cost of their own lives. In a matter of minutes, the two men who were fighting were carried away on stretchers and taken to the hospital. They might have been taken to the morgue, because there was no movement on the stretchers.

"Did you check the fat copper who was doing all the swinging?"

"How could I miss the motherfucker? He must weigh 350 pounds."

"Yeah, Woods, and he's only five foot eight. He loves using that club. He's put a lot of suckers on nut row."

It was incredible how quickly the activity on the yard resumed. The domino tables were busy as if nothing had happened and the weight lifters never even stopped their routines. There was not much to see on the yard. One handball court accommodated the entire population. In back of One Building were two shuffleboard courts and the marble games. Marbles was a big money game in Folsom. It was played a lot differently than I remembered it as a child. There were some deadeyes who could hit a marble at fifteen feet, nine out of ten times. Yet it was ludicrous to see old men on their knees playing marbles for cigarettes.

Every game in Folsom was played for cigarettes with a do-or-die attitude. Cigarettes took the place of money. You could buy food, drugs, and even assholes for cigarettes. Everything was measured with a set price in packs. Cigarettes were loaned inside prison the way money was loaned on the outside. The only difference was that the interest rate was higher and the length of the loan shorter.

The lenders were called "two for three" men. A "two for three" meant exactly that; he loaned two packs for three in return. No stories were accepted when the debt came due. However, in rare cases, a debt would be extended for no longer than a week at double the cost. If the debt went any longer it usually resulted in a stabbing. Anyone who loaned money had to be willing to do whatever it took to collect. If he showed weakness one time, the word went out and he could never get paid again by anyone. Consequently, the men engaged in this business were usually capable of collecting.

"C'mon, Woods," said Jaw, "Let's go check out the tempo of the yard."

"What do you mean, the tempo of the yard, Jaws?"

"Y'know, I like to know what's goin' on. I ain't been shot yet, and I don't intend to be. You'll know what I'm going on about if you ever get five summers in here— if you don't make that cut out of here."

We walked over to the side out by the handball court and the marble games. Jaw pointed to a lone white guy playing marbles, "You see that white boy over there?'

"Yeah," I said. "What about him?"

"See those Mexicans sitting by the TV table? They're checking him out. He's played every fuckin' game they got here already—the football line, bets on handball, now he's down there shooting marbles—he can't do any of 'em right. I hear he's borrowed money from the Mexicans to pay his bets off. I can tell he's a loser, and those guys are plottin' on him real hard, can't you see it?"

"No, I don't check it out, Jaw."

"Well, check it out for a while, man. You'll see they're looking at him real hard. C'mon, let's go over to the commissary—I don't like the thought of this, I don't like standing over here..."

"Well, I guess you know what's happenin.'"

"That's what I meant when I said I was checking out the tempo of the yard."

As we got in the commissary line, some guy got in back of us, and he was about the ugliest motherfucker I'd ever seen in my life. Jaws started up a conversation with him, and the first words out of his mouth were, "Hey Tony Curtis, what's happenin?" and this guy named Tony Curtis just nodded, "Oh, alright, Jaws." And they continued on with their conversation. I turned to Hog Jaw and whispered to him, "Man, how'd that guy get a name like Tony Curtis? Is that his real name? He looks like death on a soda cracker."

Hog Jaw chuckled, and said to me, "Man, the Mexicans

gave him that name about five years ago. Even when he got out of the joint for a while, and was back on the streets of East LA, I heard they were still calling him Tony Curtis there, and I guess it stuck—so, he's about used to it by now."

Hog Jaw and I ate lunch and then returned to the yard. It was the same thing all over again in the afternoon. The thought of spending another day on the yard was almost more than I could stand, and this was only my first day. I lined up with the Jaw to go back to the cell house.

"If I don't see you in the morning for breakfast, make the sick call line for that knee," he instructed.

Getting locked up at 2:30 was a relief. The yard was exhausting. It was like a little city where the inhabitants seemed to have only one objective: hustling cigarettes. The same people, day after day, wearing the same masks of hate and anger. Only one day inside, and I could already feel my own mask beginning to form.

CHAPTER 44

I woke up early with one thought—escape. Everything else was secondary. I knew now that escape was impossible from Folsom. I had to get a transfer to San Quentin. That was the goal. Every day, every thought, every action would be directed toward that goal. I felt out of place in Folsom and wondered why. Wasn't I the worst criminal of all? Who in Folsom could be any worse? Stealing from morning to night, everything, anything. And wouldn't I have killed Stan? So why did I feel different? What was so repulsive to me about the population in Folsom? The toughest guys from every neighborhood in the state were together hustling each other.

The water boy stopped by and handed me the religious pamphlet from Hog Jaw. "He said not to forget to use it, whatever that means."

"Thanks."

The cells were opened shortly after the water boy left and I walked to the mess hall. I couldn't see Jaw, and ate by myself. The mess hall reminded me of a James Cagney movie. Cagney had made it all seem so glamorous, but there was nothing glamorous about this.

Sick call took up most of the morning. I wasn't able to see the doctor but I did succeed in getting an appointment for the following week. I left the doctor's office and went to the yard. As soon as I got there I heard Hog Jaw's voice blaring like a loudspeaker. "What happened at the call? You see the doc?"

"Couldn't. I'm seeing him next week."

"That's better yet. Maybe you can get your knee puffed up by then."

"Like how?"

"Any fucking way we can. Hit it with a baseball bat."

"You're sure they don't operate here?"

"Not any major surgery. They sent Eddie Roth to Quentin for knee surgery and he had nine thousand robberies. Come on, I got a domino game. Can you play?

"It's not my stick." We started walking toward the domino tables, which were set in concrete in a forty-by-forty-foot area just to the right of One Building. The domino players played the game all day, seven days a week, any kind of weather. It didn't matter whether it was raining or the sun was beating down with a hundred twenty degree temperature, they played. It was easy to distinguish the players who had been at it for years by the deep lines the sun had etched on their faces.

The players were waiting for Jaw and were impatient with him for being late. "Come on, Jaw, you're hanging everybody up," one of the chess players screamed. Jaw made some remark about suckers who can't wait to lose their money, then told me he'd see me later.

I told Jaw I would be at the handball court. There was a good game in progress when I got there. There was always plenty of betting action on the sidelines. If the game was one-sided the bettors made adjustments by adding or subtracting points. There were more variations to handicapping a handball game in Folsom than there are in handicapping a horse race. I watched for an hour, then got restless.

I considered working out and headed toward the weights. Just before I reached the iron pile, I spotted Tom standing by himself. He looked so lost and defeated standing there that I felt sorry for him. I had felt that way about Tom from the first time I had seen him. He didn't fit into Folsom's society, even if he had committed a murder. He looked so totally miserable I had to laugh. Tom looked up and saw me laughing and for a moment, his face asked, "Why, why are you laughing at me?" I continued to laugh. I couldn't stop. Tom's face went from astonishment to bewilderment and then he started to laugh too. We were both laughing together, laughing so hard we couldn't stop. At the height of our laughter I wondered how I could be so uninhibited in a place like Folsom. It went on and on for three, four, five minutes. When it finally ended, we were both spent. I was the first to speak. "Motherfucker, you are pitiful. You looked like the doctor just told you that you'd have to have your dick cut off."

"Man, you caught me trippin.'"

"Trippin' my ass, you were doing it like a dog."

"Yeah, well maybe I was. I can't see getting adjusted to this place. It always feels like something is about to happen. Like that fight yesterday where the two guys got shot. Did you see it?"

"Yeah, I was right there. Take three thousand crazy motherfuckers all trying to fuck each other around every day of the year and you got a joint where something is happening or about to happen at any time."

"You're right, but accepting it is a bitch. I never know what's going to happen next. Like talking to the wrong guy in the wrong place and it's over."

"But that's the way it is outside, too."

"You can stay away from the nuts out there."

"Look at it this way. You can't get hit by a car in here."

"I'll take the cars."

"If you're going to stay out of that bag I caught you in a few minutes ago, you're going to have to get involved in something you can stick your nut sack into."

"Like what?"

"That's up to you. There's two ways to escape; one's over the wall and the other is to get involved in something so heavy it consumes you. You see those weight lifters over there?"

"Man, I'm no—"

"Hold it. I'm not saying you're a weight lifter. That's their escape. You know what's going on in their minds? When they raise out of here they can go back to the neighborhood in a tee shirt and flash, and that keeps them going. Some guys do it in school, drawing, chess players, handballers, even the guys playing dominoes are escaping."

"What are you doing to escape?"

"I can't have a horn here so I might get a guitar, write some tunes and learn some new games."

"What, you mean like stealing games?"

"No, Monopoly, motherfucker."

"You ain't hanging it up?"

"I'm a dope fiend. Come on Stuffy, let's check out the Jaw. He's playing dominoes."

When we passed One Building I heard Jaw laughing. As we approached, one of the players named Billy was standing about three feet back from the table, shaking his head.

I heard him say, "Come on, Jaw, don't fuck around." There was a lightweight commotion around the table. As I got closer I saw why. Hog Jaw had his dick on the domino table, something he did all the time when he was losing. Since everyone in prison was trying either to establish or maintain his masculinity, a dick on the table presented a problem. What do you do? Act cool? You can't pretend you don't notice it. Do you get angry? Well, Billy walked away from the table, probably the worst thing he could have done. Once Hog Jaw found out he could intimidate a person, he never let up. "Come on, Billy, it's your play. I promise not to take it out again if it gets you hot."

"Fuck you, Hog Jaw."

"No, really man, if you get excited I'll cool it. It's a nice one and some guys just can't handle it."

"Cash me in. How many games am I up?"

"You can't quit when I'm three games down, not if you want to get paid, Billy."

"I don't have to put up with your dick on the table either."

"Come on, Billy, you see it's in my pants now. I'll leave it there."

"Man, I came out here to play dominoes, Jaw."

"All right already, it's over, baby. The rod's back. Let's play."

"Yeah, well if it happens again I'm out."

"Come on, Billy."

Billy picked up a hand. The game continued but under different circumstances. Hog Jaw had broken the rhythm of the game, which was what he had been trying to do. In the next half hour, Jaw won six out of seven games, but then they quit for lunch. Jaw was grinning when he walked up to me and Tom and asked what was for lunch.

"I didn't notice." I replied. "I'm not going to eat anyway."

"Why?"

"I'm going to my cell."

"The cell?"

"Me too." Tom said.

"What is with you guys?"

"There isn't anything on this yard that knocks me out." I answered.

"You just can't get used to the yard, can you Woods?" he laughed loudly, and Tom just rolled his eyes. "You'll see, it's like that in the beginning, then in a few months you'll start loving it."

"You love it. I'm going to the cell. I'll see you tonight at dinner. You too, Tom." I left quickly to keep from hearing any more of the Jaw's comments. Sometimes he didn't know when to shut up. Shooting off his mouth and making a joke of everything was his way of doing the time. If he ever had a serious day in his life, he'd probably jump off the fifth tier. But he had a loyalty about him that took up a lot of slack, and he had access to anything that drove through the gate. Before I left, I took him aside. "Get me an outfit in my cell tonight."

"You're going to fuck it up fucking around like that."

"Just get it for me."

"It's your transfer, not mine. You're the one that doesn't like it here."

CHAPTER 45

"Did you sleep?"
"No, I read all afternoon."

"I saw the doctor's list. He put you on for tomorrow instead of next week, and I got the outfit for you."

"You are Business Jones, Mr. Jaw."

"Well, you can't take care of business in the cell. Take this outfit; it's burning a hole in my pocket. You sure that knee of yours shows something wrong on x-rays?"

"It's been on the gimp side since I was in high school."

"It better have some pathology because the sawbones you're going to is suspicious about every convict he sees. Say as little as possible and be sure to flash that religious pamphlet. You still got it?"

"Yeah."

"I saw Faulkner in the mail room this afternoon and told him to send over your mail. Did you get it?"

"Yeah, I got three letters from my grandmother and one from my old lady."

"Does your old lady write regular?"

"Once a week is all they allow her to write."

"And I suppose she's coming up the first day she's out?" Jaw said sarcastically.

"As a matter of fact, she is, asshole. She's a racehorse."

"They're all racehorse material until they have to run. None of them ever reach the stretch."

"You are a cynical cocksucker, Jaw."

"No, I just know women."

"Sure you do, with your state-raised ass you haven't been out twenty minutes since you first found out you had a dick, and you're going to tell me about women? Besides, you are an ugly motherfucker. What chick is going to come up here every week and look at that lantern jaw of yours?"

"I could have a string of bitches here, if I wanted them."

"Sure you could, Jaws."

"Waiting for some broad to show every visiting day is like a double sentence. When is she getting out?"

"A year with good time."

"By then you'll be in San Quentin. The visiting room here is like a dungeon and you got to talk over the phone through a glass door."

"I didn't know it was that tight. I was going to have my grandmother come up."

"Folsom ain't the spot for moms and grandmoms. Wait till you get to Quentin."

"You're probably right. I'll give you the outfit back in the morning."

"Don't leave it in your cell."

"I won't. I'll see you at breakfast."

"You got it."

I waited until the showers were over before I took the outfit out and examined it. I put it together and tested it with water. I placed a towel over the bed rail so that I couldn't be seen sitting on the toilet. I jabbed the needle into my knee and injected a full dropper of water. It burned a little bit but it wasn't painful. It didn't show anything, so I injected another dropperful. Still no noticeable difference. I continued; a third, a fourth and it began to swell. I stopped at ten, stood up and walked back and forth in the cell. My knee felt different but didn't hurt. The entire knee joint was swollen. I looked like I could have been an old linebacker for the Los Angeles Rams. I walked back and forth in the cell for an hour or so, feeling very pleased with myself. I lay down to read. Every few pages, I looked at my knee. It was still swollen. What a marvelous sight, all puffy like that.

When I woke up the next morning, the first thing I did was look at my knee. It was nice and big. The pass to the doctor's office, which had been delivered before I woke up, was on the bars. I dressed quickly, remembering to put the outfit and religious pamphlet in my pocket. The bar was pulled, and I was the first one out of my cell. When I reached the mess hall, Jaw was there waiting for me. "How did it go?"

"Perfect."

"Let me check it out." I pulled up my pant leg to show Jaw. "Yeah, it looks great. How does it feel?"

"I can't tell it's in there."

"What time is your appointment?"

"Eight-thirty."

"Where's your God book?"

"Oh, yeah." I produced it from my pants pocket and placed

it in my shirt pocket. "You want the fit now?"

"Yeah, hand it to me and I'm on my way. I'll see you on the yard by the handball court."

"Don't worry, Jaw. I'll hear you."

"Fuck you."

I left the mess hall and walked around the yard a couple of times before going to the hospital. I presented my ducat to an officer at the hospital door, who told me to wait on the bench. Half a dozen other men were waiting to see the doctor. There were no books or magazines to occupy myself so I read the religious pamphlet I had brought with me. About that time, the doctor entered for his appointments, but I didn't know who he was, so I continued reading. I looked up to see a tall man with a round face and round glasses peering at me as he walked past and entered the office of Doctor Rosendall. I asked one of the men who was waiting, "Was that the doctor?"

"The one and only."

I knew the doctor had seen me reading the pamphlet. I was called in by the clerk and motioned to a chair. I sat as the doctor filled in some charts. When he had finished, he handed the charts to the clerk, looked at me and said in a very professional tone, "What's troubling you?"

"I'm in constant pain with my knee, Doctor."

"Which one?"

"The left."

"Drop your trousers so I can look at it." He stood up and walked over to where I was standing. He went through the usual knee inspection, bending it one way, then another and asking questions along with his inspection. "How long has it been swollen?"

"A couple of weeks, but it comes and goes."

"You have a lot of water in there. How did you injure it?"

"When I was in high school playing football for the first time, and several years later when I was hunting with my father, I fell off a ledge and had to be hospitalized." I had never known my father and had never been hunting in my life, but I knew it sounded good, so I threw it in. "They took x-rays and said I should have an operation."

"Well, that's what we're going to do, take x-rays. I'll schedule you for x-rays next week. Try and stay off it as much as possible. Do you have a job?'

"No, sir."

"I'm going to give you a cane so it will relieve some pressure. You have quite a bit of water in there. If it gets worse, I'll remove it for you." He went to his desk and wrote out a prescription which he handed to me. "Take these pills when it hurts. I'll see you again after I've looked at the x-rays."

I thanked him and left. I knew it had gone well. I filled the prescription of aspirins and they gave me a cane. Another stage in the plan had been completed.

CHAPTER 46

A cold wind was blowing as I came out of One Building. I stood in a moment of reflection, looking over the yard, the domino tables, the bleachers. I couldn't believe a year had gone by already. It was beginning to rain but I didn't care. There weren't a lot of men on the yard, only the ones going to work. I took my time limping across the yard. There was no hurry. I had all the time I needed now. Halfway across I heard Hog Jaw yell to me. I turned slowly and stopped. "What you doing with your gimpy ass in the rain, motherfucker?"

"Trying to get to Receiving and Release so I can get away from your crazy ass."

"The doctors told me you could be the first on the list. It won't be much longer, now, Woods. Come on. Can you limp around the yard a couple of times before you go?"

I hobbled across the yard to catch up to him. "I could run around the yard a couple of times."

"Just keep limping, motherfucker, or you'll blow a year of hard-ass work. You got all the addresses written down?"

"They're all checked in."

"Good, if you can't hook it up with your old lady and have to blow Quentin on your own, give Art a call as soon as you get to a phone. Your code name is Rhino. Come to think of it, it fits. I told him if he ever got a message from the Rhino to pull out all the stops, and he will. You could even send your old lady by to see him when she comes up to visit you. She can tell him to be on the point for your call if nothing else. Well, you did it, motherfucker. You waltzed that doctor right out of his drawers. No one even knew you were here. You can take your time in Quentin, wait for the right opportunity. It's there. You're only going to get one shot, so make it a goodie."

"You don't think there's any chance they would send me back here?"

"No, just see Norman. You might have to get the operation. You ever think of that?"

"If that's what it takes. Oh, I forgot to yell you. Joe is being interviewed by the parole office, but sends his love, and you know Fat Phil's in the hospital with stomach trouble. I sent word up to him last night. You haven't cut our talks up with anybody, have you?"

"No, I haven't said anything. Joe and Phil probably know already what's going on but they wouldn't crack to anybody."

"If I make it, Jaw, I won't be in touch with anyone. If I don't make it, I'm not coming back, period. When I was out there, it was a full race affair and I had to take some chances where my life was involved, but there was a point where I pulled up, like when I tried to escape to Mexico. I almost made it, but in the last few seconds, a cop had a gun at my head and it was either get killed or pull up. After being in this pit, I'd let him shoot before I'd come back."

"You'd be better off because the next time is definitely all day. No compromises. It's over."

"Are you sticking it out here, Jaw?"

"Why not? This place doesn't bug me like it does you."

"Yeah, you know why it is this pit really bugs me, Jaw?"

" No, why?"

"I think it's because I can see this place for what it really is, a melting pot for two thousand motherfuckers whose hustle has been diminished to cigarettes and zoo-zoo's, and their lives, at least ninety percent of them, have been reduced to a hopelessness they don't recognize or understand. Two thousand motherfuckers who are lost, and don't know it.

"Sure, maybe some of them have hope, because you can't take that away completely; but the sadists have a system designed just for them called 'parole.' So, the parole board brings you up every year and tells you something, some shit like: 'We'd like to see you get involved in our landscaping program and attend some of those gala club meetings,' leading them to believe that, if they did these things, then maybe they'd have a chance the next time they appeared. When I go on the yard, and I look at those faces, is when it bothers me the most. I guess I'm afraid if I don't get transferred, the same thing could happen to me."

There was a long silence as we stood and watched the prisoners milling around the yard. For once, Jaw was at a loss for words. I turned to him and asked: "How do you hold up, Jaw? You're always laughing and smiling like this is all one big joke."

"I didn't do more than I could fade," Jaw replied.

"What do you mean by that?"

"I knew I could handle a dime. I knew, even with a string of robberies a dime was max— C'mon, Woods, I got some ducats. Let me buy you a cream before you go. You're depressing the shit out of me."

As we walked over to the commissary, I looked around the yard one last time, and saw Tom hanging out by himself on a bench.

"You know that black cat you seen me with?"

"What about him?"

"I want you to keep an eye on him for me."

"What for? You know I don't fuck around with rugs."

"Just do this for me."

"What do you want me to do?"

"Tell Burton I said to look out for him. Don't let anybody put any games on him. Tell him it's for me. He'll understand."

"I know you're not fucking him. He's too ugly. What's the hook-up?"

"Well, you just do it no matter how much it hurts you."

"All right. I guess you got your reasons." We bought our ice cream and walked back toward Receiving and Release as we talked.

"I guess I'd better check in. It's time. Thanks, Hog Jaw. I couldn't have put it together without you. I guess this is it."

"Yeah, I guess so. You take it easy, you big fruiter, and when you do it, do it right."

"I'm going to be trying my ass off." I turned and walked away quickly. I would miss the Jaw and I knew the Jaw would miss me, yet neither of us said anything more.

They were waiting for me at Receiving and Release. Twenty-eight of us were being transferred to different prisons throughout the state. The bus had pulled up ready to board. The men on the yard were lined up waiting to see who was being shipped out. It didn't matter that it was cold and raining; they stood there and watched. As I got on the bus, Jaw gave me the clenched fist sign with a quick jerky down-movement which meant "take it easy." I returned the gesture as I got on the bus. Once inside, I felt a sense of relief. The leg irons were put on and in a few minutes the bus was driving down the same eerie driveway I had entered over a year before.

CHAPTER 47

There were three officers waiting for the bus as it pulled up and stopped in front of San Quentin. We all got up to stretch, but just then an officer with a voice that could have been heard across the bay entered the bus, and said, "All right, everyone remain seated." He repeated it again in an even louder voice. It took only a few seconds for us to settle down and get back to our seats.

"Woody Woodward B63570."

"Yes, sir."

"Up front."

When I reached the door the officers motioned me out. There were two other officers waiting outside the bus. Due to the leg irons and my affected limp, it took a few minutes before I reached the ground. The officer with the booming voice pointed to an iron grill gate, and then two more officers fell in behind me, one on each side, and walked me to the gate in silence. The first officer banged on the iron gate with his keys, and a guard on the other side opened the door to let us through. At the end of the corridor was another gate and then we were inside the prison. I was directed to my right. I saw a sign that read "Control Room." We walked on in silence, and stood for a few minutes.

At the entrance to his office, the Captain stood with three other officers. He was close to fifty, about five-ten, carrying 220 pounds or more, but his body was hippy around the middle and showed lack of physical development. His eyes were close together but not so close as to appear stupid, and he held them almost closed, probably a habit formed over the years. He looked to me like he had worked for the Department of Corrections twenty years or more and had heard every story in the book. From the look on his face I could tell that bullshit wouldn't get in with him, that you could get away with telling him to go fuck himself a lot easier than saying you were sorry.

While I was waiting to talk to the Captain, two other officers entered with Stan. So that was it. It was all clear now. Was I ever going to stop paying dues to that sonofabitch? For a tough guy, Stan had sure done a flip. I looked at him, then lowered my eyes to the ground and waited. The Captain "You see your friend out there?"

"Yes, sir, I saw him."

"How do you feel about him?"

"I don't have any feeling about him one way or the other."

"You weren't thinking that way in the County Jail or in the Guidance Center. What happened in the space of a year that changed your thinking?"

"I got an all-time loser on my hands with this guy, Captain. He's not worth what it's going to cost me."

"You thought about it a lot?"

"I didn't think about it at all until I saw him standing there a few minutes ago. I realized what it's going to cost me to satisfy a revenge that's already over with. What I did to him in the County Jail was sufficient. I don't want any more of him, Captain. That's the truth. It's over."

The Captain tilted his head to one side in a pensive gesture and looked into my eyes. He'd probably used this move for twenty years to weigh a man out. "You know I believe you, Woody. I believe you've got enough sense to leave him alone. However, there are other ways to get him if you want to. Like spreading the word that he is an informer. I've got an institution full of young injustice collectors that would be happy to do the job for you just to build a reputation for themselves."

"I haven't got any control over that, Captain."

"You're going to have to because I'm going to assign his protection to you. I'm going to hold you responsible for anything that happens to him. If anything does happen, you're going to be in segregation for a long time. I mean a long time. Do you understand what I'm talking about?"

"Yes, I do."

"Do you want to talk to him while we're all here?"

"Yeah, maybe I should."

The Captain sent for Stan and offered him a seat. He started off saying, "You guys know each other?" Stan nodded. He was apprehensive and didn't know what to expect.

I sensed this and took over. "Look, Stan, whatever happened outside was yesterday, as far as I'm concerned. You and I could take this thing all the way and end up with a loser. There's no win for us." I knew he didn't want to take any kind of action, that all he wanted was to be left alone and get out of prison without being hurt.

"I would like to forget everything that we were connected with outside. From this day on, we start all over. If anyone asks me about you, I'll tell them it was a misunderstanding. I'll say whatever I have to to keep it off the yard. If anyone approaches you, tell them to see me. That would be the best way to do it." I could see the relief on Stan's face. He knew what it would be like to do his jolt with a rat jacket. Even the rats called you a rat if they could get away with it.

Finally Stan spoke. "We have to live together. We might as well get along."

The three of us engaged in trivial conversation for a few minutes, after which the Captain told Stan he could go back to work. Stan stood up and said, "I'll see you on the yard, Woody."

"I'll be there." I was pleased with the way it turned out. It could have been a disaster. This way, everyone was satisfied. Stan wasn't going to be exposed or hurt, I wasn't going to be locked up, and the Captain wouldn't have to concern himself with a stabbing or a killing.

The Captain looked at me. "Remember, we have a deal."

"I'm glad it's settled, Captain." I stood, thanked him, and was escorted to Receiving and Release to pick up my personal property.

CHAPTER 48

It was a typical San Quentin day; cold, windy and drizzling. The noon meal lined up an hour earlier in Quentin than in Folsom. There were at least a dozen lines under a tin shed, which offered little or no protection from the constant, strong winds. I stood in the chow line waiting to go into the mess hall. I was trying to find someone I knew who could tell me where Red was. Quentin was much larger than Folsom with double the population. I would get to know it in time, but at the moment I was confused by all the activity. It seemed a lot livelier than I had remembered it. There were over a thousand men on the yard, and dozens of guards.

I finally got into the mess hall and there on the steam table serving cabbage was Morrie. I had met Morrie years back when we were playing together in a strip joint. Morrie was the M.C. He wasn't hooked when we first met, but when the club folded six months later he was a "hope to die" junkie. Morrie was the only junkie I had ever known who was always immaculately dressed. Even if he was hooked to the nuts, he would get all dressed up to score in East LA. Morrie had a long line of shit that never stopped coming, but he was always straight with me and I respected him. When I saw Morrie serving food it was like I had found a long lost friend. The line moved fast so we didn't have much time to talk. "When did you get here, Woody?"

"Just now."

"Why didn't you tell me it was like this?" We both laughed.

"Where can I find Red Kelly?"

"On the lower yard playing handball. I'll see you down there when I get off work. Thirty minutes or so."

"I'll be looking for you." I took a seat and started to eat, but the food was horrible, so I contented myself with some bread and coffee. The mess hall here was much noisier than at Folsom, and I didn't like the invasion of privacy.

Outside the yard I tried again to spot someone I knew from the streets but the faces were alien to me. I was anxious to see Red, so I walked to the lower yard. I spotted him right away in a hot handball game. I could tell by the intensity of each point that there was heavy money on the game. I waited until the game ended and then walked up close enough to Red to be heard and said, "Hey, Big Red Mommy."

Red turned around slowly. "God damn, Woody! I read about you in the papers. That was over a year ago. Have you been in the County Jail all this time?"

"I've been in Folsom a year. Come on, let's take a few laps around the track and cut it up."

Red noticed the cane for the first time. "What's wrong with your leg?"

"Nothing. I faked a bum knee to raise out of Folsom. They sent me here for an operation. I got to locate a cat named Norman. You know him?"

"Sure."

"Hog Jaw said he has the juice to keep me here."

"Hog Jaw told you right. He's a heavyweight in the juice department. Norman's a very strange cat. He's the Warden's right hand man. Works seven days a week and loves it. He won't make a move for just anybody but I know him well enough to get a favor."

"Hog Jaw told me to see him."

"Then you're covered."

"Doesn't he have a murder beef?"

"Yeah. His partner shot an off-duty policeman in a market robbery. Norman was sitting in the getaway car. Poor asshole, it was the first time he ever did anything like that. They got popped two blocks away and both of them got life. Norman never saw the inside of a jail before and woke up the next morning doing all day. He went to work for the Warden the first week he was here. Warden's always got to have the closest thing to a boy scout for a clerk. There's lots of confidential shit coming out of his office every day. If he had someone in there who couldn't keep his mouth shut, he couldn't run the joint."

"And Norman keeps his mouth shut?"

"That's why he's been there so many summers. Sound like a kiss-ass?"

"Yeah, in a way."

"He's not. Anything but that. Dig what he did last week. This red-faced lieutenant who's a real pain in the cunt comes in Norman's office just before court line and asks Norman for a file on some guy, and Norman promptly tells him to fuck his mother. Well, the lieutenant just flips out, and runs into the Warden's office. His alcoholic personality is working overtime and he's screaming where everyone can hear that Norman just told him to fuck his mother.

Anyway, the Warden comes out of his office and he's pissed with the lieutenant for upsetting the office routine. He asks what's the problem. By now, the lieutenant is really in a rage. He keeps pointing his finger at Norman with a jerky movement and screaming that Norman told him to fuck his mother. The Warden very coolly asks the lieutenant to be quiet, walks over to Norman and asks what happened. 'I don't know what Lieutenant Campbell is talking about. It doesn't make any sense to me, Warden.' Norman says."

"By now the lieutenant is absolutely mad and starts screaming all over again, 'That's a fucking lie, Warden. He told me to fuck my mother. That sonofabitch told me to fuck my mother.' The Warden, as Norman tells it, stopped the lieutenant with one word, 'enough.' He then went on to say the incident was over and he didn't want to hear any more about it. But the lieutenant still had to talk to Norman because he was the only one who had the court list. The Warden was still standing there in front of his office so the lieutenant tried to act very polite when he said, 'May I have the court list, please?' Norman knew the Warden was watching and replied in his most courteous voice, 'Why certainly, Lieutenant. It's all prepared.' At this point, the Lieutenant doesn't know whether to scream or shit. The Warden finally ended it by saying, 'Alright, let's all get back to work.'"

"You mean he got away with that?"

"Sure did. Norman said when the lieutenant walked past him to the outer office, he glared at him real hard but Norman just kept typing like nothing happened. You'd have to know Norman to understand it. Norman doesn't smoke or swear and doesn't get high. His biggest vice is studying higher mathematics, plus he's been working for the Warden for seven years. The Warden didn't believe Norman was capable of saying something like 'fuck your mother,' especially to a lieutenant."

"What about the lieutenant?"

"He's never said a word. He probably figures if he can't get him thrown in the hole for calling him a motherfucker right in the Warden's office, he'd better forget it."

"Goddamn, that's a strange sense of humor, an unusual sense of rebellion."

"That's it, you hit it. He's a real rebel but no one knows it because he shuts everyone out."

"I'd like to see him. Can you set it up?"

"Tomorrow at lunch. He doesn't eat lunch but I'll get him out here tomorrow."

"Tell him I'm a friend of Hog Jaw's."

"You thought about what you want to do here?"

"Yeah, look for a hole I can crawl out of. That's what I came to Quentin for."

"Well, there are a couple of possibilities. The hospital has a weak spot, but you'd have to swim the bay at night."

"How far is it to the other side of the bay?"

"Could you make it a mile?"

"I could do whatever it takes. What's the other possibility?"

"A hideout in the industrial area. They both will take some time to check out and then putting them together will take some more time. Just relax. I know you're on your mark, but you can't rush something like this. A word to the wrong guy and you're finished. I know the people to see to hook it up. Are you ready for a Bogart move if it's necessary?"

"If I am ready to swim that's shark's cafeteria, I got Bogart covered."

"I just wanted to know."

"What are you doing here?"

"Morning bakery shift and crash handball every afternoon. I'm glad you're here. I got so much action I can't handle all of it myself."

"What kind of action?"

"A football book and a floating poker game on the weekends. They're both stickups. It costs them three to win two on the book and I cut ten percent out of every hand plus a free ante."

"They still stand for that?"

"It's my third year with the book and I've had the poker games going for three months. They go for it. That's all I can tell you."

"Do you play in the game?"

"Yeah, I sit there with a free ante and wait for a cinch."

"I didn't come here for the weather or to get rich, Red. I want to blow out of here."

"So I'll help you. We can be partners until you make your move."

"If I'm in the action I might rank the whole play."

"That wouldn't have a fucking thing to do with it; they'd just think you were settling down, finding your groove. They don't give a fuck what you do as long as you don't hurt anyone collecting your dough."

"I don't want them to know me. I got to keep the same kind of low profile I kept in Folsom."

"They're going to know you regardless of what you do. It's possible you could sneak by unnoticed if you didn't talk to anyone—I mean no one—eat by yourself, and then go back to your cell. But come on, Woody, be realistic, you couldn't book that kind of act for a week without flipping out."

"I got to put this together, Red."

"I know you do, but believe me, being in action ain't going to affect it. Besides, it's sorta nice having a bank roll when that old smackola drives through the gate. Think that one over."
Red knew the magic words, the sonofabitch.

"Hey, there's Morrie, Red. Call him over."

"We finished talking?" Red asked.

"Yeah, shit. It's you and me, you redheaded motherfucker, but no jackpots or I'm out."

Red and I observed Morrie for a minute. He was almost running around the handball court trying to find us. Red yelled out and Morrie rushed over. "Man, you could have knocked me down when I saw you drive in the mess hall."

"Morrie, your shoes aren't shined," I said to him, then, turning to Red, I added, "I used to call this cat 'Creases.' I think he even had his shorts pressed. What happened to your razor sharp ass, Morrie?"

"Man, when they busted me I had on tennis shoes and a swim suit and I haven't recovered yet."

"That's the high cost of low living." Red said.

"Nothing like a nice little heroin run to take the starch out of a player's ass," I said.

"I saw that spread of yours in the LA Times, sucker. You weren't exactly looking like Paul Newman."

Again Red interjected, "The high cost of low living,

fellas."

"Well, while we're at it, what's a good safe man doing with a gun in his hand?"

All three of us said simultaneously, "The high cost of that low living." We were all laughing and it felt good to be among friends and to be able to feel loose in the constant uptight environment of prison.

While we were laughing, a convict came up behind me and said hello. The groove was broken, but I didn't realize how much so until I turned around. My expression changed immediately when I saw it was Lee, the dope fiend I had watched set up his own cousin in East LA. "Never thought I'd see you here, Lee. How did you get here?" Before he could answer, I asked another question. "How's your cousin?"

"She's all right."

"What happened to her?"

"She went to Corona."

"That's going to be hard for her. What was she, about forty?"

"Yeah, something like that," Lee answered.

I was talking to him like he was a child, ending every sentence with Lee's name. "I liked her, Lee. Did you like her, Lee?"

"Sure, yeah, she's good people." It was obvious to everyone that he was becoming nervous with the way the conversation was going.

"Then why did you set her up, Lee? You little rat bastard."

"I—"

"Don't say nothing, punk. I was at the drive-in the night you did it to her. I saw everything, Lee."

"Woody—"

"I said not to say anything. Didn't you hear me?" I turned to Red and Morrie. "I saw this little punk set up his own cousin."

"Maybe we can sell his ass for five packs." Red said.

"Three, maybe."

Lee couldn't fight the case and knew it. The only thing

open to him was to walk. As Lee was leaving, Red yelled, "Walk slow, pussy."

"I wanted him to know I knew," I said.

"Yeah," Red said, "the joint's overrun with Lees."

"He sure got in the wind fast."

"There wasn't a hell of a lot to hang around for, was there? He probably thought Red was going to sell him right while he was standing here."

"Did you get your blankets out of household?" Red asked me.

"No."

"Let's go to the upper yard and see what's happening."

"What *is* happening, Red?"

"What do you mean?"

"Is there anything on the yard now?"

"No smack. I got some stumblers. If you want some uppers I can see a guy at dinner who's holding."

"What kind of stumblers? I haven't been high in a year."

"Don't they ever get any dope in Folly?"

"Not much, and I didn't want to take the chance."

"You *have* changed. I got some reds and yellows, that's all that's around right now. Pick your color."

"The reds have it," I answered.

"I'll bring them to the mess hall tonight. There should be some smack around this weekend. Whoever gets it will come to me first. They always do. They know I got the bankroll and figure it's better to deal with one guy. They take a little less money but a hell of a lot less heat."

Red turned to Morrie, "You think the yard will be sticking this weekend?"

"A strong possibility. There's a half dozen guys on the point."

"There goes Skinny." Red said. We turned around to see a convict walking between two guards. The guards walked about five feet from him, front and back. As the trio proceeded across the yard, a convict preoccupied with something got within a few feet of them and the guard leading the procession yelled in a loud voice, "Dead Man." The preoccupied convict, realizing he was within ten feet of a death row inmate, stepped back at once.

"That Dead Man routine's a cold move," I said.

"It's cold alright, but it gets everybody's attention. They don't want anyone passing anything to a guy on the row. Did you recognize him?"

"No, should I have?"

"Skinny Wilson."

"You serious?"

"That was him."

"He's all puffed up, looks like a heavyweight contender."

"Some guys eat up then some guys don't. He eats."

"How did he get there?"

"Killed a guy a year and a half ago right over there." Red pointed to a spot by the domino tables. "The guy was a loudmouth and had it coming. Skinny should have waited, but he got him right there in front of everyone."

"Skinny didn't look too unhappy."

"No. By the time they get you to the chamber it ain't as big a deal as it was when you first get sentenced to die. You got to keep thinking of it every day and every day they get a little more of your nut sack. When it comes time, you're ready to get it over with. But that's only my opinion. Who knows how you act when the real shit's on you."

"That's the real shit all right, no doubt about that." I said.

"Come on, let's get your blankets. I know the guy working in household. We'll get you some new ones." Red was hooked up on every level. He had every spot in the joint covered. I thought to myself how much Red and I were alike. It was going to be a good partnership.

After I got the new blankets, we lined up under the shed and waited to file in the south block. When we got to the rotunda, we separated and said our goodbyes until dinner.

I lived on the fifth tier. I could look out the dirty window and see the bay. There was a heavy wind which created a choppy movement in the sea. It looked cold and treacherous. I wondered for a moment if I would be able to swim that shark-infested body of water. I looked away and watched the lost souls filing into their prison homes, and I knew I would need whatever it took when the time came. I didn't have to worry about that now. I was with friends and comfortable, but, most importantly, I was looking forward to the dope Red would be bringing to the mess hall.

I heard men walking by my cell talking loudly. I grabbed my clothes along with my shoes and socks and barely got out of my cell before the main bar was pulled. The pills I had gotten from Red had put me down for the count. I was sleepy and uncoordinated as I dressed on the tier. I had probably missed Red and Morrie so I took my time as I walked down the stairs. Everyone had gone and I was alone.

I heard a strange thumping sound as I reached the fourth level. It sounded like someone was gasping and punching the heavy bag. It seemed to be taking place on the third tier, but I wasn't sure. Somewhere below me was what sounded like a group of guards running with keys jingling on their belts. Very cautiously I approached the third tier and saw nothing, but still heard the thumping, gasping sound. I sensed some form of danger, something unusual, so I waited and listened for a moment. I didn't have to wait long. The jingling of the keys had stopped. The guards had obviously reached their destination. Then I heard, "Give it up, Tucker. Come on now, that's enough, give it to me."

I got on my knees and peered through the iron steps affording me a view of the third landing. There was blood everywhere. It looked like three gallons of red paint had been spilled over the floor. One prisoner was sitting on top of another prisoner stabbing him. The one getting stabbed was dead but it didn't stop the man on top from continuing to plunge the knife into the body. Half a dozen guards were trying to coax him into giving them the knife, but he just continued stabbing. A guard got in too close and barely missed getting cut. After that, they backed away and waited.

They had a long wait. The blade of the knife was over seven inches long and wide, real wide. Every time the prisoner plunged it into the man's body it made a sickening sound. He was in a frenzy, his eyes were glazed. The knife kept going in and out, in and out, in and out, like a stamping machine. He had an incredible amount of energy, and when it looked like he was going to stop from exhaustion, he would suddenly get a new burst of energy and plunge the knife in even faster than before, all the while keeping his eyes on the guards standing in front of him. The strokes were getting slower and slower and he was having a hard time pulling the knife out. It seemed like he was never going to stop. Finally, unable to get the knife out, he collapsed over the dead man's body. Only then did the guards go in and take him.

I went back to the fifth tier and waited until the breakfast line had been run. When I was sure it was clear, I walked down the stairs and out to the yard. I found Morrie almost immediately and gave him a blow-by-blow of what had happened. Morrie knew the convict who had done the stabbing and figured it was connected with a homosexual play because the guy was a punk.

"That's cold, getting put in the clouds by a punk." I said.

"Clouds are clouds, what difference does it make?"

"Guess you're right. It's still cold. Where's Red?"

"He's working. He'll be out of the bakery by noon. You guys gotta meet with Norman at twelve sharp. You can't be late for Norman; he keeps a tight schedule. Red wants me to introduce you around to his runners and some of the guys that bet every week. He wants me to point out who not to take action from. Red doesn't take any bets from niggers."

"None?"

"No, none. It's too hard to collect the money."

Morrie knew the yard as well as anyone. I wondered why Red didn't use Morrie for a partner. Red was the kind of guy who never forgot it if you did something for him. I was sure he remembered all the times I had visited him in the county jail, and from what I had seen on the yard, it was obvious that it took a certain kind of guy to run the book properly. Morrie was a sweetheart, but he could fold if the pressure got too heavy.

I captured the tempo of the yard in one morning. It was high energy, unlike Folsom where everyone walked slowly and took their time with life. Practically every convict who was in action could tell at a glance what was happening on the yard. They could tell if there was dope to be had, if the money was heavy or light, if there was going to be trouble or if it was cool or hot. They seemed to have a built-in radar system and the ones who survived were never wrong.

Morrie introduced me to a group of guys standing around drinking coffee and lying as fast as they could about the murder that had taken place. They were all authorities on what had happened, yet none of them had been there. I just listened.

Morrie saw someone on the other side of the yard and told me, "Come on, I want you to meet a friend of mine."

"Who?"

"That guy over there with the plumbing tools in his hands." I looked over and saw Stan.

Morrie noticed my expression harden. "You know him?"

"Yeah, he lives on my tier. I'm not going to give you a rundown on him now, but leave him alone." I said.

"What do you mean?"

"You don't need to know anything about him, and I don't want you to be running around the yard playing detective."

"But Woody, you—"

"God dammit, Morrie, put him on hold, that's all I'm asking you to do. I'll explain it to you when I'm ready. In the meantime, just treat him the same as you always have and don't have any business with him. Can you do that?"

"Yeah, if you want me to I can."

"I want you to." The line for the noon meal was starting to form. "Come on, Morrie, let's get in line."

"Red said not to eat; he's having some good stuff delivered to the yard, something off the death row food cart. He hardly ever eats in the mess hall. He doesn't have to."

"I can see why. That food last night was a joke, but the menu looks terrific. I wasn't ready for Waldorf salad and

Salisbury steak. That Salisbury, I couldn't eat it."

"The whole fucking menu's a joke. You got to make the mess hall with peanut butter and jelly to survive."

"That's about it, isn't it Morrie?"

"Don't worry about it, Red will take care of you. He's got a good hookup for getting things out of the kitchen. There's Norman and Red by the drinking faucet. Go on. I'll see you. I got something to take care of."

"Remember what I told you about Stan."

"Alright already, it's forgotten."

If the guy with Red was Norman, he was entirely different from what I thought he would be. Norman stood well over six feet and in spite of a few extra pounds around the waist, he looked like he could have been a football player. His hair was beginning to thin and he wore glasses, which added to his intellectual appearance. His posture was erect in an almost military fashion, which made him stand out from the other men on the yard. Norman was listening to Red as I approached. His head was tilted to one side and he seemed to be completely involved in what Red was saying. When Red saw me he said something to Norman and Norman turned around.

"Hi, Red."

"All right. Woody, meet Norman."

"Hi, Norman."

"How do you do? You're a friend of Hog Jaw's, aren't you?"

"I just left him. He told me to look you up."

"Red has explained everything to me."

"He has?"

"Yes. I understand the situation."

"What's my first move, Norman?"

"You don't have to manipulate anything. Just complete the hospital procedure. I'll handle it from there."

"What about an operation?"

"What about it?" Norman asked.

"I mean, do I have to get my knee operated on to stay here?"

"Do you want your knee operated on?"

"Not exactly, you see—"

"Then don't have the operation. Red's told me all about the way you got here."

"So I don't do anything?"

"Nothing. When you're cleared by the hospital I'll take it from there. Judging from your being here, I take it your meeting with the Captain yesterday was a successful one."

"He wasn't that hard to talk to."

"Sometimes he's not, but he's the type of man who has to have things his way."

"That's the impression I got. The less I have to do with him the better."

"That's correct."

"Is there anything I can do, Norman, while I'm waiting to be cleared from the hospital?"

"Nothing. Just stay with your redheaded friend here. He'll keep you out of trouble. I've got to get back to work now, Woody. It was very nice meeting you. And again, don't worry about anything. It'll be taken care of."

"I don't know how to thank you, Norman."

"Don't try, it's unnecessary. See you later, Red. Goodbye, Woody."

"Goodbye, Norman." We watched Norman walk off.

"Did you like him?"

"Yeah. Yeah, I really did."

"I told you you would. He's a very unusual cat. Now, it's easy to see how he got away with that scene with that lieutenant. What were you talking about with the Captain?" Red asked.

"I don't know why I didn't tell you yesterday. Guess I was too excited. There's a guy here who fingered me. I busted him up in the County Jail."

"Bad?"

"Pretty bad. Yesterday the goon squad escorted me right off the bus to the Captain's office. He wanted a promise I wouldn't bust him up again, or have him busted up."

"That's no problem. We'll have a little on-the-job accident."

"We can't, Red."

"I'll set it up good, no one will know."

"Red, we can't. If anybody takes him out, drops something on him, or even so much as steps on his ingrown toenail I'll get the beef."

Red stared at me in disbelief. "So you're not going to do anything?"

"Not now. I couldn't believe Morrie knows him. He was going to introduce him to me this morning."

"This guy doesn't work in the plumbing shop, does, he?"

"Yeah, he's a plumber."

"Oh, man, he lives on my tier right next to Morrie. Morrie's been waiting for him to get minimum custody so he can make a runner out of him."

"I'm telling you this guy is good. He could deceive his mommy. He knows all the moves and talks all the right shit."

"What did you tell Morrie about him?"

"Nothing, except to keep him on ice until I explained."

"You got a plan for him?"

"Not this minute. Doing anything to him directly or indirectly would be a disaster right now for what I'm trying to hook up."

"That may take some time."

"That's all right. In the meantime, when my old lady gets out, I'll have her hustle up a saxophone and we might get lucky and put something together on the smack side. I want to do a lot of taking it easy until I get the chance to blow out of here."

"Will your old lady run something besides a saxophone?"

"Sure, if she had it, but she's getting out of the growler stone broke."

"She doesn't need any money. My brother is the man right now. He's been in action over two years. He won't bring it up here, but he'll give it to someone who will."

"Have you got a way to get it in?"

"I can get it all in one load, no cloak and dagger, either. One smooth move."

"It would have to be smooth. I wouldn't ask my old lady if it wasn't."

"When the time comes, I'll tell you all about it."

"Who knows about your brother?"

"A couple of movie stars and some musicians."

"I mean in here."

"Are you kidding?"

"Good. That's the way it ought to be."

"That's the way it's going to be. What happened to your horn?"

"What fucking horn?"

"Yeah, Harry don't let you play no horns, does he?"

"He takes it all, the same way he took away Morrie's creases."

"I know a guy in the band room who owes me a favor. What kind of saxophone?"

"A tenor, but I'll take anything."

"I'll go see about it now. What are you going to do?"

"Think I'll check out the library and lock up."

CHAPTER 49

"I raise ten, uh…"

"Call or pass. Let's keep it going," I said

"Ten dollars is a lot of dough, man. Let me think a second."

"You should have been thinking about it before he made

the bet. Come on, what do you wanna do?"

"What have I got on the books?" the caller asked.

I looked quickly at the tally sheet and answered, "Eleven bucks."

"That taps me if I call."

"No, you'll have a dollar left to raise if you want." The players all laughed.

"I call."

Winners bet and suckers call. At least playing low ball, I thought.

"Six, four," the bettor said.

"Take it down, Mr. Slick." said the caller.

I asked the caller what he had called on and he showed me his hand, which was a hard seven. "That's tough luck." I would never tell him what a sucker call it was.

Despite rumors to the contrary, there are more suckers in prison than anywhere else in the world. Where but prison would you find someone who would pay fifteen to ten just to make a bet? But cons are notorious for trying to get something for nothing, even if they have to take a three to two chance to do it.

The game was held on the fourth floor of the North block. Red had hired lookout men who were stationed at each end of the tier. The game was designed so that it could be broken up in a matter of seconds. There were no chips involved, only a score card subtracting points from the losers and giving points to the winners. If the guard ever got as close as the second tier, I would hand the score card and playing cards to the lookout man and everyone would disperse until the cop left. But most of the time, the cop stayed in his office.

I took a lot of football bets while running the card game. I wrote them down and handed them to the lookout man. The point man was paid to take the fall if the game got busted. That way Red and I stayed clear. We never kept anything—no markers, cards or tally sheets.

The quality of the players was generally so poor that it was difficult for me to be enthusiastic, but the time passed quickly and the money was good.

I was surprised one day to look up and see Red standing in the doorway. "How's it going?" Red asked.

"These guys are tough. They're killing me."

Red smiled. "Can you put the game on ice for five minutes?"

One of the losers said, "Come on, Red, don't do me like that. I'm down eight cartons."

"I'll only be five minutes. I got to go over something with Woody. Come on, Woody."

I called the lookout, handed him the tally sheet and walked off with Red.

"What's up?"

"You think you can find a vein in five minutes?"

"Oh man! You serious?"

"As serious as a heart attack. We'll use Okie Bob's cell on the third tier."

"You got the outfit?"

"I got it in Okie's cell. He's waiting for you."

My excitement was almost uncontrollable. My stomach was going up and down. When we got to the cell, Okie was waiting with the heroin already cooked up in a spoon. At a nod from Red, he took the eye dropper out of a small box from underneath his bed and handed it and a handkerchief to me. With the precision of a surgeon, I wrapped the handkerchief around my bicep and found the mark. That warm feeling, that feeling I hadn't had in over a year, took over my body and my mind. I sat on the bunk and began to rub my eyes slowly.

"You aren't going to fade on me, are you?" Red asked.

"Oh Christ, Red, that was a bitch of a jolt. That's my first jolt in over a year. Goddamn, it's good, Red." I was scratching my body lethargically.

"Will you wake up, sucker. I got one more surprise." I opened my eyes. "Look under the bunk you're sitting on."

I leaned over and looked under the bed. I saw an old beat up baritone saxophone case. I stood up immediately and then got on my knees and pulled the case out. "How'd you do it?"

"It's a long story. I'll tell you later. I can see you're not going to be worth a shit for the rest of the afternoon. Take it to the lower yard and blow your dick off. I'll run the game. Go, get out of here."

"I got ten cartons with Dallas and everyone likes St. Louis. Also, the Rams were—"

"Man, get out of here. We'll straighten that shit out later. I can't let those losers cry much longer. I'll see you tonight." Before I could say anything, Red was gone.

"Thanks for using your cell, Okie. Did you get down?"

"Red threw me out a paper."

"It's good, real good. I'm going to the lower yard, Okie, and try this sax out. I'll see ya."

"Don't scratch too much out there."

"I won't have time. Later."

I wanted to take the horn out immediately and see what kind it was, but I waited until I got to the bleachers. The case looked a thousand years old, and it revealed a decent looking 12 M Conn. As I was putting the neck and mouthpiece together, I felt the same kind of excitement I had experienced earlier when I had held the outfit in my hand. Finally, I got everything just the way I wanted it. I played softly at first, listening intently to each note. When I was sure it was in tune, I increased the volume slowly to get the feel of it. It was a good horn, not a Selmer, but a good horn, and I liked the sound. The muscles in my mouth hurt a little so I stopped and rested briefly. I looked at the horn, knowing every pad, every spring, every piece of cork.

Leaning back on the bleacher seat, I played several choruses of my favorite tune, "Round Midnight." The horn did what I asked it to do but my chops were weak. I rested again. Sitting there looking over the yard, high, free of anxiety, with my horn in my lap, I knew this was probably the best feeling about life I was ever going to have.

CHAPTER 50

"Hey, Woody. Woody, come on man, you got a visit."

"A visit?"

"Yeah, they've been calling you over the loudspeaker for a half hour. Goddamn, you look fucked up. Go put some water on your face."

I didn't know how long I had been nodding on the bleachers. I was lucky not to have been busted. "What time is it, Morrie?"

"Two o'clock. Red sent me to get you."

"I wasn't expecting a visit."

"Well, you got one. Man, you do look awful."

"How many times are you going to tell me? So, I look awful. Take my horn in for me. I got to boogie if I'm going to get there before the visiting room closes. See you tonight." On the way to the visiting room I stopped by the drinking fountain and splashed some water on my face, but it didn't help.

I didn't see her at first. She looked so tiny. She stood up slowly and gracefully moved her hand, such a delicate, sensitive gesture. The way she did those little things broke my heart. Every gesture, every move of hers was like that. I put my arms around her and touched her very gently. "You surprised me, Grandma."

"Well, I did it at the last minute. I've been planning the trip for some time saying next week, next week, always next week.

I called the bus line yesterday and they gave me directions, and here I am."

I loved her so much. She was everything decent and genuine in the world. What a gift to be a part of her life. I knew that I, too, had something different, a special kind of inner feeling that couldn't be acquired; it had to come from the bloodline. It had been wasting away in me, wasted in alleys, in institutions and in drugs, but it would always be there. She had given it to me, a special kind of soul that no one else had. The streets couldn't take it from me, the institutions couldn't take it, but the dope had gotten a piece of it. The dope had sucked and sucked; it sucked the soul she had given me and left me barren. That was what made communication with her so difficult; our souls no longer corresponded when I was loaded.

I looked into her beautiful blue eyes, eyes that never stopped searching my soul, and I knew what she saw when she looked deep into my eyes. Every gesture, every word, conveyed the hope that I would straighten out my life, but she never spoke a harsh word to me. She was like a teacher who knew the student had to find the answer by himself or the lesson learned wouldn't mean anything. So she waited with her heart aching.

"How was the ride?"

"I enjoyed it. I didn't travel all those years with the circus and not learn how to get the best out of a bus ride. You've gained some weight. Is the food good here?"

"It's good, Idah."

"Oh, you'd tell me that anyway."

"You're right, but it is good."

"How long will they keep you?"

"Maybe two more years." I didn't want to tell her the truth. Two years was a figure she could live with. After that, I would have to tell her something else.

"Have they told you so?" she asked.

"No, but it's pretty definite if I go along with everything, and I will."

She wanted to know everything about my existence there, so she asked a lot of questions. I couldn't answer them without lying. I regretted having just used heroin because it didn't let me appreciate her fully. If it had been Sylvia visiting me rather than my grandmother, it wouldn't have mattered, but my communication with her was different; we both listened to each other's every word. I never thought of her as an old woman, because in both our minds, she was forever young and vital.

After too short a time, the guard interrupted to tell us the visit was over. She got up very slowly. I put my arms around her and held her for a long time, and then I kissed her on the head.

"I'll be back again."

When she turned to walk away I watched her take each step. I hadn't realized it until then, but I was no longer loaded. I was cold sober.

CHAPTER 51

I awoke the next morning with a heroin hangover, so I stayed in my cell and slept. I felt guilty about staying in my cell because there was gambling business to be taken care of. By the time I got to the yard, Red was already there and had taken care of business. He spotted me and called me over.

"I heard Stan is borrowing cigarettes in the South block. He's in debt to Louie for eight boxes."

"That's bad news." I said. "What's the borrowing for?"

"He likes those basketball games."

"That punk is vice-ridden in every department. He doesn't need to bet basketball. He has money every month."

"Well, he did."

"How serious is it?"

"Louie gave him a deadline for tonight."

"We better bail him out before he has a dozen Mexicans swinging from his neck. You know who'll get the beef if he gets taken out. The Captain would even hold me responsible if Stan got caught getting fucked in the ass."

"You want me to see Louie?"

"I hate the thought of dealing with that greasy little money-lending motherfucker. I'd like to step on his fucking neck."

"What are you so hot at him about?"

"I can't stand his flyweight ass. He's a little nothing creep. If he wasn't hooked up with the Mexican Mafia he'd probably be sucking some guy's dick for a jar of coffee."

"So what. There's a lot of creeps around here." Red said.

"I'll tell you why I hate the greasy bastard. He used to come by my cell when he was a key man and just stand there, stand in front of my cell and expect me to talk to him. You just can't tell one of the psychopathic killers to take a walk so I'd make lightweight conversation. He got to coming by every night about seven o'clock while I was reading. He'd talk about crazy shit like how many cartons of cigarettes he had, or some fucking uncle of his who was doing time in Leavenworth, and then he started talking about the guys he had put out."

"He told you who he killed?"

"Yeah. I couldn't believe it. He even went into details. They were all done on the sneak. He'd have knives stashed all over and crawl over tiers to get to them but he always got them from the rear. Every night I had to listen to this little motherfucker tell me how he put some guy in the clouds. I was about to stab him myself just to keep him away from my cell."

"So, what did you do?"

"It ended the night he told me about dusting Carter. He went into all the details how he lured him to the laundry room on the pretense of loaning him some cigarettes, and that he wasn't mad at him because he was late in paying. He told Carter the cigarettes were in the laundry basket under a stack of blankets and when Carter reached down to get them, Louie stabbed him in the back. He said that, as Carter was dying, he kept saying, 'Holy Mother of God.' He seemed to get a real thrill out of Carter saying that. Like he had the power to make a man pray, or plead, or die. I didn't give a fuck about insulting him after that. I asked him if he thought he was going to have a chance to say a prayer when he got took out. That shocked his little jive ass. Then I followed it up with 'I have more important shit to do than to listen to someone talk about a murder involving a couple of packs of cigarettes.' He's sub-zero on the I.Q. side, but he finally got the picture. He's too dumb to insult. I tried everything before I finally laid it out to him once and for all when he tried to interrupt me while I was reading. I looked at him with a straight face and asked, 'Louie, how do you spell 'enthusiastically?' but he came back again the next night. What did it was the 'Mother of God' shit. It takes a real sick sonofabitch to get off on that."

"What happens when you see him now?" Red asked.

"Nothing. We just don't talk, which is exactly the way I want it."

"You better have a change of plans because he's over there talking to Stan right now."

"Where?"

"By the domino table, the last table."

"I'm going over there."

"I better go with you."

"You might press his paranoid button. I'll go by myself."

"Okay, I'll be close by."

As I walked over to them I could see Stan gesturing with

his hands. He appeared to be trying to explain something.

"Hey, Stanley. What's going on?"

"Hi."

I looked at Louie and nodded my head slowly. Louie acknowledged me with a slight nod, nothing more. It was obvious he resented the intrusion. I turned to Stan but before he could say anything Louie said, "We got some business, man."

"Maybe I can help you take care of it." I answered.

"It's between me and Stan." As Louie said this, he was looking in the other direction like he wasn't talking to us.

"Well, you can talk business with me if it involves Stan or dough. I handle all his finances." Louie looked at Stan but didn't say anything, then looked away. He played his role to the hilt.

"Has it got anything to do with dough, Stan?" I asked.

"Well, yeah. I owe Louie some cigarettes. We're working it out."

"He's a week late." Louie said.

"How much do you owe him, Stan?"

"Eight boxes."

"Is that right, Louie?"

Louie was still looking away with an air of complete indifference, his cigarette hanging from his mouth. "With interest, it's eight boxes."

"Where do you want them delivered?" I asked.

Louie still didn't look at us. "My cell, before the evening meal."

Stan started to say something, but I brought my hand up like a traffic cop to silence him. "I'll have them delivered in an hour. Does he owe you anything else?"

"Just the eight boxes."

"They'll be there in an hour."

Throughout the conversation Louie had not looked at either me or Stan. "I'll be there."

Stan and I watched Louie walk off. "Thanks, Woody, I—"

"Shut the fuck up."

"Woody, I was going to—"

"I don't give a fuck what you were going to do. What you're going to do is listen to me and keep your mouth shut. We had a deal in the Captain's office and you aren't living up to your end of the bargain. That over-hip Mexican you were dealing with would put your lights out for eight cigarettes and you'd never know what hit you. I didn't square the tab because I'm in love with you. If I'm going to ride the beef I might as well do the job myself, and I will if I hear any more funny stories about you in the yard. You understand the way it is with us, Stan?"

"I understand, Woody."

"Okay. Go on, get out of here." I didn't have to look for Red; he was standing almost within hearing range. "We got to have eight boxes for Louie in an hour. I said we'd bring them to his cell."

"Is he too good to pick them up?"

"That's what I thought when he said bring them to his cell. He played his tough guy role to the end. Didn't you see the way he was standing, slouched over in that East LA stance like he was doing us a favor? He wouldn't even look at me. It was beneath him to enter into the conversation."

"That's all he's got is his role."

"I'll have them sent up when I go back to work."

"You know what cell he's in?"

"Yeah."

"Hey, there goes that guy that's going to the gas chamber this morning." There were two guards escorting a black man across the yard.

"I thought you said he was going today."

"He's going to see his attorney for one last shot."

"Did you know him?"

"He was a handball player. He got hooked up in the black movement and quit talking to white boys."

"Was he all right?"

"He paid his debts."

We watched him in silence taking slow, deliberate steps as

he walked across the yard. It wasn't over yet, at least not until he got the final word from his attorney, and he was trying to hold on. Passing a group of his own people, they tried to comfort him with their eyes. One of them made a gesture with his head, a quick movement upward which meant, "What's happening?" The condemned man's reply was given with a jerky downward motion of a clenched fist, meaning it was all right. Both gestures were executed in the blink of an eye and understood by all.

I followed him with my eyes as he turned the corner and disappeared. I felt a sadness for him. What tormented thoughts the man must have had, trying to hold onto his dignity, his head high, his shoulders back and straight. "Does he have a chance, Red?"

"I don't think so. He doesn't have any dough. You can't beat the chamber without dough."

"But where do you put it?"

"Attorneys, maybe. I don't know, but I've never seen anyone get fried who had money. See that red light on top of the East block?"

"Yeah."

"When they enter the chamber it goes on. They turn it off when he's pronounced dead."

"That's another cold move."

"They're just letting us know that they kill motherfuckers around here. That's the message. Come on, the canteen is open. Let's get an ice cream." We were still eating our ice cream when we saw the man from death row return. "There he is again." Red said. "They've taken the starch out of his ass this time. Check him out."

The man was walking slower now. His shoulders were slumped, his eyes to the ground staring hopelessly at nothing. A group of blacks tried to make eye contact to offer their support, but he didn't acknowledge them. He was on his way to die, and no human support was going to make it easier. He was in the midst of over a thousand men in a beehive of sound, but his vacant stare revealed his obliviousness to everything.

He stood there like a frightened child, bewildered and confused by what was happening. He looked up at the sky, not for help, but for that one last glimpse of life, and then, as if on cue from some invisible director, every movement, every sound in San Quentin stopped. A convict walking in the opposite direction, not aware of what was happening, started a sentence and stopped in the middle of it. There was an eerie silence, and although it only lasted for a few seconds, it would always be remembered by the men who were present on that day. The spell was broken as abruptly as it had started when the death row guard said, "Let's move it." The condemned man took one step and disappeared. The guard followed him through the door. Shortly afterwards, the red light went on, and then off.

CHAPTER 52

As I came down the stairs on the way to the mess hall, I saw Red standing, waiting. Red should have been working in the bakery and I wondered if he had gotten fired. "How come you're not in the bakery?"

"Had to see you. I got someone to do my work for an hour."

"What's up?"

"We got trouble."

"With who?"

"Some niggers trying to use our line on the games and our mimeograph connection. They went to Eddie in the Education

Department and propped him. First they asked Eddie to run off some tickets and then they tried to get our line from him."

"How could they hurt us? They could just wait one day and get the line from the yard."

"You're missing the point. They're trying to move in on our territory."

"What did Eddie tell them?"

"Eddie's scared to death. He doesn't want any trouble."

"Who exactly are we talking about here?"

"Niggers. Real niggers. They use all the scum hustles. They were shaking down a child molester, making him come up every month to keep his beef off the yard. One of them got caught robbing a cell a few months ago."

"Have they got any dough?"

"They've got some kind of bankroll. Both of them work in the laundry room in the East block, and that's good for thirty boxes a month."

"You want to go talk to them?"

"Woody, I don't talk to niggers."

"Okay." I thought a minute while Red seethed. Then I had it. "Wait, I got an idea. Can you shoot a couple of guys into them to make a bet?"

"What are you getting at?"

"They couldn't know anything about football or they wouldn't be trying to hijack our line, right?"

"Right."

"Well, we'll change the point spread on one of the games, send in two or three guys to bet it and knock them in for twenty or thirty cartons. That ought to hurt them, hitting them in the bankroll. We got to set up a 'put up' cash bet."

"We could do that."

"That's the only way it will work. If we tried to collect after the bet was won, it would tip them off."

"I don't give a fuck about tipping them off. I'd like them to know who did it to them."

"But it's so much better this way, Red. We get their money and they never know what happened. This way we're totally uninvolved. If they get hit that hard the first week they're in action, they'll give up and that's our objective; to keep them out of our fucking business."

"You're probably right."

"Shit, yes, I'm right, Red. We don't want a war with anyone right now, especially with the smackola on its way."

"Are we going to keep the same point spread on our line?"

"Sure. When anyone wants to bet it you tell them we had too much action on it and had to take it off. The Bears are playing Green Bay favored by seven and take the Bears. If Green Bay wins, they'll be lucky, especially in Chicago."

"What will I tell Eddie?"

"Don't tell him anything. If he can get some dough out of them for our line, let him do it."

"And printing the tickets?"

"Let him get dough for that, too. They'll only be in action a week. We can't crack to Eddie. This way only you and I know."

"What about the guys who place the bets?"

"Be sure of them."

CHAPTER 53

I hadn't planned on going to dinner but a letter from Sylvia turned that around. She was coming up the next day and I had needed to see Red to get our business straight. We had talked throughout the meal and now the mess hall was almost empty.

"We'd better blow. I'll get a hundred from the stash tomorrow and bring it to the yard in the morning. I'll have it in a balloon and you can give it to her in the visiting room."

"What if she doesn't go for it?"

"She'll need a hundred anyway, just getting out, and we can't let it be a hardship getting back if she's got the drugs. You want her to hitchhike up here with two ounces in her cunt?" Red asked, feeling excitement at the prospect of two ounces of heroin.

"You're right. I'll see you in the morning."

"I forgot to tell you. I got twenty boxes bet with the niggers. I got it down this afternoon."

"Is Eddie nervous?"

"No. He printed the same tickets for us. We'll just change the point spread on the Bears game.

"Perfect. That's just fucking perfect. No way will they ever know."

I was up half the night thinking about Sylvia. Had she changed? And if so, how? Would she bring the dope? Would she not bring the dope? It went on and on until three in the morning. I woke up tired and apprehensive.

When I got to the yard, Red was taking action with both hands. "A dozen guys wanted that point spread on the Bears. I told them it was off the line. I got a runner holding the hundred. You might as well take it now and stick it in your chops so you get used to it."

The loudspeaker announced my name. "Shit, she's here."

"Man, she must have slept on the bus."

"Who's got the hundred?"

"Wait right here. I'll get it." Red got back before I could comb my hair and handed me the money. "Come on. I'll walk over with you. Are you excited?"

"I get spurts. It's been such a long time."

"She got out yesterday and she shows the next day. You got a racehorse, Woody."

"I know."

"How long since you've seen her?"

"Sixteen months."

"Damn, they gave her an assload for the first time. You got the phone number?"

"I got it."

"Go on out there and take care of business."

"Will you be on the yard when I get back?"

"I'll be out here all day. Good luck."

I walked across the yard trying to imagine what it was going to be like seeing her. When I reached the visiting room, I went through the usual shakedown procedure and then waited for my name to be called. The visiting room guard opened the door, let me in and informed me briefly about the visiting room rules. I was told to wait until I saw my visitor and then to take a seat at a table.

The visiting room was similar to the attorneys' room in the county jail; seven or eight rows of tables with chairs on both sides and a wooden divider down the center of the table to prevent any hand contact. The walls were covered with pictures painted by the convicts; some good, some terrible, with price tags and the artists' names at the base of the frames.

It was a different world on this side of the two doors. The absence of bars on the windows was enough to change the atmosphere, but it was the love that passed through the gates that changed things. Brothers, sisters, mothers, fathers, wives, lovers – they all came for one reason, love.

I saw her walk in. She was nervous and her face was strained. She saw me and closed her eyes for a brief second as if saying a prayer, then rushed up and put her arms around me. I could feel her shaking as I kissed her. She was startled to feel something foreign in her mouth. When she got her breath, she asked, "What have I got in my mouth?"

"A hundred dollar bill in a balloon."

"What's that for?"

"I'll explain later. You look wonderful."

"No, I don't. I gained twenty pounds."

"Well, you look damn good to me."

"Mr. Jones, you always say the right thing."

"Of course I do. That's why you can't live without me."

"I just got out yesterday and it's all so strange to me. It seems like a whole new world. I'm confused. I thought getting out would make everything alright, but it hasn't."

"Give yourself some time. You'll adjust. Are you staying with your mother?"

"Yes. She gave me two hundred dollars to rent an apartment. I had to see you so I used fifty of it to make the trip."

"You won't have to worry about dough much longer."

"Why?"

"You're going to have to do something for me. One simple little move."

"Honey—"

"Listen to me. I'm not going to put any heat on you or myself. You just got out and you don't have anything. Trying to make it on those streets flat broke will put you right back in the spoon."

"I can't go back to jail again. I couldn't stand one more day. There were girls that came in and out a dozen times while I was there and they didn't seem to mind it, but I hated every day I was there. It never got better. Every day was worse than the one before."

"I know, honey. I wouldn't ask you to do anything that could put you back in there."

"Then what is it?"

"Alright, here's what's happening. My partner in here has a brother who is dealing in Los Angeles—"

"Oh, sweetheart, you said—"

"If you wait until I've finished, you'll understand. Believe me, there won't be any risk. I know how you feel about going back to jail. I wouldn't ask you to take a risk. If you'll do exactly as I tell you there is no possibility of anything going wrong. My friend's brother, Wayne, doesn't have any heat. He only deals in big quantities, and he's never on the streets. The easiest part of the whole setup is the way to bring it in. Did you notice the visitor's toilet at the bottom of the hill?"

"I think so."

"Well, everything that goes through the sewer line is

processed through the sewage plant here. If anything is flushed down the toilet, it goes through the lines and comes out in the plant. My partner has a friend who works there and will bring it in to him. It'll all be packaged and ready to go when you see Wayne. All you have to do is pick it up from him, put it up inside of you, carry it to that outside toilet, and flush it."

"I think of using all the time. I don't know…with it between my legs, I don't know."

"We're both clean now, sweetheart. We don't have to react the way we did when we were hooked. There's dope all over the yard here, and I never use it."

"How do you say no?"

"I want more out of life, especially since I've been clean. I want my music and a life with you, and I know I can't have either one with drugs."

"It's so hard for me to say no."

"Well…I don't want to put that on you. I thought maybe if you could do it just this once, I'd be able to get a horn."

"You haven't played here?"

"I haven't played, no. I have to have my own horn to play."

"Don't they have any horns here?"

"Yes, but there's a waiting list to check one out. It seems that everyone that comes to the pen wants to be a saxophone player." Another pause, one I liked. "If it's too much for you, honey, I understand."

"I couldn't see it. I wouldn't even want to look at it."

"You wouldn't have to. It would be in a package all wrapped up."

"If I did it one time, just once to get your horn, would you promise not to ask me again?"

"I promise."

"Who do I see?"

"Call 545-8744 and tell Wayne you're Sylvia. He'll take it from there. Use the toilet on the way out so you know exactly where it is. You'll have to come right back when you get it."

"Don't worry. I don't want to hold on to it any longer than I have to."

Suddenly the guard appeared and told us the time was up,

then went back to the front of the room, leaving us a minute to finish our conversation.

"I just sat down," Sylvia said.

"I know, honey. The time passed so quickly. Do you remember the number?"

"545-8744."

"Write it down as soon as you leave."

"I will."

"Are you frightened?"

"Yes. I guess I am."

I wanted to tell her to forget it, but I couldn't. Instead, I said, "It'll be all right, honey." We stood up and I kissed her lightly.

"I love you." she said.

"I love you, too, honey."

She turned and walked away. When she got to the door she looked back at me for a moment then disappeared.

I went out to the yard and took a few laps around the track before going back to the poker game. I felt like being by myself, away from the action. I knew I had made a bad move sending Sylvia to the connection, especially in her state of mind.

CHAPTER 54

Getting back into the action of the poker game helped me take my mind off of Sylvia. While I was playing, the point man came up and gave me the Bears' final score: six to three.

That put the blacks on ice for twenty cartons. Just as the poker game broke, Morrie showed up and told me Red wanted to see me and that it was important. I had already given the score sheet and cards to the point man so I rushed out to the yard. Red was waiting by the North block.

"What's up, Red?"

"We got a little problem with the niggers. I think they woke up."

"What happened?"

"Two guys I've never seen before cut into me and asked how I did on the Bears game. I tried to be nice in the beginning. I told them I had it at seven points to start out but I got too much action so I took it off the line. Then they asked me how many guys bet it when the point spread was seven. I made one last attempt to keep out of a jackpot by telling them I couldn't remember offhand. Then this little skinny dude gets up in my face and tells me I should try and remember. I told him I remembered now; it was his mommy who made the bet."

"It's bad timing, Red," I said.

"That was the only reason I held out as long as I did. If your old lady hadn't showed up today I would have downed him right then."

"Did you collect the twenty boxes?"

"Yeah, they couldn't fuck with that. It was put up before the bet. But they know we bankrolled the bet."

"How do you know?"

"I had one of our runners pick up the cigarettes. The two that came up to me were talking to the brothers who tried to steal our line so I know they're hooked up together."

"You think they might try to make a move?"

"If they do, they're fools. They talk too much to be bad. The ones for real never say anything. They usually act as if everything is alright until they take you out. I'll check them out tonight. If they're going to be a problem, we'll make the first move."

"You think we can square it up without a war? My old lady

could be back here tomorrow."

"We can't show them any weakness. We've got to take it all the way. Fuck them. What did your old lady say?"

"She'll make the run back as soon as your brother lays it on her. She's going to call him the minute she gets home."

"All right. We'll hang loose for a couple of days. Be careful until we resolve this business. Don't go to the gym unless we're together and keep your eyes open on the tiers. I don't think we got anything to worry about, but stay alert."

CHAPTER 55

The next day I went to the yard. By noon, I had taken care of collections when Red caught up with me. We were walking up and down the yard when we heard my name called over the loudspeaker for a visit. "Damn, she did it. I knew she would."

"The guy from the sewage plant comes up for lunch. I'm going to try and catch him before he goes back to work and have him bring it in tonight."

"Oh man, you think you can catch him?"

"It won't be because I haven't tried. Go on to your visit. I'll see you when you come back."

"Where will you be?"

"I'll be around the weights on the lower yard."

"You think we'll have it tonight?"

"If I can catch this guy. Let me get going. I'll see you at the weight pile."

"You got it." I couldn't keep from feeling excited as I walked to the visiting room. I also felt real secure having Red as a partner. If Red was your friend, he would go to the wall for you, but wasn't that the same reason Red joined me? He knew he could expect the wall from me. About fifty percent of the prison population wanted to be looked upon as mud holders but in actuality, only a few could walk the walk. The joint didn't produce a lot of Hog Jaws, Reds or Normans. The ones who did keep their word and pay their debts did so to gain respect, which was what most prisoners strived for. Even the rats and punks tried to put up a front to be what was called a regular. But guys like Red were in a special bag.

I knew I was going to be rich and loaded for a long time. As I passed the Catholic chapel, I saw the two black guys that Red and I were having trouble with. They didn't pay any special attention to me, but nevertheless, I made a decision to resolve the problem as soon as I got out of the visiting room. I wasn't going to walk around having to watch my back.

Sylvia was waiting for me as I entered the visiting room. I rushed up to her and held her in my arms, but I could hardly control my excitement. I felt like screaming out, "Yes or no? Tell me quick." I made light conversation for as long as I could but finally blurted out, "How did it go?"

"It went all right."

"You saw Wayne?"

"Yes."

That's it, I thought, what a sweetheart, she did it. I said, "Did you put it in the toilet?"

This time she looked me in the eyes and after a pause said, "I got it from Wayne, but I couldn't go through with it. He gave it to me in the afternoon and drove me home. When he left I thought I would lose my mind. I walked up and down in my room, just like I did in jail. I couldn't eat and my heart was pounding. All I could think about was using it. I don't know why I didn't. When I couldn't stand it any longer, I put it in my purse and went back to Wayne's house. I handed it back to him and told him I was a drug addict and that if I took it with the intention of delivering it to you and his brother that it would never get there. I told him everything about my life with you, how I had been in jail and was scared to death to go back. That if I didn't see it, feel it, or smell it I might have a chance. I told him because I had to tell someone. I told him you would be mad at me and probably tell me not to come back." She stopped and waited for me to say something, but I didn't. I was crushed. I couldn't find the words.

"Are you angry at me?" she asked.

"You had it in your hands and you gave it back?"

"Maybe later, honey, when I have some strength I can do it. I'm too weak now. All I can think about is fixing. I even have dreams about it. I don't know what to do about living. I don't know how. Nothing means anything to me but you, and you aren't there. I'm so lonely and I miss you so much I want to die. I've been drinking ever since I left you Sunday but it doesn't make things any better. It only numbs the feelings. Please, please don't be angry with me. I tried. I tried as hard as I could."

"If you couldn't do it, you couldn't do it. What did Wayne say when you gave it back to him?"

"He opened it up and looked at it first and then he seemed to understand. Wayne doesn't use, but he understood. He said if I ever changed my mind to call him. I said I would."

"Just forget it for now if it tempts you to use. Once you're accustomed to the streets again you won't be so tempted. Most of that fear you're experiencing is from jail. You know that, don't you?"

"I guess so, honey. It terrified me to think of going back."

"You're not going to have to go back. There's nothing to go back for, especially if you're not using. What are you going to do now?"

"I'll have to stay with my mother. I don't have any other place to go. She doesn't want me there. She's afraid I'm going to start using again."

"Isn't there someone you can stay with for awhile?"

"I don't know anyone."

"What about Helen?"

"I wrote to her when I was in County Jail and the letter was returned with no forwarding address."

"What about a job?"

"Honey, I don't want to bother you with my problems. I'll make it. You're the one locked up, I'm free. I'll make it. Would you write to me every day? I need your letters."

"Of course, sweetheart."

"Your time's up," the guard said.

"Man, it's always up."

"I'll be back, honey."

I stood up and kissed her. "I love you," I said and started to walk away.

"I love you, too. Please, don't forget the letters."

"I won't."

Watching her walk out of the visiting room, I felt a twinge of guilt for her helplessness, but the guilt was short-lived. "Goddamn, it didn't have to be this way," I thought to myself. "If she had only listened. Why couldn't she have made that one simple move? Everything would have been wonderful. What a fucking time to get self-righteous. She hasn't got enough money for the price of a pair of drawers. She could have had real money. Red and I could have had the dope. Oh, God— and she had it in her hands."

There were three cops waiting for me when the door opened. The first cop motioned me to one side and told me to strip. I complied and was given a thorough shakedown and then told to sit on the bench. I sat as the other men were released to the yard. My mind was racing with things that could have caused this kind of shakedown. I knew it couldn't be anything serious because I hadn't made any serious moves.

"You can put your clothes on now," the guard said. I complied without saying anything. "Take a right turn when we pass the gate. We're going to see the Captain." I led the way with the three guards in back of me. The Captain's office was next door to the visiting room so it only took a few seconds to get there.

There were half a dozen men waiting to be interviewed by the Captain and he was talking to someone as we approached. He saw me and stood up immediately, dismissing the inmate he was talking to. He motioned me in with a wave of his hand. My prison sense told me that something very serious was going on. I entered his office and was told to take a seat. He seemed to be preparing himself for what he had to say, waiting a moment to speak. I was now certain that this was no routine bust. "I've got some bad news for you, Woody. Your partner, Red, was killed while you were in the visiting room."

"Oh my God, oh Jesus Christ," I thought, in shock.

The Captain let it sink in before going on. "I'm sorry, Woody. I know you were close to him." I couldn't talk, I felt out of breath.

"The tower guard said it was two black guys," he continued. "They beat him with a weight bar. With your help, we can get them. I've called a general lock up. Every man in the prison is in his cell and the two men who killed Red might still have blood on their clothing. All I need are their names, and I promise you I'll put them on death row."

So that was why he was being so nice, I thought. I paused, and then spoke for the first time since I had entered the room. "I'm sorry. I don't know who they are, Captain."

He looked at me hard for a full minute. "They killed your friend. Am I wrong in assuming he was your partner?"

"We were partners, but I don't know who those guys were."

"You ran the book together and the poker games. You ate breakfast and dinner together. You were always together, and now you sit there and try and tell me you didn't know he was having trouble or that maybe both of you were in trouble?"

"We didn't take any black action."

"You didn't have to take any of their bets. It could have been something else."

"I don't know who it could be."

"You going to play it that way, right to the end, huh? You ever been in segregation, Woody?"

"No."

"Well, you're in for a treat. You don't have to work; you don't have to do anything. They'll bring you your meals three times a day and you even get a shower once a week, but don't take over three minutes. You'll have a nice little cell all to yourself. It's the same in there day after day, there's never any change. But after a while, you'll get used to it. I hope you'll get used to it because you're going to be there as long as I'm Captain in San Quentin, unless you give me the names right now." There was silence. He waited for me to answer; five, ten, twenty seconds. "Well?" he asked finally.

"Well, what?"

He stared at me then motioned one of the officers into his office and said, "Permanent seg."

I stood up and followed the officer out, defiantly looking straight ahead.

CHAPTER 56

Segregation was another world, a prison inside of prison, where contact with the yard was virtually impossible. The unit consisted of twenty-four cells, mostly occupied. At the front of the tank was a grill gate where the guard stayed. There was talking back and forth between prisoners, but since everyone knew the guard was within earshot, all the conversation was at a bullshit level.

I didn't know anyone there and didn't try to get acquainted. The only other source of information was the convict on the food cart, but he was a known rat so I had no contact with him. I knew that if I kept my mouth shut, they would eventually have to let me out. Somewhere down the line, I would get out of there. I made up my mind to wait patiently.

Every day with increasing obsessiveness and hatred, I shaped and reshaped my plans to kill the two men who had murdered Red. I worked out every detail. I would get them the minute I was released from segregation. I would pick up the hatchet Red and I had stashed in the paint shop and go directly to the White room in the East block where they worked. I would get both of them at the same time, but I wouldn't take them out right away. I'd hit them in the legs first to put them down. Then, I'd take them apart methodically a little at a time. A hack on the arm, a couple of fingers, a leg chopped off, but nothing in the head; that would be too quick. The two would watch each other's pain, would watch death coming. These thoughts of revenge kept me going.

The days passed slowly. I lived inside myself, speaking to no one, seeing no one. I was in segregation for two months before I discovered that I could order books from the state library. From then on, I requested stacks of books at a time and read incessantly. I read Thackeray, Thomas Mann, Proust, Wolfe, Dostoevsky, Milton, anything that caught my fancy. At first it was a struggle getting through some of them. The passages I didn't understand I would read to myself out loud over and over again until I got the meaning. The first time I read out loud, I was startled by the sound of my own voice. I had not spoken to a soul in two months.

I changed the segregation routine and created one of my own. I would read all night until breakfast and then sleep most of the day. When I got up, I would exercise for two hours. A thousand sit-ups and a thousand pushups were my routine. I knew I had to be in perfect condition the day I was released.

Six more months of isolation passed. Then one morning waiting for my breakfast, I looked up to see a new man on the food cart. When I picked up my tray from underneath the door, I discovered a note. I waited until the guard was out of sight before I opened it. The note was from Morrie, brief and to the point. The guys who killed Red had been shipped out, one to camp, the other to Chino. Both had escaped and one had been shot and killed in a robbery. The other was still at large. Morrie had been unable to find out anything about when I was to get out. He had checked with Norman, and if Norman didn't know, no one knew. Just as I finished reading the note, the cart man walked by. I gave him a little nod of thanks. I was unable to read for a week after I received the note. I was angry that one of Red's murderers had been killed. I had wanted to kill both of them. Now, fate had taken away half of my reason for living.

Segregation allowed letters to and from the outside so I kept in constant contact with my grandmother and Sylvia. My grandmother's letters were always uplifting and full of hope. In my letters to her, I tried to convey a sense of hope I didn't feel. I wrote less often to Sylvia, telling her the truth about my situation. Her letters to me were full of self-pity and sorrow over our being separated, and seemed to have been written under the influence of alcohol.

The days were getting longer. I could no longer sleep through them as I had during the first six months. Now I could only be unconscious a few hours in the afternoon. The monotonous existence of segregation was closing in. Every day became harder to get through. My life consisted of my books, my exercise, my letters, and my hatred. I held on a day at a time, sometimes an hour at a time. Then one morning without any warning or indication, I was told I was being released. I had been in segregation over fourteen months.

CHAPTER 57

After well over a year of artificial light, I found natural sunlight blinding. I had never thought I would miss the cold damp weather of San Quentin, but it felt good on my cheeks. I was starved for conversation and wanted to talk to everyone, but I retained my prison mask—the mask that said, "I've been down for over a year and made it. I'm self-sufficient and need nothing." The time in segregation had affected me deeply. I had lived entirely inside of myself for fourteen months. Although I was happy to be out of isolation, I was still filled with hate.

My first step was to pick up my blankets. I was by myself for the first few minutes, enjoying the things in life I had always taken for granted. Things like the sky, sun, birds, the everyday things of life. As I emerged from Household with my blankets, I saw Norman standing in front of the Education Department.

"Norman!"

"I've been waiting for you."

"How did I get out? Did the Captain have a heart attack?"

"He almost did when he found out you were getting released."

"He didn't release me?"

"No, the Classification Board did. Your case went before them last week. The Captain was furious. When he found out you were getting out, he scheduled you himself."

"Soledad?"

"He's setting you up to get killed. It's a black and white war zone down there, just like the civil war all over again. Every week someone gets stabbed or killed. Everyone in the system knows Red got taken out by the blacks. They also make it their business to know who his running partners were. When they find out you're coming there, they won't wait around to see what your attitude is. They'll make their move before you can establish yourself. The Captain knows all of this. He could have recommended Folsom just as easily. It's a death sentence."

"Have I got a move?"

"You could smack a cop. That would send you to Folsom, but you know what they would do to you there."

"Yeah, I know. Anything else?"

"Besides good boys, the only others who get out are nut cases and suicides."

Norman's words suddenly gave me an idea. "How long have I got?"

"A couple of days, maybe three or four. No one knows you're going to reclassification except me."

"Am I going back to the fifth tier in B section?"

"Yes."

"Do you know Des?"

"Yeah, he's the tier man on five in B section."

"Is he all right?"

"As far as I know. Why?"

"I got a plan. I haven't worked it out yet. If I could put it together, I'd have to be able to trust him."

"I'd trust him."

"That's all I wanted to know. One more thing before you go back to work, Norman. What's the guy's full name and number?"

"James Sims. His number is B9600."

"Thanks, Norman."

"What are you going to do?"

"Shit, I don't know yet. I got to locate Des. That's my first move."

"You don't have much time."

"What about talking to the Warden?"

"Dead. The only one who knows you're going up for transfer is me, and the Warden wouldn't get involved in the Captain's business. They work together."

"Just a thought. Go on back to work, Norman. I'll be here for the weekend, won't I?"

"You won't go before Monday."

"I'll see you sometime before then."

"I wish there was something I could do," he said to me.

"Don't sweat it. You've done plenty. At least I know and I got a little time to put something together. Have I got any heat?"

"No, you're clean. The Captain figures he's got you all packaged up and ready to go. He won't fuck with you now."

"Okay. I'm out of here. I'll see you—well—I guess I'll see you when I see you."

"Be cool."

"You, too."

I made a thorough inspection of the upper yard; no Des. I stopped by the Education Department and checked the school list. Still no Des. I didn't ask anyone, I just kept looking. My last stop was the lower yard where I spotted him sitting on the bleachers reading a book. Des was a quiet, nice-appearing guy, a first-rate gem burglar out of Chicago who knew his stuff. His only prison vice was chess, which he was reading about when I came upon him.

"Hey, Des. How you doing?"

"All right. How are you?"

"I'm okay."

"When did you raise?"

"About twenty minutes ago."

"They kept you there a long time."

"Yeah, the yard seems different."

"It was too bad about Red. I know it was hard for you."

"Yeah."

"Did they ever nail anyone for it?"

"Not to my knowledge. I need a favor, Des. You want to help me?"

"Ah, Woody, Red and I were friends and I like you, too, but I can't get involved in heavy action. I just want to do my number and get out."

"I know, Des. I know where you're at and I wouldn't ask you for warfare support. This is totally different. It hasn't got anything to do with Red or the trouble I had. It's one simple little move that won't take any of your time or put you in any kind of cross."

"I don't know, man." Des looked uneasy, but I went on talking, explaining what I wanted him to do for me that evening.

About an hour before the graveyard shift went off duty, there was a quietness in San Quentin that was almost peaceful. All the guards assigned to the block had finished making their rounds and were sitting in the office on the first floor waiting to be relieved by the day shift.

The tier men were released from their cells and started to gather at the end of the tier to fill their buckets with hot water. Des moved slowly and sleepily down the walkway. Looking around, it was difficult for him to distinguish one cell from another because the lights hadn't come on yet. When he got halfway down the tier, he stopped and peered into my dark cell. He stood there for only a second, then turned and ran as fast as he could back in the direction he had come from. He shouted frantically for the guard. "Guard! There's a man hanging on five in B section." By the time he had repeated the words, I could hear the guards running up the stairs.

"Where is he?" a guard asked.

"Half way down."

"Show me where. Come on, God dammit, move it."

Half a dozen guards trailed Des and the first guard. They heard a loud crashing racket which ended with a heavy thud of something hitting the floor. Flashlights bounced back and forth off the walls of the cells. One of the guards in the rear shouted, "He's back here!"

Two guards entered my cell. The others gathered in front, pointing their flashlights, trying to get a look. "He alive?"

"I don't know. I'm trying to get a pulse. I got a beat. I got a pulse. He's alive. You want to sit up, fella? Get a fucking nurse up here. I feel a pulse, but he ain't moving. You want to sit up, fella?"

I had a torn blanket tied around the light conduit. It must have been broken.

"He was hanging when I called for you," Des said.

"Yeah, I can see the rope burn on his neck. He's a big sonofabitch. His weight pulled the whole fucking conduit off the wall."

"That was the crash we heard. How do you feel, fella? You want to sit up?"

"Leave me alone, leave me alone," I muttered in a slow monotone.

"Come on, we want to help you."

"Leave me alone."

"Where's that fucking nurse?"

"Fuck that nurse. Come on, give me a hand. We'll take him to the hospital ourselves."

The two guards in the cell struggled to pick me up. They had a difficult time because I was unmoving, dead weight. Once they got me out of the cell, I suddenly came alive and bolted for the rail, making a move to jump off the five-story tier. I completely surprised the guards who, for a moment, just stood there, but Des jumped in, grabbed me around the waist and held on until the guards regained their composure. They took over roughly and carried me spread eagle down the stairs.

When they got me to the hospital they made me take my clothes off and sat me on a wooden bench. I sat with my eyes to the ground, staring vacantly. A nurse arrived, put a bandage on my neck and gave me a healthy jolt of Thorazine. A few minutes later, I was taken to the strip cell in the hospital.

CHAPTER 58

The psychiatrist didn't look like a psychiatrist. He was heavy set with bulging eyes and thick lips, and his clothes looked as if they had been bought at the Salvation Army. Just before he started to talk, he would arch his left eyebrow, purse his lips and, breathing very heavily, look straight into my eyes. "I am Doctor Russell. I've been asked by the hospital staff to talk to you." He waited, hoping for some reaction before he continued. "How are you feeling now?" I shrugged my shoulders very slightly and continued to look at the floor.

"Would you like to tell me about what happened?"

"Why?"

"I'm sure it would make you feel better."

"Who said I wanted to?"

"Come now, Mr. Woodward. You're a comparatively young man. You have a lot to live for."

I didn't answer. "You seemed to get through segregation for over fourteen months. What happened after you were released that changed your mind about living?"

"Nothing. Nothing changed. I just never had the guts to end it before."

"But you didn't end it, did you?"

"If it hadn't been for that rat tier man, I would have."

"You'll thank him some day for saving your life."

"Look, I didn't ask to see you. There's not a fucking thing you or anyone else connected with this nut house can say that will change the course of what I have to do."

"I could if you'd let me."

"Don't waste your time. It's over. I won't miss the next time."

"Why do you feel that way, Woody?"

"Doctor Russell—" The psychiatrist leaned forward, thinking I was ready to explain myself. I looked him in the eye. "Go fuck yourself." The psychiatrist said nothing in reply and was noticeably quieter after that.

I was pleased with the way the psychiatrist reacted. He knew that someone who had just attempted suicide wouldn't care about what anyone thought about him. What I hadn't realized was how good it was going to feel to say "fuck you" to an authority figure. I hated institutions and the people who ran them and I would never allow them to get a piece of my nut sack. No fucking "yes, sirs" or "pleases" from me. Especially from that pear-shaped Captain with all of his little games and plots going, trying to run lives from his office. But I could play the game, too. A little sandpaper on the neck for the rope burn, pulling the light conduit off the wall so the guard thought my weight had broken it. But the best move was having Des grab me off the rail when it looked like I was going down five flights. Des was beautiful; he had made it look so natural. Without his help it could have never gone down that smoothly, and he might even get a commendation in his jacket for saving a man's life.

All the time I had been thinking, the psychiatrist was busy gathering up his papers. When he left, he said goodbye, but I didn't answer. I kept my eyes straight ahead as if in a trance.

Shortly afterwards, the guard appeared and took me back to the strip cell. It was lunchtime when I got back. My food was given to me on a paper plate but I didn't touch it because I didn't think it would be appropriate for someone in my state of mind to have an appetite.

All the blue chips were in the pot now. I had played my hand out to the limit. It was in the psychiatrist's hands from this point on. Whatever he recommended would be final.

Three days later, the guard came to my cell, and told me that I was being transferred, and to be ready in an hour. He didn't say where and I didn't ask, I knew. Just before I left, the nurse came in and gave me a shot of Thorazine for the road. They had treated me like a suicide case and I played it to the end.

I was escorted across the yard by one guard. I kept my eyes straight ahead, not looking at anyone, but when I got near the chapel I saw Morrie and Norman standing by the door. I looked at them and winked. I saw a hint of a smile begin to form on their lips and in a few seconds, I was gone.

Part Five
FREEDOM

CHAPTER 59

Vacaville was more like a hospital than a prison. It was where they kept the nuts and suicide cases. Convicts and guards had a softer, more human countenance than at Folsom or Quentin. Vacaville was definitely what convicts called a hot water joint. The floor plan for the entire prison was one long corridor with living units that extended half way down on each side. The hospital, mess hall, control room, and gym occupied the other half of the corridor. It was a prison built for tight security, yet it had a loose feel to it. I knew I could be comfortable here.

I was given my property at R & R and then escorted along with a handful of other convicts to my assigned unit. Arriving at P wing, I, along with four others, was checked in by the officer and assigned to cells. We were given cell keys and directed to Household to pick up blankets, sheets, and rule books.

My cell was on the second tier, two doors from the TV room. I put my blankets away and decided to watch television. I took a seat in the back and started reading the rule book. Before I had read two pages, I saw a friend of mine named Geno come into the room. Geno was a bitch of a drummer in San Francisco who I had played with around LA. He was in his early thirties, and had a lot of experience playing with the heavies, but his drug addiction and constant trips to jail had kept him from making it big. He was arguing with someone in the front row. I couldn't hear what they were saying, so I stood up and walked toward them. When I got closer, I saw it was for real. Geno was talking to some guy who outweighed him by fifty pounds.

"Man, I put my comb on the seat when I went to take a shower." Geno said.

"There ain't no comb here."

"Well, you're probably sitting on it."

"There ain't no comb here, man."

"You going to up my seat or not?"

The big guy stood up and said, "I ain't giving up no seat unless you take it."

"Man, what kind of style is that?"

I was now standing in back of the big guy. I put my foot on the seat and shoved it the length of the day room. When it crashed into the wall it sounded like the whole room was going to fall apart. Then everything got real quiet. "You want the seat that bad, punk?" I said, looking straight into the big man's face.

"Who are you? I don't know you. This is between me and Geno."

"No, it's between you and me now."

"Hey, Woods," Geno said with a surprised look on his face. "I can handle this."

"I know you can, but you know how I love to fist fight, Geno. What about you, big man, you love to fist fight?" No reply came from the big man. "Well, do you? If you do, let's hook it up; if you don't, why don't you get the fuck out of here." I walked up close to him. "Well, big man, which one is it going to be?"

The big man turned around and walked out without saying anything. There were only a few men in the day room and they sat very quietly.

"Come on, Woody, let's take a walk on the yard," Geno said, walking down the stairs, "Well, I see you haven't changed any. You almost got in a hassle over nothing."

"What do you mean, nothing, Geno?"

"Man, that guy's a child molester. He pulls that tough guy shit all the time."

"Are you serious?"

"Yeah, the joint's overrun with nuts and child molesters."

"You mean I'm in a nut house?"

"Light weight, but it's a good joint. You can do your time here easy. When did you drive in?"

"Twenty minutes ago."

"And already you're in a hassle. Man, Woods, you are a bitch. You got to drop that bully hand here or they'll give you a bus ride. This place is more like a hospital than a joint. Everyone who isn't on the work crew goes to therapy and is under the supervision of a psychiatrist."

"Are you on the work crew?"

"Yeah, I work in the record office."

"What do you do there?"

"As little as possible. It's where the records are kept on every convict doing time in the state."

"You got access to them?"

"I work there."

"You can find out where any con is in the system?"

"If he's in any joint, I can find him."

I then told Geno everything that had happened in Quentin—Red's murder and the suicide fake-out to get to Vacaville.

"You've been making a lot of moves, Woody."

"These joints take a lot of moves. My next move is to find that guy."

"Do you know the guy's number?"

"Like my own name: B9600. His name is James Sims."

"What do you want to know about him?"

"Everything. He escaped from a Quentin camp six months ago. I want to know what joint he goes to when he gets caught. I want to know where his mommy lives. I want a rundown on his brothers, sisters, cousin. If he's got a dog, I want to know that, too, so I can shoot the motherfucking dog."

"Damn, Woods, I know he killed your partner, but you're

sticking pretty heavy with that revenge gig. Hating a guy like that will put you in the gas chamber."

"If I can get Sims the way I want him, the gas chamber wouldn't be a bad tab. I'd kill the motherfucker in front of a police station. Wherever I see him, he's dead."

"I guess you and Red were pretty tight."

"That's a lot of it for sure, but the way they did it, I can't get that out of my mind."

"How did they do it?"

"Red was on the lower yard doing bench presses and they tipped up on him and hit him in the head with the weight bar. Then they pinned him with the weight he was bench pressing with and beat his brains out of his head."

"Where were you?"

"In the visiting room. I saw them lurking around the Garden Chapel on my way in. I should have known something wasn't right, but my old lady was supposed to run something in that day and I was in too much of a fucking hurry to go back and tell Red."

"You sound like you blame yourself."

"Not entirely, but I should have gone back to Red and told him."

"If you really want me to, I'll check his file tomorrow, but—"

"Just check the file."

My hatred for Sims was so strong it put Geno off balance and made him feel uncomfortable so he switched the subject to music. "Where's your horn?"

"The only horn I've had since I've been locked down was a state horn Red got for me in Quentin. I had to leave it there when I left."

"Are you going to get another one?"

"Now that I'm here, I'll figure something out. I can't rely too much on my old lady. She's barely making it. What about the money here?"

"It's loaded. Everybody has dough."

"Do they play cards?"

"All the time and it's legal."

"Good games?"

"Everybody's got dough."

"Maybe you can cut me into one of them."

"You need at least twenty to sit in."

"I didn't come in with anything. I'm busted."

"I got twenty in ducats, but it taps me. Can you make any moves?"

"Of course. I'd move on Nick the Greek with the case twenty."

"There's a game in J wing every afternoon. I'll give you my ducats and you can sit in. I got to work for a few hours. Come on, I'll take you up there now."

When we got to the game, it was already in full swing. Geno handed me his ducats and motioned with his eyes. I asked if there was a seat open and was told to sit down. After a few hands, Geno left for work saying he'd be back if he got a chance, otherwise, he would see me back in the wing.

CHAPTER 60

"Don't tell me. I already heard about it." Geno smiled. "Who said what?"

"They said you were one lucky sonofabitch, that you won six bills."

"You got that right. I didn't have to make any moves; every

hand I picked up was either pat or a one card draw in good position."

"You want to part with four of those twenties? A guy in J wing has four papers for sale."

"Has anyone you know used any of it?"

"Yeah, it's good."

"Why don't you see if you can buy all he's got."

"Four papers is all he's got."

"Are you sure?"

"I'm sure. Besides, you got horn money now, don't blow it."

"When can you do it?"

"He's waiting."

I peeled off four twenties and then a hundred dollar bill. "Here, take this extra dough."

"He said—"

"I don't care what he said. Hundred dollar bills have a way of getting to the real shit quick. Take it and flash, just in case." Geno took the money in a rush and was back within five minutes.

"Already?" I asked.

"Call me 'Swifty'. He went for the hundred, too. He said he had them promised to his cousin and that—"

"Sure, Geno. He's got a sick aunt, too."

"Come on, we'll fix in my cell. There's less action on the third tier and it's further away from the heat." When we reached Geno's cell, I told him to prepare the stuff while I pointed for the man.

"Put enough in for two jolts so we don't have to cook up twice." I said.

"It will have some of my blood in the dripper."

"Big deal. You got leukemia or something?"

Geno was quick. He had the shit out of the paper, into the spoon, cooked up, and drawn into the dripper in less than thirty seconds. He didn't even tie up when he hit, he just held his arm tightly against his body and fired it like a spear gun straight into his main line. "Whoeeee! Oh, Damn! Woody, this is good shit." He handed the eye dropper with the remainder of the heroin to me.

"Will you quit 'whoeeeing,' motherfucker, and let me in the cell."

Geno came out of the cell rubbing his face and eyes and I stepped in. I injected the stuff so fast that I was out of his cell a second or two before it hit me.

"What do you think, Woods?"

"It's good. It's real good. My fucking system is so clean I could get high on baby powder. God, it's been a long time. I don't feel like walking around. I want to enjoy it completely."

"You're a dead give-away, Woods."

"Yeah, both of us. We'd better get off the scene. You going to the mess hall for dinner?"

"I don't think so. I can't hit my ass with both hands."

"I'm not any better off. I got to get to my cell, Geno. If I had to say hello to the cop, I'd have a case. I'll see you later on. Should I hold the dough on me?"

"It's cool; just don't be nodding at count time. I'll give it to my old lady in the visiting room this weekend and she can send it to your woman to buy you a horn."

CHAPTER 61

Why did any contact with the outside world make me so nervous? Ever since Sylvia said she was coming to see me, I hadn't been the same. Her visit didn't fit in with my routine. In prison, I could manipulate every situation to my advantage. My con sense and cunning were always directed toward positioning my freedom within the prison. I never did anything I didn't want to do. Any form of responsibility was pressure. The visiting room represented pressure because it was outside my world. Visiting Sylvia, I would be forced to talk about outside things, see outside people and face the outside world I knew nothing about.

Geno stopped by my cell to check on me. "Did you take all the whites?"

"Of course." I said.

"Man, you're going to be wired. Your eyes already look like saucers."

"I'm telling you, they aren't doing it. I don't feel a thing."

"When did you take them?"

"Twenty minutes ago."

"Hang in there. They'll hit. You're showered, creased, and foo-fooed. Man, are you foo-fooed. You're going to take her down with that aftershave."

"Too strong?"

"Did you use the whole bottle?" I went to the sink and ran some water over my face.

"There you go," Geno said, "now at least she's got a chance."

We could hear my name being called over the loudspeaker.

"Hey, hey, there she is."

"I think the pill just hit."

"Go on out there, Suave Jones, and kill her. I'll see you when you get back."

The pills weren't taking away the nervousness. I was still uptight as I walked into the visiting room but I faked it as well as I could. When Sylvia saw me, her face lit up. She had a look in her eyes I had never seen before.

"You look great, honey." I said.

"You, too."

"I feel great, baby." I said, feeling a flash from the pills.

"I brought your horn. Just want to set your mind at ease. I

knew that's the first thing you were going to ask."

"Not necessarily." We both laughed. "Did you have any trouble with Sal?"

"No, I just told him I had three hundred and fifty bucks and wanted to buy a new Selmer. He said to come over with the three-fifty and I got it. It's never been played. It's still got cork holding the keys down."

"Jesus, my dick just got hard."

"Honey, you're crazy."

"Did you give a hundred to my grandmother?"

"Yes, and I told her not to say anything about it when she writes."

"How is she?"

"She's okay considering she's seventy years old. She takes her daily walks and wants to know everything about you. I called her last night and told her I was bringing your horn. It made her happy. The one thing she never asks me is when you're getting out. I think she's afraid of the answer."

"It's not as bad as it could be. At least I've got some time in back of me now, and a couple more years might do it. What about you? How are you doing?"

"I'm fine. My life has never been better."

Without me it's never been better, I thought to myself. "What are you doing these days?" I asked.

"Just working and going to AA meetings."

"AA?"

"Alcoholics Anonymous."

"What's a nice dope fiend like you doing going to a lush meeting?"

"When I got out of the county jail, I had to escape from my head but I was too afraid to use drugs because I didn't want to go back to jail, so I drank. Drinking gave me some relief but after a few months, bad things started happening to me. I kept losing jobs. Someone gave me a black eye."

"Who?"

"I don't know, I was drunk. Then I got a 502 but the arresting officer didn't show in court so it was dismissed. I was finally getting the message I couldn't drink when a girl I knew who had been a drunk, asked me if I would like to go to an AA meeting. I went to a meeting with her and I've been sober ever since. I haven't used anything in over a year."

"That's good, honey."

"I mean nothing. No alcohol, drugs, pills, nothing."

"That's great. So, you don't take anything?"

"No. It's the only way the obsession is taken away."

"Are you comfortable with the natch?"

"I wasn't in the beginning."

"What about now?"

"It gets easier every day."

"I suppose you got me all mapped out for when I get out."

"Not really, but I've said some prayers that you will get it."

"Get what?"

"The willingness to stop using."

"I'm not using."

"I don't mean just heroin. I mean using anything."

"Well, maybe I could do that when I got out, but if I get a chance to get high in here, I will. Escape outside is different than escape inside. Any time I can forget about a day or even a minute in here, I'm going for it."

"I understand. I just hope that some day you won't have to escape from anything."

"Come on, you're talking to me like I'm some kind of cripple."

"I don't mean it to sound that way."

"Well, let me get out first."

"Do you think that once you're out you can play those bars and not use?"

"I might have a few drinks, but I can play gigs and not use."

"But if you start drinking, you'll eventually start using again."

"Who made up that fucking rule?"

"It's a fact. It's a drug addict's dream when he quits smack that he'll be able to stay high and never go to jail or be sick again."

"Where do you get all these facts?"

"From the meetings. They have them here, too. I asked the officer at the desk when I came in. Why don't you go to one and maybe you'll see what I'm talking about."

"The meetings wouldn't be the same in here."

"Meetings are the same all over."

"You haven't been to one in here."

"Neither have you." We both laughed which broke the tension that was beginning to mount. "If you feel like it, go to one," she said.

"Yeah, okay, I'll check it out, honey."

We both kept the rest of the visit light. I tried to get sexy by telling her how I'd like to put it in. She responded for a while but then got cold. When I asked her what was wrong she said she didn't want to leave me with her pants on fire. We went to the guard at the front of the visiting room and I asked if I could pick up my horn. He said he would check out front and see if it had been cleared. In a few minutes, he came back and handed me the horn. "You know the rules on it, right? No loaning it to anyone."

"I understand." I answered.

Watching me look at the horn, Sylvia sensed my excitement. She knew I wanted to check it out so we said our goodbyes and kissed. It wasn't a dramatic exit. I didn't know if that was good or bad. I had always rather liked her dramatics. It was a different kind of visit than I had anticipated. Sylvia had changed a lot. It wasn't just that she looked different, but I could tell she felt differently about herself. I wondered if it was because she was sober. I started pondering about that, but then decided not to dwell on it.

Geno was waiting for me when I came out of the visiting room. "I see you got the ax."

"It's brand new, never been played."

"Crack it open, let's check it out."

"Let's get out of the hall first. There's too many lames around." We both started walking down the hall together.

"The whites still working out?"

"They get me edgy."

"You won't be long. I got you in my pocket."

"What are you holding?"

"The real shit."

"You jiving?"

"Two papers. I know you're going to ask me so I'll let you know in front, there's no more."

"How are you so sure?"

"I was there when it was cut up. The guy only scored for a gram. We were lucky to get the deuce."

"You got the outfit?"

"It's in the wing."

"Well, let's do it." After we fixed, I showed Geno my horn and took the cork off the keys so it was playable. We went to the One yard and I played until count time. I was once again just the way I wanted to be—comfortable and content with a horn in my hands and heroin in my veins.

CHAPTER 62

For the next few months, life in Vacaville was good and easy, as good if not better than it had been on the outside. I had my horn, money from playing cards, and an abundance of dope. At last, I had a goal to work toward and my time was valuable. I practiced every day for at least four hours. Because of my drug usage, I had never practiced consistently, but I had had enough foundation in music to know what it took to become a motherfucker. Now, I thought that getting busted might have been for the best. The way I had been going when I was outside, I never could have played the way I wanted to, but now, I had the opportunity. Geno and I played every morning for two hours. We liked playing music by ourselves because we could communicate so well together. We also played in the joint "big band" which wasn't any fun because the majority of musicians were so awful. But according to the Supervisor of Education, in order to be allowed the privilege of playing two hours by ourselves we had to play in the band.

We had packed up and were on our way to lunch when Geno reminded me that the big band was scheduled to play for the AA banquet that night. Despite my promise to Sylvia, I hadn't given AA a thought since her visit. I felt a little guilty about it, but now with the banquet, I would be able to semi-truthfully tell her I had gone to a meeting.

That night, Geno and I went to the banquet early to set up the instruments. The band was to play music as the guests arrived, and then throughout the dinner. We had specific instructions as to what kind of music to play—nothing loud or in the jazz vein. The banquet was being held in the visiting room with dinner accommodations for twenty guests, six speakers, and fifty or so convicts who were members of AA or knew someone who could put their names on the dinner list.

The convicts came mainly for the food and a glimpse at some real women. There was also a long line of "goody-two-shoes" waiting to get into the banquet hall for the after-dinner meeting. I saw nobody I knew, and didn't expect to either. Most of these punks were playing the Game: meetings, no more drinking, no more drugs. It all looked good to the parole board.

The banquet was to start at seven-thirty, but we started playing as soon as Geno got his drums tuned and set up. The guests all arrived at once, took seats and talked with the convicts. There were two guards stationed at each end of the large room but they remained unobtrusive. I always played with my eyes closed, so I didn't see the visitors until they were already seated. When I opened my eyes, I saw someone smiling at me with his head moving up and down and I realized it was Tom, my black friend from Folsom. Tom laughed as he saw the surprise register on my face. He left the people he was with and came over to me. "Hi, Woody."

My surprise at seeing Tom must have showed in my face. Tom saw what I was thinking. "I made parole the first time I went to the Board."

"I thought you were doing a murder beef."

"It was manslaughter."

"And they let you out the first time, man, that's fantastic. What are you doing here?"

"I started going to AA in Folsom after you left and I've been going ever since."

"You mean you don't fuck with that 'loud talk' anymore?"

"No, Lord!" We both laughed.

Geno left his drums and came over to me and Tom. "Geno, meet my friend, Tom."

"Hi, Tom."

"Hello, Geno. Good to see you. You and Geno in AA?" Tom asked me.

"We're playing here. That's all."

"You ought to check it out. They're your kind of people; you'd like them."

"Maybe I'll give it a play down the line. Did you come all the way up here from Los Angeles?"

"No, when I got out, I took my parole in San Francisco. — They're starting to eat; I'd better sit down. But I'll see you after. Are you going to stick around?"

"I'll stick."

After dinner, each speaker got up and spoke for fifteen minutes. Tom had the best story, but there were three others whose stories I could recall: a young man in his twenties, a well-dressed woman in her fifties, and a distinguished-looking man in his early sixties. The young man told about selling pills in high school, drinking wine every day, being busted but avoiding trial somehow, and ending his run with three DUIs which led to a sentence of six months, and three years' probation with the stipulation that he attend AA while on probation. He had ended up living in his car, but now had a room, a hot plate, and a job in a machine shop. No girlfriend yet—"but I'm working on it," and next week, two years clean and sober! Blah, blah, blah. He had an energy and enthusiasm for life, which I found nauseating.

The next speaker was even better. She was this well-dressed attractive looking fifty-ish woman, and I was amazed when she told this story of how she had done a two-year bit for passing bad checks. She told of how she had fucked "half of San Pedro," but then got a DUI which led to a sentence of eighteen more months plus two years of AA meetings. I was impressed with her honesty and the changes that took place in her life, but was turned off by her so-called transformation as a "do-gooder." I felt she could have found better things to do with her life than coming four hundred miles to confess to a bunch of cons.

The last speaker to come to the podium was elegantly dressed, had a strong baritone voice and a confident manner that bordered on the arrogant. It seemed like his story would never end. He went on about how his brother was his original sponsor, who insisted that he go to five meetings a week. He did that for a year while cutting down, somewhat, on his drinking. After lots of build-up, he told how his brother then took him to an exclusive club that his father had helped found, and he recounted the advice that Dad had given him when he was trying to get sober.

"It's simple. When the waiter comes by and asks you for your drink order, you just say: 'I pass.' It all started for me with those two words: 'I pass.'"

Well, that about did it for me. I was ready to puke at that point. I had never heard anything so ridiculous in my life. What a smug, conceited bastard. What did he know about the real world? Him and his fancy clothes and his daddy's exclusive club! I couldn't wait to get back to my cell after that.

I didn't get much time with Tom after the talks, because the dinner and the meeting had taken longer than expected, and the two guards hustled everyone out. The other musicians had left, but I stayed with Geno and helped him pack up his drums. The guards were standing at the end of the hall waiting for us to get our equipment so they could leave. We finished packing, and then headed down the hall back towards our wing.

"The old lady coming up this weekend?" Geno asked.

"Yeah, she might move to San Francisco."

"Does that mean you'll go there when you get out?"

"I'll go where she is."

"You know, you could just get lucky when you go to the Parole Board next month."

"No way."

"You never know, Woody."

"They'd have to make a mistake."

"They do that sometimes."

"Oh my God, Geno! What's he doing here?"

Geno followed my eyes. "He's the new warden here, Woody."

"That's the asshole Captain from San Quentin that put me in segregation." There wasn't time to avoid him. I wanted to put my eyes to the ground and walk past, but I couldn't. We looked at each other. The Captain glared, I didn't look away. It wouldn't have done any good. I was almost past him when he said, "You been having a good time down here?"

"I'm doing my number."

"You're going to be doing it back in San Quentin, so get packed." He then turned around and rejoined the Supervisor of Education as if nothing had happened.

"Was he on the square?" Geno asked.

"You better believe it."

"Go see your therapist. He can hold you here."

"It's the Warden, Geno. Nobody out-clouts him."

"Your old lady's coming up Sunday. Have her stay over and talk to him. He can't transfer you out of here before

298   VERDI WOODWARD

Monday."

"Don't bet on it. We got a thing going. He hates my guts and I hate his. My old lady talking to him isn't going to do any good."

"You don't think there's anything you can do?"

"Nothing except get some pills for the trip."

"I'm sorry, man."

"That's life in the pen."

Two officers came to my cell at count time and took me to Receiving and Release. I didn't get a chance to say goodbye to Geno or to get any dope for the trip.

Thirty minutes after the Captain spotted me, I was in the staff car on the way back to San Quentin. It was almost like getting busted all over again.

CHAPTER 63

I arrived in Quentin a few hours after the evening meal and was taken to a cell on the fifth tier. I was too tired to think about anything so I went right to sleep.

Waking up in Quentin the next day was like a bad dream. On top of everything else, my trick knee was out again. After my cell door was opened, I took my time walking to breakfast, trying to find someone who might have some dope, but I saw no one to ask.

I ate by myself in the mess hall and then went to the yard. There had been a big turnover in the population, and I found few men I knew. I picked a spot to stand by at the North Block. It was where Red and I always took bets and it was the last place we had been together. I hated the reality of being back in Quentin, but it would give me a better shot at Sims. If I could get Sims, nothing else would matter.

I turned around and saw Stan walking toward me. I hadn't thought about Stan in a long time, but seeing him brought back all the misery the bastard had caused me. It would be easy to take him out because, in spite of his street sense, he didn't know how to protect himself in prison. But there was the chance I would get nailed doing it, and that would ruin my chance of getting Sims. First, it had been the Captain; now Sims ranked the play.

Stan approached me like a long-lost brother. "Hi, Woody. When did you get in?"

I looked at him feeling a cold hatred. Stan sensed it and stiffened up. "The Captain's gone, Stan. Get out of my face. Stay out of my face."

"I don't want any trouble, Woody."

"Then make yourself scarce."

"I can do that."

"Good. Why don't you do it now?" Stan nodded, turned and walked away.

Once Stan was out of sight, I heard a lilting voice in back of me. "Hey, Big Boy, would you like some head for two packs?"

I turned around quickly to see what new fruiter was working the yard and found Morrie standing with his hand poised on his hip. "You motherfucker, Morrie."

"What're you doing back here? You couldn't stand prosperity?"

"That fucking Captain got me again. Goddamn, Morrie, I'm glad to see you here."

"I'm not glad to see me here."

"You know what I mean, sucker."

"Did you do any good down there?"

"I got the dough together for a new horn and stayed fucked up every day."

"That's doing a lot of good. Norman told me you were coming in last night."

"Doesn't Norman ever miss anything?"

"Not much. I see your boy Stan found you right away." Morrie said.

"Yeah. I told him to get in the wind."

"What if he goes to the man on you?"

"What's he going to tell him?"

"I don't know yet. You know that little short bean over to the right of the drinking faucet?"

"Yeah, why?"

"He keeps looking over here."

"He's okay. He's just the warden's houseboy."

"Well, he just keeps looking over here." The Mexican started to walk in our direction. When he got within fifteen feet, he stopped and used his eyes to call Morrie over. "I'll be right back, Woody."

"What's up?"

"I don't know. Hang tough a minute."

I watched Morrie approach the other con. I didn't sense trouble but I knew there was something cooking. After a few minutes, I was tired of waiting and decided to leave for R & R when Morrie and the Mexican finally came over to me.

"Woody," Morrie said, "this is Topo." Then Morrie looked at Topo and said, "You can ask Woody about Stan. It's his friend."

"What do you want to know, Topo?"

"Can I trust your friend Stan?" Topo asked.

"Why?"

"He wants me to do something for him."

"Like what?"

"He's on minimum custody and works on the outside plumbing. He did something with the plumbing on the Warden's house on the hill, some kind of time that shuts off the water. He wants me to call control on a certain night and tell them the plumbing is fucked up."

"Why?"

"He said his chick would meet him out there and give him some pussy, and that he'd give me fifty bucks if I make the call."

"What are you worried about?"

"If he's a wrong cat and he gets busted, he could say I helped him."

"When is his girlfriend supposed to show?"

"Next week."

"Make the call, Topo. It's an easy fifty."

"Alright, Woody. Thanks a lot."

"Anytime, Topo."

When Topo left, Morrie said, "Man, Woody, why didn't you run Stan's pedigree down to Topo?"

"We got a week before anything happens. I want to check Stan out."

As we started walking to R & R, Morrie noticed my limp. "What happened to your leg?"

"It's out for real this time. It looks like a fucking basketball."

"What are you going to do about it?"

"See the doctor. Maybe he can drain it. I don't know. I may have to have the operation this time for real. Are you going to see Norman?"

"I can." Morrie said.

"Tell him I want to see him."

"He's a busy cat."

"I know. Just tell him I have to see him. Is there anything on the yard?"

"It's bone dry except for some stumblers."

"Can you get the stumblers?"

"I think so."

"I'm broke. You'll have to front me."

"I'll cover it."

"What about the games in North Block? Are they still

going on?"

"I'm not sure. I'll find out."

"Who's got the book?"

"There's two or three of them going. The Mexican Mafia has one."

"See if you can find out about those games. I'm going to need some dough around here."

"I'll check on it when I go back to work."

When we reached R & R, I got my property and gave it to Morrie to take in for me. "I'm taking my ax to the lower yard and practice, Morrie." I said.

"Okay. The games, stumblers and Norman, right?"

"Right." I answered.

Later, limping down the stairs on my way to the mess hall, I saw Norman waiting in the rotunda. "If I'd known you were this bad, I'd have called for a stretcher. What's happening with the leg?" Norman asked.

"It's out. I might need the operation for real this time. Did you come to eat with me?"

"No, I got to get right back to the office. I'm breaking in a new clerk for the Captain and I have to show him how to do everything."

"Anything on Sims?"

"He got arrested in St. Louis for burglary."

I felt a surge of excitement but I tried to control myself, asking, "What are they going to do with him?"

"They dropped the charge. They're going to let California have him back."

"When?"

"San Quentin has thirty days to pick him up."

"When will he be here?"

"There's two officers in charge of transporting prisoners, but they're booked solid so it will probably be toward the end of the thirty days."

"Is there a chance he could be released if they were late?"

"They're never late."

"What's the procedure when he comes back?"

"He'll go to the isolation cell for twenty-nine days for escaping."

"Anywhere else he could go?"

"If isolation's full, they put him on deadlock in the South Block."

"I'm going to need your help." I said.

"For what?"

"You know what."

"You really going to give it all up for that guy?"

"All of it."

"I'll go for you to a point, Woody, but I haven't worked all these years to get out and then—"

"I know, Norman. I wouldn't put you in any kind of cross."

"I don't approve, but if it's what you want, all I'm going to do is tell you when they go for him. The rest is all on you."

"That's all I need. I'll take it from there."

"By the way, I saw your name on the Parole Board list. You could lay the groundwork for next year. They're always going to be here."

"Thinking about the Parole Board next year isn't real at all to me, Norman."

"What happened to the clean cut kid that went to Vacaville?"

"You didn't believe that shit, did you?"

"Well, you have changed. I've got to get back or that clerk will have the office in a mess."

"Alright, Norman. Thanks." Watching him walk away, I realized that no one really knew Norman. His style kept him a notch away from revealing himself. He had both the convicts and the guards on automatic, preferring the company of books over anyone except a select few. The straight hardworking role he played with the Warden enabled him the luxury of privacy from the majority of the population. He hated institutions and their policies, but no one would ever know that.

Norman knew the convict well, probably better than anyone because of his position, which was why he remained aloof. No one would get any help from Norman without first proving himself, but he would extend himself to the limit for a friend and even take a chance that could ruin everything he had worked for. It was this part of Norman's character that I was attracted to. In a world of misfits and con men, it was a privilege to have his friendship.

CHAPTER 64

The intense fear of being before the Parole Board begins months before the actual meeting, at two in the morning, alone in a cell; the convict wondering what chance he will have, what to say if they ask this question, what to say if they ask that question. By the time he's finally called to make an appearance, he has answered a thousand questions in his head and has become a nervous wreck. The atmosphere in the boardroom is like the county jail booking office, only more intense. The four parole members sit behind a long table and pretend to be engaged in an evaluation of possible release. Usually only two members ask questions. The other two members are busy working up the next case.

The questions asked and the answers given are on the most superficial level; "Do you think you can make it out there if we give you a chance, Mr. Jones?" "Oh, yes, Mr. Parole Board member. I will never come back."

The Parole Board members are appointed by the governor,

which means a convict can draw a dentist, a councilman, or a cop. He could even go before a supermarket cashier if the cashier knows the governor. There aren't any qualifications for appointment to the Board and under the indeterminate sentence law, these people have complete control; no one supersedes them. They realize their power, and with rare exception, develop the same abusive hate and contempt that characterizes the prisoners. Since the answers one gives have no direct bearing on a release, it's best to keep it as light as possible. The main objective of every convict appearing before the Board is to conceal his hatred and anger. Angry men do not get paroled.

Going to the Board that day, I knew all this, but it didn't make things any easier. I was still nervous and frightened. My case was the last one to be heard in the afternoon. I had to wait from eight o'clock in the morning and by the time I was called in, I was close to numb from anxiety. The Board members were overly polite, almost condescending in the first few minutes of the interview. They talked about my drug addiction, my crimes, and my arrest record. I thought it was nearly over when one of the members who had not said anything spoke to me, "You know, we're building a new maximum security prison."

"I didn't know that, sir." I responded.

"How much time do you have in now, Mr. Woodward?"

"Five years and three months."

"Well, Mr. Woodward, your sentence has only just begun as far as I'm concerned. You'll be at the top of the list to go to our new prison."

I glanced at the name plate in front of the man. "Mr. Edwards, I am aware of my bad record, of the crimes I committed and my drug addiction, but I've had five years in which to change. I've got a job to go to and a woman who has waited for me all these years."

"Why were you transferred back here from Vacaville?" the Board member asked.

"The Warden there transferred me." I replied.

CHAPTER 65

I had not seen Sylvia since Vacaville. Taking care of business in San Quentin had kept me occupied, so I hadn't been able to give her much thought. She had promised to visit me the first chance she got, but now, as my name was being called over the P.A. system I wondered to myself why she always caught me at the wrong time.

I was so loaded it was an effort for me to keep my eyes open, and that was where she would look first. It was almost like visiting a cop. I tried to collect myself, but had to sit on the bed again. I looked down at my feet and saw that I had no socks on. Getting my shoes off, socks on and shoes back on was an ordeal. I had a bitch of a time standing up. Then, hearing the officer who was waiting at the end of the tier call my name, I hurried out the door and waved thanks to the guard. The cop left, and I sat down on the tier where I attempted to tie my shoes. Somehow, I got to the yard where I fell out on a bench and sent for Morrie. After what seemed like days, Morrie showed up. "Motherfucker, you are pitiful. You better get off the yard."

"I need some speed. Who's got it?"

"There's some in the East Block."

"Would you go get it for me?"

"Why don't you just go to your cell?"

"Because I got a visit."

"Man, you'll never—"

"Just go get it."

"Boxy's got it."

"I don't give a fuck who's got it, just get it."

"All right, hang here and try to look respectable. I'll be back as soon as I can."

"Hurry!" I sat with a glazed look on my face, staring straight ahead, trying to look like I had some sense until Morrie returned.

When he came back, he looked at me and shook his head. "I got twenty spatulas. How many do you want?"

"Give me all of them. And Morrie—"

"Yes?"

"Would you try and locate me a hot cup of coffee?"

"You're a bitch, a real bitch. Yeah, I'll be right back."

"Hurry, Morrie." Things were looking up by the time he got back with the coffee. The spats were doing their job.

"Here you go, a little booster. How long ago did they call you for a visit?"

"Shit, I don't know. It seems like I've been waiting for you all day."

"It's two fifteen. You better get out there if you're going to have any time with her." I stood up rather perilously. "You gonna make it?"

The walk to the visiting room gradually brought back the feeling in my legs. When I walked into the room, Sylvia was smiling. Then she did a quick doubletake. I could tell she knew I was loaded and was disappointed in me.

"You look great, honey." I said.

"Thank you. How do you feel about coming back to San Quentin?"

"Well, since I've been here, there's been two stabbings, an attempted escape, one heart attack, and a sea gull shit on me. Outside of that, I've been fine."

"Are you loaded right now?"

"No."

"You haven't got anything in your system?"

"Well, a few reds."

"That's loaded."

"Not to me, it isn't."

"It's not clean," she said.

"Damn, you're so fucking straight lately. You make me feel uncomfortable."

"I don't mean to."

"Then lighten up on me. It's always something; will I go to a meeting, am I loaded— All those questions and then checking my eyes out every chance you get. It's not exactly a picnic in here. If I get loaded once in a while, what does it hurt anybody?"

"If you don't stop in here, you won't stop outside."

"That's horse shit. Ever since you started going to those fucking meetings, you've been on a soapbox. I don't need a soapbox. I need some support."

"If you come out the same way you went in, what chance do you think we have of making it?"

"I'm changing every day, and don't worry about us making it. We'll be all right."

"You used to tell me it would be all right when half of the Los Angeles police force was looking for us. Saying it's going to be all right doesn't make it all right."

"What do you want me to do?"

"I love you. I always have. I try to con myself into believing it will be different when you come home, but I know it won't. My life is real now, maybe not exciting, but real, but I still live in a dream world where you're concerned." Her voice trailed off and she looked away from me. I felt a tremendous gulf between us. Both of us were reflecting on what we had been through together and where we were heading now. She wanted to change the subject. "What did the Board say?"

I looked at her and knew that she didn't deserve to be lied to, didn't deserve to be led on with the hope that we could have a life together. I knew there was no chance for us. "What does it matter what they said? I'm booked solid. It's a bad deal. You're not the same, I'm not the same."

"I don't want to be the same. Is that the way you want me to be? The way I was when we were using? I'll never be that little girl again. She's gone."

"I'm going to be totally honest with you so you'll have a choice. I don't intend to ever stop using drugs inside or outside. Whenever the opportunity to get high comes up, I take it.

Always. If you can't accept me on those terms, then I don't want you to come up here again."

She wouldn't look at me and there was a long pause. "I can't be part of those terms," she said.

"Then you can't be part of my life."

"Are you sure, absolutely sure, that's what you want?"

"What I want is for you not to come here anymore."

She still didn't look at me. Her eyes were cast down toward the floor. As I stood up, I saw her tears falling gently on the table. I looked at the top of her head affectionately for a second, then said goodbye and walked out.

I stood outside the visiting room reflecting on what I had done. It had finally ended. She was gone, out of my life. I should have ended it the day I got arrested. I felt like I had always, from the very beginning, deceived her. I wondered what she would think if she knew I was planning to kill someone. She thought I had principles and character. She wanted me to be as good and generous of heart as she was. I felt a painful epiphany, but I repressed it with the conviction that I would have to learn to exist without her.

CHAPTER 66

I needed to get back to the action of the yard to take my mind off Sylvia. There was important business to take care of, and now I could put everything into it. I made a quick survey of the yard trying to find Morrie and discovered him standing by the domino tables sweating out a game.

"Man," Morrie said, "how you got through that visit I'll never know. You looked like a wild wolverine on your way out there. How do you feel now?"

"I'm good. Come on, I've got to talk to you."

We walked down to the lower yard where there was always more privacy. Morrie noticed that I had to walk slowly because of my knee. What're you going to do about your wheel, sucker?"

"I'm gonna see the doctor about it."

"You think you're going to need an operation?"

"I don't know. It's no big deal either way. What's happening with Topo? Did Stan give him a date?"

"It's on for tomorrow."

"Did he give Topo the fifty?"

"Yeah."

"Then it's obvious he's looking for something more than getting his nuts out of hock. That motherfucker's got plans on moving out."

"Of course he has, but he ain't going nowhere." Morrie said. "What are you going to do?"

"I've had it all worked out in my head since the day I talked to Topo but I have to talk to Norman to polish it."

As we were talking we walked to the center of the football field. I wanted to make sure no one could hear what I was about to say. I paused for a second then turned to Morrie. "I need you to help me with something else. Sims is coming back."

"When?"

"Within thirty days. Norman will let me know the day they pick him up in St. Louis. I need five Hoosiers willing to go to the growler for five days.You think we can get them for two cartons each?"

"You can buy assholes for two cartons. Why do you want them?"

"If all of the cells in the hole are occupied, they'll put Sims in the South Block. That's where I want him."

"You going to take him out?"

"I need some gasoline. I'm going to barbecue his ass."

"That's real risky, Woody. Lacquer thinner would do the job, and you could get that out of the hobby shop."

"That's a good move, Morrie. I know I'm leaning on you heavy, but I'm going to need some brushes and paints to make it look like I'm an artist. That way I can keep the thinner in my cell. Can you put it together fast?"

"Yeah, but I thought you had thirty days."

"I want everything ready before Sims even leaves St. Louis."

"Do you know how you're going to do it?"

"Yeah, walk up to his cell, throw it in and light a match."

"You're going to have a bitch of a time getting out of there without being seen. I don't think you can pull it off clean."

"But I can pull it off."

"Maybe if he was sleeping you could pour the thinner in his cell and be gone before he wakes up."

"I don't want him sleeping. I want him to see me. I want him to know who's doing it to him. I don't give a fuck if he screams. I want to watch him."

The next day I got up early, my head buzzing with thoughts. I was focused now, concentrating on my plans for Sims. I had already set up a morning meeting with Norman. Because of Norman's wish for discretion, we were to meet in the library. I arrived a few minutes early. As usual, Norman was right on time. He seemed especially animated, a wide grin on his face as he walked up to me.

"Hi, Norman. You look happy."

"You will be too when I tell you the news."

"Well?"

"Your boy in St. Louis has TB."

"How do you know?"

"It came in on the teletype this morning."

"But will they still bring him back?"

"TB won't change the wheels from turning. They'll put him in the TB ward at the hospital. You'll never see him in the main population again." Norman smiled and expected a smile from me. I considered what Norman had said, then asked, "Can I get into the TB ward?"

"That's not difficult, but why bother? It's been taken care of for you. He won't last long. The teletype referred to his case as terminal."

"He ain't going like that, not after what he did."

"What are you going to do, kill him twice? He's almost dead now."

"When will they bring him back?"

"Next week."

"Do you know that for sure?"

"For sure."

"Let's forget about it, that's settled. There's something else I want to talk to you about."

"You're serious, aren't you? I mean about dusting Sims?"

"I've never been more serious about anything in my life." I said.

"It's a real loser, Woody. I suppose you know that."

I didn't respond. My mind was settled on Sims. It didn't matter if Sims was dying. Tuberculosis had no place in my plans. I continued speaking calmly as if we were talking about the weather. "I got Sims covered right now, but I need some other information. How many convicts are outside the walls after the evening meal?"

"Three in the snack bar, that's all."

"What about the maintenance plumber?"

"There's two of them, day shift and night shift."

"Stan Singer's the night shift?"

"Yeah, he just got the job."

"Who sends the plumber out?"

"I do, or the Captain's clerk."

"One more question. Is the patrol car out there all night?"

"They come in at four in the morning."

"Stan's got plans to leave tonight."

"How do you know?"

"I know."

"What are you going to do about it?" Norman asked.

"I'm putting the motherfucker under the jail."

"How are you going to do that?"

"I got it all worked out, but I need your help."

"You keep me in jackpots around here. You've always got some kind of move going on."

"I'd never ask you to do anything you couldn't get away clean on."

"It's got to be clean. You know I'll say no if I don't like it." Norman said.

"I'd want you to if you didn't like it, but if you're in, I'm going to count on you."

Norman and I ate dinner together that night. I was too preoccupied to eat much, but watched him as he dug into a huge meal. We saw Stan enter the mess hall, but neither of us paid any attention to him. At the end of dinner, we stood up and talked, then Norman went back to the office and I returned to my cell. I tried to read but couldn't concentrate. I looked at my watch then turned the light out and tried to relax. My part was done, now things were out of my hands. I closed my eyes, picturing to myself what was going on in the control room. It was already seven-thirty. Now, all I had to do was wait and let the plan unfold...

Norman's at his desk typing, glancing at the wall clock. Just then the phone rings, and he waits for it to ring twice before picking it up. "Hello, Warden's office. I'll get one out there right away, no problem." Norman hangs up the phone and walks into the Captain's office to where his new assistant Lansky, is sitting behind his desk working on a crossword puzzle. "The Warden's plumbing has broken down." Norman says. "Get a hold of both maintenance plumbers right now. We can't keep the Warden waiting."

"I'll take care of it, Norman."

Norman waits a few minutes and then raises the blind on his window from where he can see anyone leaving the institution. As he glances out, something catches his eye. He sees Stan walking by the chapel with a toolbox in his hand. A moment after Stan passes by the window, Norman hears him knock on the heavy iron door to let him out of the prison, then hears a guard open and then close it. After a couple of minutes, a tall man carrying a toolbox walks by. Norman hears him also leave the prison, and after a few minutes, he goes back to the Captain's office and asks Lansky, "Did you get the plumber out there?"

"Sure did. They're both already on it," he eagerly replies.

"You sent both of them out?"

"Yeah, that's what you said to do, isn't it?"

"I said to call both plumbers. You call them both, then send out the first one you get a hold of. That way there's never a delay. But you never send both out at the same time."

"Am I in trouble?"

"It's just not procedure, that's all. I thought you knew that."

"Well, maybe I oughta phone the tower and have the patrol car bring one of them back."

"You could do that."

The lights throughout the cell house had already been turned off. Most of the men had gone to sleep. I was still lying on my back with my hands behind my head. My mind was racing: "What if that wet motherfucker does manage to get away? It is possible. There's always a chance of something going wrong. What if Norman has a problem with Lansky? What if Stan slips by everyone? He's capable of it…" I looked up and saw Norman peering into my cell. I jumped up and was about to say something but Norman lifted a finger to his lips in a gesture to keep it down.

"Jesus Christ, Norman, it seems like three days since we were in the mess hall. What happened?"

"It was busy tonight."

"For fuck's sake, Norman, is he popped or isn't he?"

"You're asking me if Stanley was apprehended in the act of an attempted escape?"

"Goddamn, Norman, will you stop being cute and give me the story?"

"I got the call from Topo at 7:30 and then flat-stored Lansky into sending out both plumbers. He still thinks it was his idea."

"Then what happened?"

"I went back to my office and did some paperwork. Oh, by the way, you have a ducat to see the doctor at ten tomorrow."

"Norman, fuck the doctor tomorrow. What happened?"

"I waited until I saw both of them leave the institution. I waited three minutes and then went back to talk to Lansky the lop."

"What time was it then?"

"I had four minutes."

"Wasn't that cutting it thin?" I asked.

"I had to do it that way." Norman said.

"Go on, what then?"

"Lansky called the tower and they sent out the patrol car to bring back one of the plumbers. When they got to the Warden's house, Stanley wasn't there so they went looking for him. Then I didn't hear anything."

"What do you mean?"

"I didn't hear anything for an hour and a half."

"Oh, for Chrissakes, Norman, did they get him or not?" Norman stared at me then slowly broke into a sly boyish grin. "Whoeee, motherfucker!" I burst out. Norman gestured for me to keep it down, but was himself excitedly laughing and hopping around. "Run it down. I want to hear it all."

"The patrol car went looking for him but missed him the first time around."

"Those open-fly cops couldn't catch a cold. Who was in the patrol car?"

"Brown and Whiteside."

"Whiteside? Oh shit, tell me they lumped him up."

"They caught him just as he was getting into the pick-up car, so they got the driver, too. And you know Whiteside."

"Did he get into his bully bag?"

"You know it."

"Stan finally out-slicked himself," I said, smiling.

"Yeah, he slicked himself into another one-to-ten and some knots on his melon he won't be able to wash off for a while."

"What about Topo?"

"Everyone loves everybody. The whole thing went perfectly. Lansky loves me for catching the mistake in time. Topo's clean and fifty up. Whiteside had a workout, and the night lieutenant loves everybody because he'll be credited with the bust. If you want to see your boy for the last time, he'll be leaving tomorrow morning at eight."

"I wouldn't miss that for the world."

"I've gotta get out of here. I'll see you after breakfast by the Catholic chapel."

"Norman, you are beautiful. Answer me one question before you go. Did you have fun?"

Norman answered with a straight face, "Just following orders."

A light steady morning rain was falling over the nearly empty yard. The mood was subdued because of the weather and most men had elected to stay inside. I stood by myself under one end of the shed. After sending word to the kitchen for Morrie to meet me, I waited, trying to stay clear of the windy sprays of rain. By the time Morrie arrived, I was soaked. "Man, where in the fuck have you been?" I asked.

"I just got your message. I came right out. Damn, man, why're you standing out here?"

"They popped Stan."

"Hmm! That's sweet. Was it clean?"

"Clean as a new penny. It couldn't have gone down any better."

"Couldn't you have just sent me word that everything worked out instead of bringing me out in this monsoon?"

"I thought you might want to see him being carted off. They're taking him to the Marin County Jail right now."

I looked up as someone approached in a yellow raincoat and hat, but it was now raining so hard I couldn't tell if it was a guard or a convict. When the figure got closer, I realized it was Norman. "Come on," Norman said, "they just went to pick him up."

The three of us crossed the deserted yard and came to the Segregation Unit where Stan was being held. We were just in time to see a raincoated guard open the chain link gate. The guard stepped out, followed by Stan and a second guard. Stan was led forward, walking slowly with his head down. After a dozen steps, he raised his eyes and spotted me, Morrie, and Norman standing by ourselves. His eyes were questioning, darting around the yard, as he wondered why we three were the only ones in the area. Then his eyes locked on me, and I stared back with cocky defiance. I raised my hand, pointing my index finger at Stan then wagged it back and forth the way a teacher would to admonish a naughty pupil. Stan was confused at first. He looked into the smiling faces of Morrie and Norman and then back at me and realized that, somehow, we were responsible for his predicament. His head tilted down again as the guards escorted him around the corner of the Segregation Unit building.

We stood quietly in the pouring rain, then I began to laugh. Morrie looked at me and shook his head. "Man, that was heavy, heavy, heavy. And when you shook your finger at him that was the final fucking capper. I thought that punk was going to start crying." We were now all cracking up openly, looking at each other and breaking into new waves of laughter. Norman had completely lost his cool, jumping up and down, slapping his leg. We laughed without interruption for several minutes in the empty yard while sheets of rain poured down on us.

CHAPTER 67

I picked up my ducat for the doctor and headed toward the hospital, which was connected to the South Block. The bay encompassed the hospital on two sides, affording me a depressingly spectacular view of the Bay Bridge and San Francisco. The unending line of cars crossing the bridge looked like a column of ants. It was only a few miles away, but for me, it might as well have been the moon. I stared up at the guard tower as I passed into the front entrance. I showed the officer my ducat and was told to report to a Doctor Grossman. Walking through the hallway of the old dirty building, I noticed the faint unpleasant smell of disinfectant and saw a scattering of mouse droppings.

Most of the doctors in San Quentin had been working there for centuries and had developed a cynical, almost hateful attitude toward the prisoners. I was, therefore, very surprised to find my doctor to be a warm, friendly man. Doctor Grossman was a non-resident orthopedic specialist who only entered the institution to operate and make evaluations. He was a handsome man in his late forties who dressed immaculately and spoke very precisely. It was obvious his work was the most important thing in his life and he didn't waste words. However, he did take the time to enjoy a sense of humor and was a pleasure to be around.

"Your x-rays show you have some cartilage that should be removed," he said.

"What would happen if I didn't have the operation?"

"It would build up more deposits and get worse. How does it feel now?"

"It bothers me a lot. If I turn it a certain way, it goes out." The doctor had me lie on a table when he examined me. After moving my leg back and forth and from side to side a few times, he decided that I definitely needed an operation. "How long before I could walk?" I asked.

"I would say in a couple of days you'd be up and around. But you wouldn't be playing any tennis for a while."

"When would you operate? You see, my aunt is coming in from St. Louis sometime next week to see me and I wouldn't want her to see me in a wheelchair."

"I have tomorrow morning free. I could do it then."

"And I'd be up in a few days?" I asked.

"I'm quite sure you would be."

I was issued a robe and pajamas and assigned to a bed in an open ward on the hospital's third floor. I sat on my bed and stared at the dirty white walls. Now that I was committed to having the operation, I began to have second thoughts about it. The doctor had said I would be walking in a few days, but what if Sims got back before I could walk well enough to do what I had to do? I could always wait a few more days, but what if they really fucked up the operation and I couldn't walk for a long time? My thoughts were interrupted by the appearance of a male nurse who held a razor and a pan of water. "You're Woodward, right?"

"That's me."

"You're the one with the bad knee?" I nodded. "I'm Russell," the nurse smiled as he spoke. "I have to get you ready for tomorrow. Would you roll up your pant leg there?"

As I carried out the request, I noticed that one of the nurse's eyes blinked every few seconds in a nervous twitch. Although he smiled constantly, something about the smile made me uncomfortable.

"Boy, that's really swollen. This shouldn't take too long." The nurse began to lather my leg. I looked down at him. Russell was in his forties, bald and thick around the waist. His eyes were close together and intense, like they never missed a thing. He had a very thin upper lip which seemed to stay fixed while the large fleshy lower lip moved. He continued to smile and chatter as he shaved my leg. "I noticed on your chart that you're a dope addict. You don't get anything right now, but tonight you get a sleeping pill and tomorrow morning before they wheel you in for the operation, you get a nice big shot of Demerol so you'll be on cloud nine." The nurse was taking longer than he had to. I stood up, feeling an intense revulsion. "Don't you want any alcohol on your leg? I'll rub it down for you." Russell said.

"That's all right."

"I guess that's it then. You get your sleeping pill from the next shift nurse, so I'll see you in the morning. You sure you don't want an alcohol rub before I go?"

I let down my pant leg and turned away without answering. The nurse was still smiling as he gathered up his shaving basin and razor and continued on his rounds.

Hospital restrictions were fairly lax and patients were permitted to roam around their floors. I went for a stroll, trying to get the feel of my new surroundings. After realizing that the cops were generally unaware of what floor each patient was assigned to, I slipped up to the fourth floor where the tuberculosis ward was located. It was virtually empty except for one patient on the general floor, an old man sleeping. As I walked past him, I noticed that he had no teeth and was breathing with great difficulty, probably dying, I figured.

I moved toward the two doors at the end of the hall. One was the linen closet door; the other had a sign that read "TUBERCULOSIS WARD: KEEP OUT." I looked into the glass peephole and seeing nothing, tried the door. I was surprised to find it unlocked. I stepped into the ward, which was about thirty feet long with a row of six cells on one wall and two windows on the other. I stood without moving for a moment, then walked down the hallway, peering into each cell. I saw only two patients. Both were sleeping with hospital masks over their faces. When I came to the final empty cell, I tried the door and found that it was locked.

I had seen everything I needed to see, so I turned and retraced my steps. On my way out, I looked back to see if the old man had noticed me coming and going. He was still motionless except for his hard breathing. I walked out quietly and returned to my floor. Everything was clear. It would not be difficult.

CHAPTER 68

"Come on, dope fiend, roll up your sleeve and I'll give you what you've been waiting for." I was startled out of my deep sleep. Russell, the nurse, was standing by my bed with a hypodermic syringe. I blinked, unsure of where I was, till groggy from the sleeping pill I had been given the night before. "I've got to get you ready. They'll be coming for you any minute." I sat up in bed, pulled the sleeve to my hospital gown up, and the nurse injected me with 200 cc's of Demerol. "That should put you on cloud nine for a while and you'll be getting it every four hours from now on so you should be as happy as—"

I got up in the middle of the nurse's sentence to go to the bathroom. I was thankful that when I returned, he had gone. I began to feel the Demerol and was surprised that a measly 200 cc's could make me feel so euphoric. I lay down, closed my eyes and waited to be taken to the operating room, wanting to get as much mileage as I could out of the Demerol. It was almost like a jolt of heroin, the same kind of rush, the same kind of drowsiness and feeling of well being.

She was leading me by the hand. A strong, warm, wind was blowing and the sidewalk was covered with autumn leaves. I didn't know what movie we were on our way to see but it didn't matter. I wanted to show her how fast I could run and she indulged me. She smiled, and let go of my hand. I dropped to one knee, then rose and began to run. My arms pumped up and down and my heart beat hard. The cool air filled my lungs and felt good; then it began to hurt. Because she was watching me, I ran even harder until finally I reached the end of the block. I pulled up exhausted and looked back expectantly at her. She smiled and told me I had run like the wind.

"We're ready for you, Woodward." I opened my eyes to see two convicts wearing masks and green surgical clothes. They helped me onto a hard gurney and rolled me away.

As I entered the operating room, I felt disoriented, but not frightened. The anesthesiologist turned me on my side and gave me a spinal injection. In a few minutes, I was numb from the waist down. They wheeled me into an adjoining room where I saw the surgeon for the first time. The doctor came over and put his hand on my shoulder. "How do you feel?"

"I'm fine."

"Good. It's going to go just fine." The surgeon pulled a screen up in front of my face and began the operation.

CHAPTER 69

I woke up feeling uncomfortable, not so much because of the operation but because I wasn't high enough. The Demerol had started to wear off, and I didn't like the idea of being sober. My knee was slightly numb but not painful. My system yearned for another jolt. I turned to a neighboring patient and asked him to find the nurse to see if I could have my medication early. The neighbor, a slightly built man named Lane, left his bed, returning a few minutes later.

"Did you ask him?"

"Yeah."

"What's he say?"

"Nothing. He just looked at me."

I leaned back and waited. I glanced at the clock and was relieved that it was almost four o'clock, the time I was scheduled for my shot. Four o'clock came, then four-ten, four-fifteen, four-seventeen, four-twenty. I looked over at Lane, who was reading a newspaper. "That's all he did was look at you when you asked him?"

"Yeah, I asked him twice."

"Would you go see if you can find him again?"

"I don't think it'll do much good." Lane said.

"Well, where is that asshole? He's twenty minutes late."

"You're dead, man. Russell knows you're a dope fiend and he's got a perverted sense of humor. He'll make you wait as long as he can."

Finally the nurse entered the ward. He started on his rounds, passing out medication. He took his time, chatting off-handedly with patients. He glanced occasionally at me, but it seemed to take him forever to move down the row of beds. After an eternity, he stood in front of me. He flipped through my papers and looked at the bottles on his medicine tray. I waited, hiding my impatience and anger, knowing that a jolt was coming momentarily. Russell checked a label on a bottle then moved to the side of the bed and took hold of my wrist to take my pulse.

"Can't I get my medication? I'm in a lot of pain." I said.

Russell acted as if he hadn't heard me. He frowned and double-checked my pulse, then scratched his head and took my blood pressure. He duly recorded the information, then turned to me and smiled, "How do you feel?"

"I told you, I'm in a lot of pain."

"Well, the doctor will check you tomorrow in the morning.

I'm sure it's normal so soon after the operation." Russell paused. I knew he wanted me to ask for the shot, to beg for it. I could have killed him right then. After a prolonged silence, he glanced again at my chart. "Oh, you have a shot coming, don't you?" I didn't reply. He idly picked up the syringe and administered the Demerol.

The next day I rested, occasionally lifting myself out of bed to stand. I started getting accustomed to using a cane to walk. My limp was heavy and fairly painful at first, but gradually eased up. Both the doctor and I were pleased with my rapid progress. Things were going smoothly, helped along by the shots of Demerol that were doled out every four hours.

In the late afternoon, Morrie came to see me. We chatted for a couple of minutes, then Morrie suggested we exercise my knee. I grabbed my cane and we walked to the end of the ward where we were out of earshot of others. "I got some news on Sims. The transportation officers are picking him up on Friday. He'll be here Saturday morning."

"What's today?" I asked

"Thursday."

I paused for a moment, thinking. "I've been up to the TB ward. I can get in and out without any problem."

"You gotta get by anybody?"

"Just some old man. There are two other guys in the cells, but it won't be a problem."

"He'll scream when you set him on fire."

"Nobody'll hear him. The door on the front of the ward is three inches thick and so's the one at the TB ward. I'll close both of them before I make the move."

"Man, the hospital is going to have some heat. There'll be a fucking investigation you won't believe, and it's going to lead right back to you."

"It can lead anywhere, but they won't be able to prove it and that's all that counts."

"Be real careful not to get any thinner on you or your clothes; that would give them a case. How do you want to get thinner up here?"

"Have Norman send me a ducat to the Catholic chapel tomorrow at three o'clock and I'll meet you there. Can you get it to the chapel?"

"I can get it there. You want it in a hot water bottle or a coffee jar?"

"You can't get enough in a coffee jar. Get me two hot water bottles."

"Two? One's enough to barbecue an elephant."

"I want two of them."

CHAPTER 70

My Demerol sleep was dreamless. I woke early in anticipation of my next injection and of my three o'clock meeting with Morrie to pick up the thinner. I had every detail mapped out. There was no need to think about it anymore. Everything was set for Sims' arrival. One more day.

At 11:30 I saw the nurse enter the ward. I was pleased that he was early for once. Russell came directly to me. "You have a visit."

I was puzzled at first, then broke into a big grin. Sylvia was back. I had always known the depth of her love for me, and now she was proving it. She would accept me and love me for what I was whether she approved of what I did or not. It would never be over. "Could I get my shot before I go to the visiting room? It's due in twenty-five minutes."

"I'm sorry. I don't pass out medication early. You won't be in the visiting room that long anyway."

"I'll just wait because my knee hurts me now."

"You'll have to go now. They called for you. Those are the rules."

"Can't you make an exception? I just had major surgery."

"You could pass on the visit." I looked up at Russell. He took a step back, frightened, then shrugged like a silly, adolescent girl. "It's up to you." He turned and walked away, half expecting me to come after him. But I didn't move. I controlled myself, feeling like a whore for putting up with the nurse's taunting.

I dressed quickly and left the hospital. My knee was stiff but with the cane, I was able to make my way. By the time Sims came in tomorrow, I was certain I would be able to move well enough to take care of business.

It took a long time to cross the yard. When I passed the North Block, I spotted Morrie playing dominoes and he motioned to me. "Where're you going with your gimp ass?"

"The visiting room."

"Sylvia? I thought that was over."

"When you're irresistible, motherfucker, it ain't ever over." Now I was feeling cocky and floor-showing for Morrie. I was so happy that she was back, I felt like doing cartwheels.

"I got the business taken care of." Morrie said.

"You got the thinner?"

"Yeah. It's all ready. I got two hot water bottles stashed in the band room. You want to take it back with you, I'll go get it and wait for you."

"Can you get to it quick?"

"Real quick."

"Leave it in the band room until I get out of the visiting room. Go on back and play dominoes but keep watching for me. When I come back from the visit, you can pick it up and I'll take it from there."

"I'll be watching."

"I can't be limping around the yard on this jive knee, so keep your eyes open."

"I told you, I'll be watching."

I nodded and approached the visiting room gate. When I spotted her, for an instant, I didn't fully recognize her. Although it had only been a few months since I had last seen her, I had grown accustomed to the memory of her rather than the reality. I immediately noticed the small details that had been second nature to me for so long they had become blurred. She came back to me vividly and forcefully. I rushed up and held her and kissed her passionately and somewhat awkwardly. I felt her body start to respond, but she was reserved, and subtly pulled away. She had an unfamiliar expression on her face. "I've missed you. It seems like a long time." I said.

"It seems that way for me, too. What happened to your leg?"

"Knee operation."

"When?"

"I had it on Tuesday. It will be better now. I needed the operation."

"Are you in the hospital?"

"Yeah."

"Is that why it took you so long to get here?" She was distant, almost aloof. I had never felt that from her before. There was no enthusiasm in her eyes or voice. My pride was upset that she was less than thrilled to see me again. After all, she was the one who had made the first move. I hadn't written to her begging her to come back. She knew that wasn't in my character so she had come back to me on her own. Perhaps now she wanted me to reassure her to ease her back.

"How's your job?" I asked.

"Good."

"And your meetings?"

She nodded but made no attempt to open things up. I waited for her, sensing that she wanted to say something to me. The way she turned away made me think that she must have fallen in love with some lop and came because she felt she owed me an explanation. "What's on your mind?" I asked. "You come here to tell me something?"

"Yes." She paused. "I didn't want the institution to tell you."

"What is it?"

She had difficulty finding the words. My exuberance suddenly disappeared, and I was prepared for anything she might say. "Well?"

"Your grandmother died yesterday."

"How?"

"Cancer. She had it for some time. She just never told you."

"You knew when you were here the last time?"

"I've known for some time."

"Why didn't you tell me?"

"Would it have made it any easier?"

"I guess not. Was she in pain?"

"She never complained."

"How did you find out?"

"I was at the hospital with her."

I closed my eyes. My stomach felt weak and I thought I was going to throw up. I tried to summon enough strength to hold myself together. I knew instinctively that no one could help me deal with this; that no one, not even Sylvia, could possibly console me because no one knew what my grandmother had meant to me, what she had always represented in the foundation of my being. "Thank you for coming here to tell me. I love you very much for that. Would you come back some time and talk to me?"

"I would like that."

"I have to go back inside now."

"Couldn't I help in some way?"

"Just come back soon." We stood up. I put one hand on her shoulder and the other on her cheek. My head was tilted down, eyes closed. We stood for a moment. We felt an intimacy we had never shared before. No one had seen me like this, no one else had ever known me like this, but she had always known.

I left the waiting room. There was a glaze over everything. There were no guards, no convicts, no prison. No words could be said by others or to others. No one could help me now. I was by myself, crying, the tears running down my cheeks as I walked through the yard.

Somehow I reached the bleachers on the lower yard and sat down. It was drizzling and my whole face was wet. The one thing I had dreaded from the time I was a young boy had happened. There had never been such a profound pain and sorrow in my life before. Kicking a habit cold in a jail cell was nothing, going to San Quentin or Folsom was no tragedy. Those things were tabs to be paid for living the kind of life I had led. I longed for the faith I once had as a young boy, a faith that believed in life after death, where death was not a permanent end and loved ones were reunited.

But her life was over. She was gone. And the memories I was left with were fitful and unsatisfactory. When she had needed me, I had been on the streets hustling dope, and in the last hours of her life, I had been in prison putting my revenge deals together. She had always been there for me, yet I had never been there for her. I knew her heart and soul forgave me, but I could not forgive myself.

I sat on the far bleacher corner all day, unaware of time and my surroundings. It was still raining when the count whistle blew. Programmed by thousands of count whistles, I automatically rose and started back towards the hospital. When I reached the upper yard, I heard someone call my name. It was Morrie. He ran over to me, out of breath. "Man, where the hell have you been? I've been holding up the domino tables all day. I had to get the thinner out of the band room. I got it on me in two hot water bottles." I looked at him, barely hearing his words.

"What did you do, score something? You look wiped out. What do you want me to do with the thinner? Should I hold it in my cell or do you want to take it back to the 'pital?" I continued to look straight ahead. "Are you all right, motherfucker?"

After a long pause, I spoke. "Get rid of it."

"Get rid of it? I hustled around here like a Fifth Street whore putting this shit together and you tell me to get rid of it? You going to take him out some other way?"

"It's off."

"What the fuck is going on? What happened since I saw you this morning?"

"I gotta get back to the hospital." I walked away, leaving Morrie bewildered.

My clothes were soaking wet when I got back to the hospital. I undressed quickly and got into bed and pulled the covers over my head before anyone could talk to me. Sleep would have been a blessing, but I was cold and wet and couldn't get warm enough.

"Well, now. Where has the dope fiend been all day?" The nurse shook the bed. I uncovered my head and looked up. "You want your medication or did you get something better on the yard?" Russell smiled at me in a repulsive manner. He was exercising his narrow power, taking his daily revenge. He spoke with casual, calculating impatience. "Come on, give me your arm if you want your Demerol. I don't have all day." I stared silently, thinking to myself, Give you my arm. Give you my arm, you said. I've been giving you my arm all my life; rolling up my sleeve, getting my jolt, waiting for you to come back and then giving you my arm again. My head felt light and my body was trembling. The nurse standing before me was a vague blur. "I said, I ain't got all day. Give me your arm."

"I pass." I said.

"What?"

"I pass." I said again. I had no idea where those words came from, but they sounded strangely familiar as though I'd heard them in a dream. "I pass," I said again. "I pass." The words seemed new and effortless. The blur at the foot of the bed mumbled something and moved away. "I pass," I continued, "I pass."

I stayed awake, lightheaded and shivering, saying those words over and over to myself. They were an incantation to some power I couldn't see clearly and didn't fully understand. But I felt something enter my being that had never been there before; some power my instincts told me was transcendent and liberating. I didn't know it at that moment, but with those simple words, my soul had been given back to me, and for the first time since I was a young boy, I was free.

EPILOGUE

W hen I finally got out of the penitentiary, I went to a few
meetings, but I didn't do the work necessary to stay
sober, so I lasted about four months. Then I came back to
meeting, and I managed to stay sober eleven years. I went to
school to learn wallpapering, and worked as a painter, too.
What I really wanted to do was play music, but I didn't get to
do a lot of playing because it was really hard to make a living
and play at the same time.

Then, a few years back, I was going with a terrific woman
who taught writing at UCLA. She had black hair and Irish
green eyes, and she thrilled me. She loved the stories I'd tell
her about the joint, and asked me to write some of them down.
I told her I didn't think I could write. I had a fifth grade
education, and couldn't spell worth a shit. But she said, "just
write 'em down." Well, I put her off until finally it came down
to where I wasn't going to get any more privileges in the
bedroom if I didn't comply with her wishes, so I wrote one
down for her, and she was impressed. I wrote three more
stories, and each time I brought one to her she complimented
me so much I started thinking maybe I could write after all.

So I sat down one day and wrote at the top of the page:
Father, I don't know what I'm going to write about, but if you
give me some help, I'd sure appreciate it. And I started writing.
My girlfriend would type them for me, and this continued as
long as we were together, about six months. I had about a
hundred pages written when we broke up. By that time I had

the writing bug, and, due to all her compliments, I got to thinking maybe I could do this thing on my own. So I kept writing and writing and writing. I don't know how I did it, to tell you the truth. I had a couple of other friends who would type for me, and I just sort of struggled for years to get it done.

When I finally finished, I found an agent who loved the book. She submitted it to several publishers, who commented that they already had someone writing in that vein. So I gave up on getting it published though I had always thought it was good. I figured, well, if it's not getting published, maybe there's something wrong with it, maybe it's not that good.

I finally lost touch with the agent, but a friend of mine named Bob Levey was in town to support his father, who was dying. We spent some time together during his father's last days. Bob asked me, "What are you doing with yourself these days?" I said, "Well, I've just been practicing, that's about all I want to do. But I did write a book."

He said, "Let me see it." So I showed it to him, and he took it with him to read on his flight back to Colorado. That was on a weekend. He called me the following Monday, and said, "Woody, I love this book, and I'm going to give it my friend Artt Frank, who used to play drums with Chet Baker. If he likes it, he's going to give it his friend Tim, who's a publisher." I waited for about four or five days, and then Artt called and said, "I'm going to give this book to Tim. He'll love it."

And that's what happened. Tim came to LA to meet me, and we got a strong relationship going as we revised the book. It was lacking some things, so he showed me how to build up parts to make it stronger and delete parts that weren't necessary. We went through it a dozen times page by page, word by word, and it reads much better now.

I'm very happy with the book, and I hope it will help and inspire people who read it, because it's about an outrageous alcoholic and addict who finally saw the light. That's really the message of the whole book. Currently, I have seven years, and they've been the best years of my life. I'm playing a lot, and I guess my claim to fame is that I haven't been arrested in over forty-five years! That's a miracle in itself.

So that's the story of this book. It goes to prove how the Father has His hand in everything, like my accidental reunion with my old friend Bob Levey, who I played with a long time ago—he's a drummer like his dad, the great Stan Levey. The Father works in strange ways. The book was just sitting there, but then Bob takes it to Artt, and Artt takes it to Tim. It started out with the Father's works, and it's ending with His works. Now, it'll be up to Him to see how it sells!

ACKNOWLEDGEMENTS

An Eskimo and an atheist are sitting in a bar in Anchorage. They're both drunk, and are having a serious conversation about the existence of God. The Eskimo, who is a Christian, asks the atheist, "Why don't you believe in God?"

"I'll tell you why," the atheist replies. "I was stuck in a blizzard a couple of years ago and I got down on my knees and prayed to God to save my life."

"What are you complaining about?" says the Eskimo. "You're here, aren't you?"

"God didn't have a damn thing to do with it," says the atheist. "Some dumb Eskimo found me and showed me how to get home."

I first heard this story from Bobby Earlee in 1970 when I was still in prison. He had come to the prison to speak on addiction. I remember the story as well as I will always remember Bobby, because he was responsible for saving my life six months after my release.

I also want to thank Sylvia Magdaleno Daly, who is probably one of the most spiritual people I have known in my life. It was Sylvia who introduced me to the program and helped me stay on it. Without her help I would have died years ago. She's at the top of my list of true friends; I would do anything for her, and she would do anything for me.

Then there's Susan who spent hours with me in the hospital when I was suffering from stomach problems. She grabbed me by the shoulders saying, "Motherfucker, you're not going to die on me!" That gave me the strength to hang in there until the doctors finally diagnosed what was wrong. They were able to help me, but it was Susan who gave me the strength to hold on. She is one of my dearest friends and I will never forget her.

How could I forget Jerry Chamalis? When I couldn't play my horn due to dental problems, Jerry gave me the number of his dentist. The dentist said it was going to cost five big ones. I told Jerry, and he took care of it. But beyond paying for my chops the real reason care about Jerry is that he is a real gentle man and he helps people. He's always in my prayers.

There are so many people who have helped me through the years. I have countless friends who are a big part of my life, and I regret I can't name every one of them, but I'll close with the two bright spots in my life—my sons. Taylor is twenty-three and Danny is sixty.

Danny, my oldest, was born when I was a teenager, but I didn't get to see him until he was thirty-five. It was difficult for both of us. He'd suffered from the same problem I had, but he has been sober now for over twenty-five years. When I had knee replacement surgery he called me every day from Shanghai where he is musical director and drummer at the Ritz-Carlton. I've come to love him just as much as my younger son Taylor, whom I raised from birth.

Taylor's a born entrepreneur and has the same problem Danny and I had, but he's off the hard stuff now. I was unprepared for the effect he had in my life when he came into this world. I was fifty-eight. He was my only concern. I'd stand by his crib for hours just looking at him. His mother and I got divorced when he was a year old, and when we talked on the phone he'd always say, "I love you Dada." He still ends every talk we have with, "I love you, Dad." You have to be a father to appreciate that I have such a large feeling about myself knowing that he loves me.

V. W
April 2006

BIOGRAPHY

Verdi Woodward is a fully recovered addict who has not had so much as a parking ticket in over forty-five years. A jazz saxophonist and counselor for recovering addicts, he lives in Los Angeles, and is at work on a sequel to HOPE TO DIE.